NEW CLINICAL REALMS

Pushing the Envelope of
Theory and Technique

NEW
CLINICAL
REALMS

Pushing the Envelope of
Theory and Technique

Salman Akhtar

JASON ARONSON INC.
Northvale, New Jersey
London

The author expresses his gratitude for permission to reprint the following:

Chapters 1 and 7 are reprinted, with permission, from the *International Journal of Psychoanalysis* (81:229–244, 2000 and 79:241–252, 1998 respectively). Chapter 3 is reprinted, with permission, from *Changing Ideas in a Changing World: Essays in Honor of Arnold Cooper*, ed. J. Sandler, R. Michels, and P. Fonagy, pp. 111–119, London: Karnac Books, 2000. Chapter 4 is reprinted, with permission, from *Contemporary Marriage*, ed. D. Goldberg, pp. 215–240, Homeswood, IL: Dow Jones-Irwin. Chapter 8 and 10 are reprinted, with permission, *Psychoanalytic Quarterly* (63:265–288, 2000 and 71:175–212, 2002). Chapter 9 is reprinted, with permission, from *Mental Health in India 1950–2000: Essays in Honor of Professor N.N. Wig*, ed. R.S. Murthy, pp. 2–8, 2000.

This book was set in 11 pt. New Baskerville by Alabama Book Composition of Deatsville, Alabama.

Library of Congress Cataloging-in-Publication Data

Akhtar, Salman, 1946 July 31–
    New clinical thinking: pushing the envelope of theory and technique / Salman Akhtar.
      p. cm.
    Includes bibliographical references and index.
    ISBN 0–7657–0335–1
     1. Clinical psychology.   2. Psychology—Practice.   I. Title.

RC467.95 .A347 2002
616.89—dc21

2002026058

Printed in the United States of America on acid-free paper. For information and catalog write to Jason Aronson Inc., 230 Livingston Street, Northvale, NJ 07647-1726, or visit our web site: www.aronson.com.

To

VAMIK VOLKAN

With affection and gratitude

CONTENTS

PART II: UNRECOGNIZED PERSONALITIES

PART III: UNCELEBRATED PARTNERS

PART IV: UNFAMILIAR PROCESSES

ACKNOWLEDGMENTS

My good friends, Drs. Jennifer Bonovitz, Ira Brenner, Axel Hoffer, and J. Anderson Thomson Jr., read parts of this book and gave me meaningful feedback. Drs. Arnold Cooper, Burton Hutto, Otto Kernberg, Peter Schou, and Shahrzad Siassi discussed some chapters in their earlier, presentation forms and made useful input for the development of my ideas. Mss. Liedwin Geertjen and Panna Naik, as well as Drs. Wendy Jacobson, Andrew Klafter, George Klumpner, William Singletary, Julian Stern, and James Youakim, pointed out references that would have otherwise escaped my attention. Dr. Jodi Brown gave me permission to include our co-authored paper on animals in this book. Drs. Gregg Gorton and Michael Vergare, respectively my partner in running Jefferson Medical College's adult psychiatric outpatient clinic and my departmental chairman, provided me the administrative leeway and collegial warmth necessary for creative work in the midst of day-to-day academic medicine. My patients honored me by their trust and my family and friends supported me with their love. Two sisters-in-law, Mss. Maryann and Melissa Nevin, provided exemplary secretarial assistance to me. To all these individuals, my heartfelt thanks indeed.

PREFACE

This is my fifth book in the realm of psychiatry and psychoanalysis. My first book, *Broken Structures* (1992), attempted to synthesize the vast literature on severe personality disorders from the perspectives of clinical psychoanalysis and descriptive psychiatry. My second book, *Quest for Answers* (1995), sought to resolve the dialectical tension between a psychoanalytic student's need for clarity and his teacher's equally understandable concern about oversimplification. My third book, *Inner Torment* (1999), brought diverse psychoanalytic traditions together in order to facilitate deeper understanding of psychopathology that arose from areas between those of psychic conflict and mental fragmentation. My fourth book, *Immigration and Identity* (1999), addressed the interface of clashing cultures and personal identity, and the mourning process mobilized by a radical change in one's culture and psychological environment.

While I was fortunate to travel through the conceptual trajectory of these topics, other matters of clinical significance kept drawing my attention as well. Pulling some of this latter material together, refining it, and adding some new pieces to it has resulted in this book.

Five parts, composed of two chapters each, constitute the book. Part I, titled "Unexplored Problems," opens with a chapter on mental pain. In it, I argue that mental pain consists of a wordless sense of self-rupture, longing, and psychic helplessness that is diffi-cult to convey to others. I note that mental pain usually follows the loss of a significant object, a loss that results in the laceration of an unconscious, fused self-object core. Abruptly precipitated discrep-ancies between the actual and wished-for self-states add to the genesis of mental pain. Issues of hatred, guilt, and moral masoch-ism, as well as fantasies of being beaten, can also be folded in the experience of mental pain. The next chapter of this section addresses the phenomenon of writer's block. It delineates the various forms and intensities of such inhibition as well as the complex and varied affects that are associated with it. Bringing the early writings of Freud, Greenacre, and Bergler together with the contemporary contributions of Britton, Olinick, Bergman, and Inman, the chapter elucidates the multiple factors leading to this symptom. These range from the non-specific element of an eco-nomically burdened ego to the specific anxieties pertaining to narcissism, separateness, and guilt-ridden oedipal issues.

Part II of the book is titled "Unrecognized Personalities." One of its chapters maps out the phenomenological and psychostructural characteristics of the less recognized shy type of narcissistic person-ality and underscores the theoretical and technical significance of such diagnosis. The other chapter, written while I was a candidate in psychoanalytic training, reports on a small cohort of female patients who sought my help because of problems in their being involved with married men. The colloquial euphemism for labeling the syndrome does not preclude my seeing it as a situation with complex social and psychological etiologies including erotic despair, ideali-zation, need for omnipotent rescue, masochism, and oedipal trans-gression, to name a few.

The third part of the book is titled "Uncelebrated Partners" and comprises essays on the developmental, psychopathological, and technical significance of man's inner relationship with animals and inanimate objects. The first chapter catalogues the remarkable ways human psychopathology enlists animals for encoding, contain-ing, and conveying its anguished message to others. The second chapter traces the significance of inanimate objects in the personal-ity formation from the early reality constancy and object permanence through transitional objects to the adult's material acquisitions and realistic use of the physical surround. It also highlights various psychopathological syndromes involving inanimate objects and the technical significance of such knowledge especially vis-à-vis gift exchange within the therapeutic dyad and the occasional development of dehumanizing experiences in the clinical situation. Clearly, in writing these two chapters, I have been inspired by Freud's histories of Rat man, Wolf man, ad Little Hans, as well as Winnicott's and Searles' devoted attention to the growing child's involvement with the ecological surround.

Part IV, entitled "Unfamiliar Processes," elucidates two sequences of events. One pertains to the way associative material and affective experience evolves during the psychoanalytic treatment of individuals with defective object constancy. The other involves the manner in which a complex and flexible amalgamation of diverse clinical orientations occurs in the analyst's mind. The first sequence is called "from simplicity through contradiction to paradox" and depicts the gradual organization and layering of the psychic material initially presented in a sequestered ad simplified way by the borderline patient in treatment. The second sequence is named "from schisms through synthesis to oscillation" and highlights the clinically attuned and developmentally anchored perspective on the coexistence of "romantic" and "classic" visions of psychoanalysis and their respective yields toward its technical armamentarium.

Part V, "Untapped Potentials," takes up the important but neglected topics of mentorship and forgiveness. The two essays represent the growing psychoanalytic interest in healthier sectors of personality and are firmly located in the tradition of Kernberg's work on love, Kohut's on wit and wisdom, and Volkan's on conflict resolution. The first delineates the psychosocial role of a mentor, distinguishing it from the potentially overlapping developmental contributions of teachers, fathers, lovers, and analysts. The second elucidates the phylogenetic and ontogenetic foundations of the capacity to forgive, various psychopathological syndromes associated with forgiveness, and the role of forgiveness in the context of psychotherapeutic and psychoanalytic dialogue.

The novel nature of these topics has necessitated that the tone remain specifically attuned to them. Thus some chapters (e.g. the ones on mental pain and forgiveness) are more psychoanalytic in their vantage points while others (e.g. the ones on the shy narcissist and animals) are more representative of descriptive psychiatry in their style. However, these differences in emphasis do not preclude the inclusion of both the psychoanalytic and psychiatric perspectives throughout the book. That has been my manner of thinking and writing anyway. The surrender to my third "tyrant" (i.e. poetry) to use Freud's wry designation of psychology as his muse, is also evident here. This tripartite paradigm composed of psychiatry, psychoanalysis, and poetry is what now constitutes my "voice." Finding this voice has taken time, but the discovery is a source of deep joy. I know that after finding one's voice one has to continually find new songs to sing. This book contains some of this new music!

Part I

UNEXPLORED PROBLEMS

1

MENTAL PAIN

At first glance, the term *mental pain* appears a bit of an oxymoron since it is the body and not mind that is generally regarded as the site of pain. Yet the expression has wide currency. Poets seek to clothe it in words. Politically oppressed people "celebrate" it in their uprisings.[1] Patients complain of it. Psychiatrists dealing with suicide use terms like *psychache*[2] (Schneidman 1993) and psychoanalysts (Freud 1926, Joffe and Sandler 1965, Joseph 1981, Khan 1979, Klein 1940, Kogan 1990, Laplanche 1981) struggle to delineate the precise nature of pain and its role in loss and mourning.

DEFINITION AND PHENOMENOLOGY

Freud (1926) insisted that "it cannot be for nothing that the common usage of speech should have created the notion of internal, mental pain" (p. 171). He introduced the concept in psychoanalytic

---

1. The *ecstatic pain* described by Bleuler (1930) as occurring in states of martyrdom belongs in this context.

2. Though similar sounding, *psychalgia* refers to "discomfort or pain, usually in the head, which accompanies mental activity (including obsessions, hallucinations, etc.) and is recognized by the patient as being emotional in origin" (Hinsie and Campbell 1970, p. 662).

literature under the rubric of *Seelenschmerz* (literally, soul-pain). He
acknowledged that he knew very little about this affect and fumbled
in describing it. He referred to a child's crying for his mother and
evoked analogies to bodily injury and loss of body parts. He also
mentioned a sense of "longing" and "mental helplessness" (pp. 171,
172) as being components of mental pain. Subsequent analysts
continued to use words such as *pining* (Klein 1940, p. 360) and
longing (Joffee and Sandler 1965, p. 156) in association with mental
pain. They also resorted to somatic analogies and metaphors.
Wheelis (1966) referred to the "furtive pain around the mouth"
(p. 161) and Joseph (1981) noted the frequency with which physical
allusions appear in associations to mental pain, with

> the patient locating it often in the lower part of the chest, and yet he
> or she knows clearly that he is not describing a physical condition;
> it is not hypochondriacal or psychosomatic; it is known to be mental.
> It is experienced as on the border between mental and physical.
> (pp. 88–89)

Joseph emphasized that mental pain is "not experienced as guilt
in relation to impulses, concern about objects, or the loss of an
object; it has not this clarity" (p. 94). The vagueness is perhaps due
to its location on the psyche-soma border. Indeed, in mapping out
the affective world, Pontalis (1981, p. 31) placed pain "at the
frontiers and juncture of body and psyche, of death and life."
   Difficulty in defining mental pain also arises from the fact that it
frequently occurs in amalgamation with other feelings. Gitelson's
(quoted in Szasz 1955, p. 187) concept of *pain-anxiety* and Amsterdam and Levitt's (1980) notion of *painful self-consciousness* are
especially pertinent in this context. Another admixture was brought
to my attention by a patient who, whenever I pointed out her anger
at our separations, insisted that she was not only angry but also (and,
more importantly) pained. Together we ended up designating her
response as consisting of *paingry* feelings. Such admixtures make it
hard to properly delineate the phenomenon of mental pain.
   Of the five major psychoanalytic glossaries (Eidelberg 1968,
LaPlanche and Pontalis 1973, Moore and Fine 1968, 1990, Rycroft
1968), only two contain entries on "pain." Eidelberg recognizes
psychic pain as an entity and describes three steps in its evolution.

First, there is little distinction between physical and mental experiences and all unpleasantness is felt as pain. Then, with further maturation, anxiety and pain become distinct with the former related to object-based concerns and the latter relating to self-based concerns. Still later, with a greater shift of psychic interest from the subject's body to object relations, psychic pain becomes consolidated as a specific affect "experienced when the cathected love object is lost or fails the individual" (1968, p. 291). Rycroft considers the definition of *pain* to be context-based "referring *either* to the familiar instinctual tension *or* to distress associated with instinctual tension, the latter being, according to pleasure-pain principle, the condition which instinctual action attempts to relieve" (1972, p. 110). He goes on to state that in Freud's writings "physical pain is 'Schmerz' and mental pain due to tension is 'Unlust' which Strachey translates as unpleasure." Rycroft's rendering of Freud seems erroneous since the latter explicitly uses *Schmerz* in connection with mental pain on more than one occasion (Freud 1917, 1926, 1950).

Highlighting the nosological imprecision in this realm, Ramzy and Wallerstein (1958) note that the term *mental pain* is used in both a narrow and a broad sense. In the narrow sense, the term applies to one specific feeling among the broad category of dysphoric affects. This is how Freud (1926), Weiss (1934), Joseph (1981), and Kogan (1990) use the term. In the broad sense, *mental pain* includes all unpleasant affects. Using the term in this way, Ramzy and Wallerstein (1958) include fear, anxiety, guilt, and mourning, under *mental pain.* Valenstein (1973, p. 368) further dilates the definition of mental pain to include "diffuse emotional states of an uncomfortable, unpleasurable, and distressful nature." My own preference is for the narrower usage of the term, which defines *mental pain* as a sharp, throbbing, somewhat unknowable feeling of despair, longing, and psychic helplessness.

Mental pain, thus defined, needs to be distinguished from anxiety. Freud (1926) suggested that anxiety results from anticipating the dangers caused by object loss while pain is a direct response to the loss itself. Szasz (1955) suggested that anxiety is an affect arising in the context of ego-object relationship while pain is an affect arising in the context of ego-body image (hence, self) relationship. Spiegel (1966), however, posited that anxiety is a response to the loss of a "*transient* external need-satisfying object" while pain is a response to the loss of a "*permanent* (constant) external object" (p. 83). Gitelson (quoted in Szasz 1955) suggested that at the dawn of psychic life, pain and anxiety are indistinguishable. Later the two become separated and follow different economic pathways. This line of thinking is also implicit in A. Freud's 1952 statement that in the beginning of life any tension, need, or frustration is probably felt as pain. From all this it seems that while there is overlap between pain and anxiety, the two affects are distinct. Pain is more immediate, lacks readily available discursive content, and is a response to a trauma that has already taken place. Anxiety is an evolving sensation, replete with fantasy, and is a response to a trauma that is anticipated in the future.

CAUSES OF MENTAL PAIN

Freud discussed the processes leading to mental pain on three occasions. In the "Project" (Freud 1895a), he suggested that *Schmerz* (pain) resulted from a marked increase in the quantity of stimuli impinging upon the mind. This, in turn, caused "a breach in the continuity" (1895a, p. 307) of the protective shield. Pain was a direct result of such shock trauma. Recall of a trauma created *Unlust* (unpleasure) and not pain. In "Mourning and Melancholia," Freud related pain to object loss and said that the complex of melancholia behaves like "an open wound" (1917, p. 253). It was, however, not until an addendum to *Inhibitions, Symptoms, and Anxiety* (1926, pp. 169–172), that Freud linked his economic explanations to his object-related hypothesis regarding the origins of mental pain. He suggested that where there is physical pain, an increase in narcissistic cathexis of the afflicted site occurs. Similarly

the intense cathexis of longing which is concentrated on the missed or lost object (a cathexis which steadily mounts up because it can not be appeased) creates the same economic conditions as are created by the cathexis of pain which is concentrated on the injured part of the body. . . . An object representation that is highly cathected by instinctual need plays the same role as a part of the body which is cathected by an increase of stimulus. The continuous nature of the

cathectic process and the impossibility of inhibiting it produce the
same state of mental helplessness . . . the feeling of unpleasure
which then arises has the specific character of pain. (pp. 171–172)

In illustrating his ideas through the situation of an infant
separated from his mother, Freud implied that the object loss
leading to mental pain occurred at a psychic level of ego-object
undifferentiation. Weiss (1934) made this explicit by stating that

> pain arises when an injury—a break, so to speak, in continuity—
> occurs *within* the ego. . . . Love objects become, as we know,
> libidinally bound to the ego, as if they were parts of it. If they are torn
> away from it, the ego reacts as though it had sustained mutilation.
> The open wound thus produced in it is just what comes to expression
> as mental pain. (p. 12, author's italics)

Thus was born the notion that mental pain is not an accompaniment of any object loss but only of that object loss which leads to an
ego rupture. Grinberg (1964) posited that such loss is experienced
as an attack upon the ego in the unconscious fantasy. The intensity
of this perceived assault varies with the amount of aggression
mobilized by the trauma leading to pain. Green (quoted in Prego-
Silva 1978, p. 520) took this a step further and stated that "psychic
pain does not refer exactly to the problem of loss, but to the
problem of hate and narcissism." Kogan (1990) also concluded that
mental pain results when an actual trauma gets associated with
underlying fantasies of hatred and destructiveness.

Additional features of mental pain connected to loss were pointed
out by Joffee and Sandler (1965). They suggested that situations of
loss invariably result in a discrepancy between the actual state of the
self and the desired, ideal state of well-being. Since that depends
heavily upon the lost object, the affective value of that object is
greatly increased in the mind. Longing and pain then ensue.
Pontalis (1981) added that such a highly desired object, while
seeming to be irremediably lost, is eternally clung to in the unconscious: "where there is pain, it is the absent, lost object that is
present" (p. 90).

The nature of such an object-relation and—until the time it is
disturbed—its "success" in keeping the psyche stabilized drew

Joseph's (1981) attention. She suggested that mental pain arises when a particular type of relationship with an object is altered and a previously well-balanced state of affairs is threatened. The individuals prone to mental pain

> have in common the employment of their important objects to contain parts of the self. This is sometimes achieved in a fairly total way, as with perverts who project themselves mentally or bodily into fetish objects like a rubber suit or a woman's body and thus keep free from anxiety and relating: it is sometimes achieved in a powerful but more limited way as when large parts of the self are projected into other people and not experienced as belonging to the self. (p. 89)

Such individuals have achieved peace by the use of this particular type of relationship with their objects, which protects them from actual emotional experiences. "When this type of pathological tie breaks down, what they experience is new and unknown and is what they . . . are calling 'pain'" (p. 89). Joseph's view implies that mental pain is not ubiquitous and that only those with "important areas of psychotic anxieties" (p. 89) have such a propensity.

Perhaps there is a quantitative dimension involved here. The experience of pain, developmentally speaking, arises in the context of undifferentiation. And it is the rupture of this undifferentiated core, upon which self and object constancy (Mahler et al. 1975) are later built, that causes mental pain. To the extent that some individuals are more governed by undifferentiation in their object relations, the vulnerability to mental pain would indeed seem variable. Nonetheless, all individuals would possess it since the undifferentiated core is universal.

Two other factors suggest ubiquitousness in the capacity to experience mental pain. First, pain, along with some hopelessness and mourning, is a constant in the course of development. Indeed, it is the "archaic admittance of suffering" (Tahka 1993, p. 35) that lays the groundwork for renouncing infantile omnipotence and tolerating the frustrations inherent in mastering higher levels of functioning. Second, to the fundamentally pregenital base of mental pain are grafted more sophisticated object-related experiences and fantasies from later phases of development (Valenstein 1973). Thus biting, smearing, and penetrating fantasies (and their passive counterparts) give further texture to mental pain. Guilt, emanating from various sources, and associated fantasies of being beaten, can also be condensed here. Pain, an experience of the ego, can thus come to serve the purposes of a cruel superego.

All in all, it seems that mental pain has many roots. These include (1) psychic overstimulation due to a rupture in the protective shield, (2) loss of a much needed object that is experienced as fused with the self, (3) loss of the object complementary part of the self, (4) discrepancy between the actual and desired state of the self, (5) threat to projective mechanisms through which aspects of self have been deposited into others, (6) activation of pre-existing hostile fantasies by a trauma and the resulting aggression's turning against the self, and (7) guilty self-flagellation in view of disturbing fantasies from various psychosexual levels. In other words, mental pain, while pregenital and simple at its core, is actually a complex phenomenon. Within the clinical situation, its *simplicity* (Akhtar 1998) is affirmed by the seeming self-evident nature of the experience and by its powerful emotional resonance in the countertransference. Also, its complexity is revealed as benevolent skepticism and waiting for fantasies and memories to emerge permits interpretation and reconstruction.[3]

DEFENSIVE MANEUVERS

There are many defensive operations aimed at minimizing or controlling mental pain. Some of these defenses seem more healthy than others. Joffee and Sandler (1965) include indignation, de-idealization, and enhanced individuation among the healthy responses to pain and the attitude of hopelessness and helplessness among the pathological responses to it. Phenomenologically speaking, matters might actually be less categorical. The various defenses might not be so separate from each other. Moreover, all of them might lead to healthy or pathological results, especially on a temporary basis and depending upon the overall psychic economy as well as the interpersonal and cultural context.

---

3. The two levels of pain have been eloquently designated by Khan (1979, p. 216) as *blank pain* and *the pleasure-pain of "the story,"* respectively.

With this caveat, I propose that there are essentially four defensive operations against mental pain. Each can have an adaptive or maladaptive outcome. Transiently deployed, each can be a way station to mourning, which requires a more *mentalized* (Fonagy and Target 1997) scenario of loss than the throbbing "unknowness" (Joseph 1981, p. 94) of mental pain.

Psychic retreat and self-holding

A frequent defense against mental pain is withdrawal. This withdrawal can be variously termed detachment of libidinal cathexis from the external world and its investment into the ego (Freud 1914a), regression into a schizoid position (Fairbairn 1952), formation of a second ego skin to prevent further psychic bleeding (Bick 1968), and self-holding to firm up a destabilized self (Kohut 1977). The effect of such withdrawal can be pathological or healthy depending upon a number of variables. If withdrawal in the face of pain is accompanied by a sense of futility and a generalized inhibition of drive and ego functions, then the outcome has certainly been pathological. Such temporary relief is not accompanied by a wish for recovery, which would require facing pain, locating its source, understanding one's own contribution to it, and mourning the breach in self-continuity. Under such circumstances, "the experience of pain is not yet heartache—though felt often to be related to the heart—but it contains the beginnings of the capacity of feel heartache" (Joseph 1981, p. 95).

In contrast, if the withdrawal is transient, focal (i.e. does not spread to all ego functions and object relations), and is accompanied by an effort to psychically sort out the ego impoverishment that has resulted from pain, then the outcome is not so bad after all. Such withdrawal, even with regression to a level of psychic organization lying beneath that of object-relatedness—Balint's (1968) *area of creation*—can be ultimately replenishing for the ego. It is as if the "badness" of the pain-causing object is taken into the recesses of a pre-objectal world, reworked, and returned to the ego surface in the form of a creative product. "The pining for the lost love object also implies dependence on it, but dependence of a kind which becomes an incentive to reparation" (Klein 1940, p. 360). Creativity mobilized by loss constitutes such a reparative gesture toward the self and its objects.

Denial and manic defense

Another way of managing pain is through *manic defense* (Klein 1940) and *denial* (A. Freud 1965). Here the ego's predominant effort is to move away from the laceration of psychic reality. Denial can result in *psychic numbing* (Kogan 1990) and manic defense in crowding the ego breach with *transitional fantasies* (Volkan 1973) and frenzied behavior. Alcohol and sedative drugs can be used to induce psychic numbness. Alternate sensations offered by psychedelic agents and sexual encounters can also be aimed at blunting the sense of inner pain.

In general, these mechanisms are pathological since they repudiate parts of the self, diminish knowledge of what is going on in the internal and external reality, and thus lead to ego impoverishment. However, if the manic defense involves only the unaffected sector of personality, so to speak, then it can serve as an umbrella under which the pain-ridden part can carry out its work of mourning in a piecemeal fashion. For instance, intensified effort at work while facing dejection in love, or a rejuvenated erotic life in the setting of a mature relationship while wrestling with professional setbacks, can, at times, facilitate the management of psychic pain through mourning.

Extrusion of pain and its induction into others

Mental pain can also be defended against by extruding it and by inducing pain in others.[4] Joffee and Sandler's (1965, p. 156) "discontent and resentment" are essentially such measures. Self-protective indignation, protest, and even rage, which can exist without hatred (Akhtar 1999, Pao 1965), thus constitute adaptive defenses against mental pain. Problems arise if the habitual way of

---

4. The turning of guilt into hatred (Jones 1928) follows a similar route by which a burden of the ego is transformed into the suffering of the Other.

dealing with pain, especially if there is characterological vulnerability to frequent pain, becomes hatred of others and cruelty toward them. Kernberg (1992) has eloquently delineated the identificatory and transformational mechanisms involved in the evolution of mental pain into characterologically anchored hatred.

Changing the form or function of pain

Mental pain can also be managed by the ego's effort to change its form or function. Such alterations can yield both pathological and healthy outcomes. Among the former are *concretization* (Bergman 1982) through acting out, and *physicalization*, that is, substituting physical for mental pain. The gross self-mutilation of a heart-broken borderline and the delicate self-cutting of a pubertal girl facing the menstrual point of no return into femininity are examples of turning mental pain into physical pain. Another problematic situation is constituted by *libidinization*, that is, finding "pleasure in pain" (Fenichel 1934, p. 308), as happens in moral masochism[5] (Freud 1924a) and traumatophilia (Joseph 1982). Note in this connection Khan's observation that "in all masochistic fantasy or practice there is always a kernel of psychic pain, that has been lived and lost, and instead, proliferations of screen-fantasies take its place" (1979, p. 217).

At the same time, "milder forms of pain, playful debasement, and humiliation (form a) part of normal sexual relations" (Kernberg 1992, p. 47). The capacity for sublimation also involves mastery of hardship and a healthy

> capacity to derive satisfaction and accomplishment from self-induced, self-dosed pain. . . . The pleasurable fatigue after a day's work, the ecstasy of an athlete's exhaustion, the dogged pursuit of distant goals, the willingness to cling to a seemingly absurd ideal—all of these represent constructive uses of pleasure in pain and a source of creative energies. (Cooper 1998, p. 125)

---

5. See also Glenn (1984) for intricate connections among loss, pain, and masochism in children.

POETRY AS AN OINTMENT

The relationship between object loss, a frequent precipitant of mental pain, and creativity has drawn considerable attention (Hamilton 1969, 1976, 1979, Pollock 1975, 1977). While other forms of creativity (e.g. music, art) do figure in this dialectic, poetry seems to occupy a special place in the ego's efforts to manage, mourn, and master mental pain. There are three ways in which poetry accomplishes this.

Utilization of defenses

Poetry utilizes a complex mix of all four defenses mentioned previously: psychic retreat, manic defense, change of function, and induction of pain into the Other. Reading or writing a poem, while in pain, necessarily requires some withdrawal of attention from the realistic surround and a calming down of the dialogue with troubling inner objects (*psychic retreat*). Engagement in such mental work allows the individual to turn passivity of suffering into the activity of creation (*manic defense*). The hitherto traumatizing event becomes the nidus of cognitive embellishment, mastery, and pride (*change of function*). And, creation of empathic resonance in an actual or imaginary audience leads to a sharing of private anguish (*induction of pain into the Other*).

Libidinal aspects of the poetic form

The formal and structural aspects of poetry themselves have libidinally gratifying and mentally healing effects. Prominent among these aspects are meter, rhyme, alliteration, simile, allusion, metaphor, and onomatopoeia. *Meter* refers to the rhythm achieved by using a fixed count of syllables in a given utterance. By thus creating a near musical tone, a line (meter's basic unit) produces the affect of pulsating perceptual input. Closely related is *rhyme* or the repetitive occurrence of phonetically similar words at the end of each line. The resulting nodal sounds are both distinct (different consonants) and familiar (same vowels). This evokes "a dualism on the one hand and magically overcomes that very dualism on the other" (Faber 1988, p. 377). Thus, separation is both acknowledged

and denied. With its developmental prototype in maternal lullabies
and nursery rhymes, such phonetic reoccurrence exerts a reassuring
effect upon the mind.[6] *Alliteration*, the clustering of words beginning
with the same consonant, is the mirror image of rhyme and
performs a similar psychic function.

Other formal components of poetry also have salutory effects
upon an inner sense of object loss and ego impoverishment. *Simile*
and *allusion* link two sets of images and ideas. More covertly,
metaphor performs the same function. It presents "one thing in the
semblance of another . . . (and) operates at the depth where
deep, but opposite truths are paradoxically valid and are reconciled" (Gorelick 1989, pp. 151–152). *Onomatopoeia*, the naming of a
thing or a function by using the sound associated with it, fuses the
sense experience and thought as well as the inner and external form
of words in language (Simopoulos 1977).

Common to all these literary devices is the aim of fusion, linkage,
and bringing things together. No wonder then, in poetry, primary
and secondary processes come together[7] and the literal and the
figurative acquire an optimal synergism (Rogers 1973). Contradictions are reconciled. Sense and thought merge. The reassuring
predictability of alliteration and rhyme strengthens object constancy
by playing a lexical peek-a-boo with the psyche. Allusion and metaphor exert a *depth-rendering* (Akhtar 1998) impact on the mind in so
far as they arrange the message being conveyed in a multi-layered,
figure-ground sort of architecture. Acting in unison, the various
formal constituents of poetry thus induce an increase in the
libidinal cathexis of links, bonds, and connectedness. In turn,
the symbolic value of this (i.e. mother–child unity) serves to bridge
the milkless abyss of separation from primary objects.[8]

---

6. For the transitional object-like functions of sound, see Sobel (1978) and
Weich (1978).

7. An optimal mixture of primary and secondary processes characterizes good
poetry. Excess of primary process makes it idiosyncratic, while excess of secondary
process makes it flat and didactic.

8. Turner and Poppel (1983) suggest that there might be neurophysiological
grounds as well for the soothing effect of poetry. The "musical and pictorial powers
of the right brain are enlisted by meter to cooperate with the linguistic power of the

Mentalization and the poetic content

Relying heavily on the prosodic qualities of language, poetry also seems to have an uncanny and direct access to the deepest layers of psyche, which is where mental pain usually originates and resides. If reading prose is like taking pills for arthritic ache, then reading poetry is akin to that of a steroid injection directly into an inflamed joint. In other words, poetry speaks to the unconscious and facilitates the *mentalization* (Fonagy and Target 1997) of the nonverbal substrate of the psyche. Reading poetry informs one about the inner state of affairs, enhances empathy with the self, and therefore facilitates mourning. Writing poetry involves self-holding, illusory though omnipotent manipulation of objects, discovery of the internal source of anguish through its mentalization,[9] and a mastery of pain through "self-dosed" (Cooper 1988a, p. 125) suffering and surviving that suffering. However, the poet not only gives expression to his own nebulous fantasies and unexpressed emotions, he also provides others an opportunity for vicarious venting of their unarticulated emotions by reading and co-creating, as it were, his artistic product. The poet becomes the "community's daydreamer" (Arlow 1986, p. 58) who uses not only delicately strung together words but also carefully placed omissions, and pauses to conduct the dialogue between his and others' deepest layers of psyche. Knights (1980) notes that

> all poets who make use of, say, the slightest of end-of-line pauses, no less than those modern poets who make typographical arrangements for silences, for pauses in the reading aloud, know how much can be achieved by it, provided, that is, that they have the art to obtain the reader's collaboration. (p. 127)

---

left; and by auditory driving effects, the lower levels of the nervous system are stimulated in such a way as to reinforce the cognitive functions of the poem, to improve the memory, and to promote physiological and social harmony" (p. 306).

9. Poets frequently find out what they were writing about only after they have completed a poem. The Nobel prize–winning Irish poet Seamus Heaney's (1995, p. 5) comment that in writing poetry, there is a "movement from delight to wisdom and not vice versa" refers to this very point.

This linguistic art of revealing via concealing and concealing via revealing lies at the heart of the poetic enterprise, especially in the realm of the unconscious fantasies being communicated via a particular poem.

TWO CLINICAL VIGNETTES

The first clinical vignette involves the psychologically beneficial use of a particular poem by an analytic patient. The second reports upon a *countertransference poem* of mine in response to a patient in analytic psychotherapy. Together, these vignettes should help clarify the foregoing elucidation of mental pain and the healing power of poetry vis-à-vis this affect.

It comes in waves

> No one, but no one, would have
> ever known what ails me
> But for where my eyes
> came to rest upon the book of verses.
> (Asad Ullah Khan Ghalib [1785–1869])[10]

A 40-year-old, married, child welfare attorney recalled the profound role played by a poem in her emotional life around 14 years of age. She was born in England and, from the beginning of life, was raised in an extremely affectionate foster family. At age four, she was reclaimed by her biological parents, who were equally loving and who were by then living in South Africa. Separation from her beloved foster mother was especially painful. The three-week journey by ship to South Africa did little to ease the little girl's anguish except that it led to the association of sea waves with waves of grief and tears. More problematically, her biological parents, while loving in all other regards, prohibited her talking about her foster mother. Lacking the "containing" (Bion 1987) and processing

---

10. Translations of the two couplets by Ghalib, arguably the greatest poet in the nearly 500 years of the history of Urdu language, are mine. Their amateur quality unfortunately might have robbed these verses of their stunning beauty.

function of maternal reverie, the little girl's pain went into an inner psychic exile.

Then at age 14, the patient had to separate from her biological parents in order to go to a boarding school; the family was living in a small town that had no good high school. Preparing to physically separate from her parents at a time when an ego move toward inner disengagement from them (Blos 1967) was also on the horizon stirred up severe pain in her. Memories of separation from her foster family also started to flood her mind.

Around this time, the patient discovered Alfred Tennyson's (1842, p. 165) poem "Break, break, break," a mournful lament of loss written on the death of his friend, the poet Arthur Hallam. The poem reads as follows:

> Break, break, break,
> On thy cold gray stones, O Sea!
> And I would that my tongue could utter
> The thoughts that arise in me.
>
> O well for the fisherman's boy,
> That he shouts with his sister at play!
> O well for the sailor lad,
> That he sings in his boat on the bay!
>
> And the stately ships go on
> To their haven under the hill;
> But O for the touch of a vanished hand,
> And the sound of a voice that is still!
>
> Break, break, break,
> At the foot of thy crags, O Sea!
> But the tender grace of a day that is dead
> Will never come back to me.

Reading the poem over and over again, with tears in her eyes and a lump in her throat, she attempted to master the pain of separation currently facing her, as well as the reawakened anguish of her earlier loss. The poem especially affected her since it is built around breaking ocean waves, an important associative element in her childhood separation trauma. However, associations to the sea were not restricted to the journey by ship to South Africa. In the patient's own words: "For me, the poem evoked the pain of the loss of my foster family at age 4 and, at the same time, the memory of the lost voices and the lost touch . . . In England, we lived near the harbor hence the significance of the sound of the sea—where my foster brother and I played together."

It seems that the patient had established a *nostalgic relationship* (Geahchan 1968) with the poem.[11] Like the bittersweet pleasure of nostalgia, reading the poem made her re-experience the childhood loss while also creating a fantasized reunion with the now idealized, lost objects. It provided a psychic space for the necessary mourning of the current pain of separation and, at the same time, for mastering the long dormant, earlier trauma. In giving voice to her hitherto mute agony and in witnessing her pain, the poem functioned as a good mother and a good analyst!

Raindrops falling on a river

> To lose itself in the bosom of river:
> a drop's ecstasy
> To become a remedy of its own sort:
> the outer limit of agony
>   (Asad Ullah Khan Ghalib [1785–1869])

A socially withdrawn, divorced accountant in her mid-40s was persuaded by her sister to seek help for a marked depression of about a year's duration.[12] This was precipitated by her being abruptly left by her married lover of quite some time. Since then, she had been pining for him, crying, and contemplating suicide. Her childhood background was one of much parental disdain, cold neglect, and occasional physical abuse. She could not recall a single pleasant experience with her mother and was generally scared of both her parents.

---

11. In this connection, it is interesting to note that the first ever psychoanalytic paper on the affect of nostalgia (Sterba 1940) was based upon the immigration experience of a four-year-old girl.

12. Certain other aspects of this case have been previously reported (Akhtar 1994).

For a long time, our work remained focused on her recently broken relationship. Session after session the patient spoke of this man. They used to meet for a set number of intoxicating hours each week. They laughed, played, talked, and made deeply satisfying love. Theirs had been an "ideal relationship" and now she was unable to let go of it. Indeed, she had held on to everything associated with him, including the pillow case on which he last rested his head, a newspaper he had left in her apartment, and so on. Her place— indeed her heart—was a shrine and he a god. He was all to her: "mommy, daddy, teddy bear, friend, lover, everything." As these details unfolded amid heart-wrenching crying, all I could do was to be a *witness* (Poland 1998), affirm her experience, and empathize with her loss.

It was during this phase of treatment that the following exchange between us took place. The patient entered the office as usual in a state of pain and near tears. I began the session by informing her that unfortunately on a rather short notice, I had to take the next week off from work. The patient nodded and soon afterward broke into tears. I waited quietly and as the crescendo of affect began its downward curve, I leaned forward and said: "It seems that my telling you that we would not be able to meet next week has really upset you, caused you pain." The patient looked at me with tear-filled eyes and said: "I have drowned in a river and you are talking to me about rain?" I felt stung by her sarcasm and her mocking devaluation of my comment. I also felt inwardly ashamed at my lack of empathy and the failure to recognize my relative unimportance (at least, on the conscious level) to her. Settling farther back in my chair (withdraw- ing from her?), I began to think and gradually became aware of the defensive purpose of her devaluation of me as well. She would not allow herself to be left again since she had been so traumatically left by her lover; I was to remain a nobody for her. Now I became aware that what I had failed to recognize was not my unimportance to her but her need to minimize my importance to her.

In the days that followed, her retort kept haunting me. Perhaps, being myself familiar with traumatic losses and unempathic helpers, I identified with her too much. That I also envied her brilliance in coming up with the image had not yet dawned upon me. Then a personal event, in which I felt quite shabbily treated by a friend I was seeking some help from, shook me up. I felt pain and, a few hours later, wrote the following poem. I gave it the title "To an impotent rescuer of my soul" (Akhtar 1993, p. 46).

> I lie on the floor of the ocean
> Wrapped in a green shawl of algae.
> My eyes loosened from their sockets
> >   float near my navel.
> My skin bloated.
> My finger nails, hors d'oeuvres for crustaceans.
> I lie on the floor of the ocean.
> Poemless. Long dead. Gone.
> And, you ask me
> If I am worried about the rain that is coming tonight?
> If I need a raincoat, an umbrella?
> How considerate of you.
> How thoughtful!

The amalgamation of the patient's pain and my pain, the incorporation of the patient's imagery and its embellishment by me, and the scathing union of her and my sarcasm, suggest a deep and profound *concordant identification* (Racker 1957) in countertransference. I became her and she became me. As though by resorting to a vocabulary of anguish, our separation was undone and the breach of empathy between us magically repaired. We now understood each other, it seemed. The "bad I" who did not understand her and the "bad Other" who did not empathize with me now became a fused target of our regressively joined bitterness. Also, in embroidering her metaphor with the graphic sequins of my imagery, I co-opted, indeed stole, her creativity; this awareness put me in touch with my envy of her smartness in making that remark.

The poem I wrote thus acted as a catalyst in self-analysis and helped me master the pain caused in me by her sarcasm, the pain I felt in identifying with her pain, and the pain I had felt in the real-life event unrelated to her treatment. After writing the poem, I became more peaceful about all three pains. Reading the poem informed me of my identification with her, my envy of her, as well as my angry competitiveness with her. It is as if I was trying to assert that she was not the only one who has suffered; I had suffered too.

Looking at the poem some days later, I also discerned the separation ("eyes loosened from their sockets," fingernail being removed) and closeness ("wrapped in a green shawl of algae," body parts being devoured by crustaceans) themes in it. Through all this, I came to know that the patient and I were dealing with loss, envy, paranoid regression, splitting, and predatory impulses to cannabilize the lost object. Writing the poem thus became "an act of peace," to use Pablo Neruda's (1977, p. 137) words regarding the enterprise of poetry in general. Not only did it diminish my pain, it also brought me greater knowledge about what was going on within and around me. The poem worked like an analyst and a supervisor.

CONCLUDING REMARKS

What these clinical examples have in common is that, in each instance, a poem enhanced the ego's processing of mental pain. Suffering was not put away or denied. Instead, the capacity to tolerate pain, to understand its external and internal sources, and to mourn was increased. Worthy of note in this connection is Bion's (1963, p. 62) emphasis upon the need for "the analytic experience to increase the patient's capacity for suffering even though the patient and analyst may hope to decrease pain itself." Joseph (1981), too, underscores the necessity to not retreat from pain but to suffer it, since only then is there a gradual awakening of interest in what has internally and externally been going on. Kogan (1990) voices a similar sentiment. And, long before these contributors, Ferenczi (1928) had emphatically declared that "It is not within the capacity of psychoanalysis entirely to spare the patient pain; indeed, one of the chief gains from psychoanalysis is the capacity to bear pain" (p. 90).

In essence, the examples provided previously demonstrate that poetry, far from being merely a psychic anodyne, can have an impact upon pain that is akin to a psychoanalytic intervention. While this seems a reasonable hypothesis, it is also true that the foregoing explication of the healing effect of poetry vis-à-vis mental pain remains far from exhaustive. It does not account for the variables of social class, intelligence, serendipity, individual differences in receptivity to poetry, and the talent for writing.

It also does not address three other important matters. First, the material presented here involves reading and writing poetry and not listening to poetry and reciting it. Although some space needs to be left for individual aesthetic and temperamental preferences, it is possible that auditory and visual pathways of a poem's entry into the psyche do not have similar effects. Similarly, reciting a poem might serve discharge and mastery functions additional to those served by writing it.

Second, it seems that certain cultures (and subcultures) are more receptive to poetry than others. In the words of the Nobel Prize winner, Russian poet Joseph Brodsky

> In the republic of ends
> and means that counts each deed
> poetry represents
> the minority of the dead. (1973, p. 136)

The reasons for differing cultural attitudes toward poetry seem complex and wide-ranging. On the one hand, economic and historical factors might play a role in whether poetry becomes a prevalent form of expression in a culture or not. Societies built around industry, consumerism, and production might have little "cultural space" to accommodate poetry. They might even deride it as the domain of little children, sentimental adolescents, and deranged psychotics. In contrast, societies based upon communal affiliation, faith, and celebration of rituals might find poetry psychosocially quite rewarding. Fundamentally "paternal" (emphasizing instruction, search, autonomy, and pragmatic mastery) versus fundamentally "maternal" (valuing affirmation, soothing, relatedness, and psychic consolidation) nature of cultures, in so far as such generalizations are possible, might also lead to an overvaluation of prose over poetry respectively. More to the point of this paper is the question of whether it is possible that the "poetry-receptive" cultures encourage mentalization of psychic pain while other cultures encourage self-dosed physicalization of it via a premium on athletics. This, too, deserves more thought, especially since it might enhance the analyst's empathy with pain-ridden patients from different cultures (Akhtar 1999a).

Finally, the dialectical relationship between culture and mental pain needs to be recognized. Culture can provide ready-made "container(s)" (Bion 1967) for the processing of mental pain (as in the first clinical example) and mental pain can result in creativity which adds to culture (as in the second clinical example). Pain and culture thus come to exist as loving cousins who often have significant things to offer each other.

2

WRITER'S BLOCK

In *Creative Writers and Day Dreaming*, Freud (1908a) wrote:

> A strong experience in the present awakens in the creative writer a
> memory of an earlier experience (usually belonging to his child-
> hood) from which there now proceeds a wish which finds its
> fulfillment in the creative work. The work itself exhibits elements of
> the recent provoking occasion as well as of the old memory. . . .
> The writer softens the character of his egoistic daydreams by altering
> and disguising it, as he bribes us by the purely formal—that is,
> aesthetic—yield of pleasure which he offers us in the presentation of
> his phantasies. (pp. 151, 153)

Such dilution makes it possible for the readers to connect their
own, similar fantasies with those of the writer and draw vicarious
gratification from the creative product. Thus the writer becomes the
"community's daydreamer" (Arlow 1986, p. 58).

Freud's scheme posits a three-step process in creativity. First,
there is the "strong experience in the present," that is, the mobili-
zation, usually sudden and unexpected, of powerful affects and
the fantasies under the influence of an environmental, external
trigger. This stage is passively experienced; it happens. Second is the
"wish" that Freud says proceeds from this feeling state. The wish
presumably is to find a release of the tension, a solution of the

problem now faced by the mind, or at least to master the passively experienced intense affect. Finally, there is the step involving "creative work," that is, the ego's effort to give some palatable and even enjoyable shape and form to the different wishes and fantasies mobilized by the entire experience. Freud hints at the nature of such creative work by talking of softening, altering, and disguising of the underlying wishes.

To put it in a poetic metaphor, the situation is akin to the ocean throwing a shell on the beach, a toddler's picking it up and carrying it to his mother, and finally, the mother's cleaning it up, putting a thread through the shell and turning it into a necklace. Clearly, psychic freedom is needed and much ego activity is involved here. Many things can go wrong in this process. What if the ocean spits a shell out on the beach and there is no child to pick it up? What if the child picks the shell up but cannot find his mother? And, so on. Such hurdles constitute the dynamics of writer's block.

DEFINITION AND PHENOMENOLOGY

The term *writer's block* was introduced by the prolific psychoanalyst, Edmund Bergler (1899–1962) in 1947.[13] Coined to denote the drying up of a writer's wellspring of creative imagination, the phrase gained wide currency owing to its brevity and self-evident nature. A closer examination of the situation reveals that many subtle phenomena are involved here. First, while the term suggests a total stoppage of productivity by a writer, the fact is that many lesser degrees of inhibition can also be subsumed under it. A writer's feeling distracted in the course of his work, finding writing hard, and being less prolific than usual are also manifestations of writer's block. However, writer's block must be distinguished from the refractoriness or "lying fallow" (Khan 1983) that almost invariably happens between episodes of intense creativity. The former is emotionally turbulent, the latter peaceful. Second, the term *writer's block* subtly implies transience to the inhibition of creativity. It seems

---

13. The history of this term, like all history, is difficult to unravel and the credit for having located its first usage (Bergler, 1947, p. 455) must go to Leader (1991).

to say that creative force is blocked today but will be free-flowing tomorrow. This excludes the more permanent sort of blocks some writers develop. For instance, there might occur a gap of years and, at times, decades between the two books of a writer. Henry Roth, for instance, could not write for nearly six decades following the publication of his highly acclaimed novel *Call It Sleep* (1934). Another author (e.g. Ralph Ellison) might write only one novel and seem utterly unable to write another one. Third, the writer's block might be of a focal sort. In other words, it might apply to one and not another genre used by the author.[14] Fourth, many types of dysphoric affects accompany writer's block. These include shame, helplessness, anxiety, depression, and even despair. The relationship among such affects and writer's block is complex. In "primary" writer's block, the creative inhibition is the cause of these emotions. In "secondary" writer's block, a major psychiatric disorder, for instance, severe depression (Styron 1996), is at the base of the inhibited creativity. While difficult to make, such distinctions are important in selecting therapeutic strategies. Fifth, the unpleasant emotions accompanying writer's block might mobilize defenses that further complicate the clinical picture. Prominent among these defenses are denial (e.g. forcing one's way through and producing contrived material) and rationalization (e.g. claiming to be otherwise busy or physically unwell).

While all this expands the phenomenology of writer's block, it still leaves some questions unanswered. For instance, what is the relationship between creative impotence and excessive drinking? Certainly, the "drinking-writing symbiosis" (Nelson 1993, p. 71) has been both disastrous and salutary. There have been writers (e.g. Charles Baudelaire, Tennessee Williams, and Anne Sexton) whose careers were destroyed by alcohol and there have been those (e.g. Edgar Allen Poe, John Berryman, and Dylan Thomas) who continued to produce excellent work while drinking excessively. Another question pertains to gender. In other words, does writer's block

---

14. The renowned Indian poet, Majrooh Sultanpuri (1919–1999), could not write a "ghazal" for years while producing a steady flow of made-to-order songs for the Bombay film industry. I remember to this day when, some 35 years ago, one morning he arrived at our house, in a state of near manic excitement, to tell my father that he had finally been able to write a "ghazal"!

differ in frequency, form, intensity, or duration among men and women? Or, does writer's block in women have different origins than in men? Leader (1991), in a detailed historical account of the difficulties faced by women writers, suggests that the origins of such blocks are "neither strictly 'psychological' (as in oedipal or object-relations scenarios) nor strictly literary-historical (as in influence anxiety)" (p. 238–250). Nelson (1993), a woman, differs and stresses that the blocks faced by women writers reflect the internalization of socially disparaging attitudes toward them. Clearly, further investigation is needed here.

The phenomenological variations of writer's block across the life span and across cultures also remain to be elucidated. Yet another area that needs to be explored is that of the various rituals and conditions that seem necessary for a writer to accomplish his or her work. Some writers need to listen to music in order to write. Others require a specific type of pen or paper. Still others have to sit in a particular place or drink a set number of cups of tea or coffee. Such practices seem unconscious attempts at creating a holding environment for the self so that it can become raptly absorbed in the playful state necessary for creativity.

Finally, there is the amusing paradox of writing about writer's block. The writer, actor, and performer Spalding Gray has written a hilarious monologue called *Monster in a Box* (1992) about this matter. Utilizing the ocean–toddler–mother metaphor mentioned in the beginning of this chapter, my poem titled "Writer's Block" (Akhtar 1985, p. 36) chisels the outlines of a damned-up imagination from the dark rock of creative paralysis:

> From the Boardwalk
> I glance at the beach
> The little boy who gathers shells vigorously
> And his mother
> To whom he brought these gifts proudly, and
> Who turned them into
> Named pets
> Frozen stories
> Are no where to be seen.
> Just the udders of the ocean searching the grip of familiar hands
> are visible.

I look with interest, faint sadness.
For I know the touch of my worldly hands
Will turn the soft tissue into bone
For I know that I am not the little boy
Or his mother. Not right now.
Right now I can only glance at the beach
From the boardwalk
And wait.

This delineation of the descriptive features of writer's block prepares the ground for delving into the etiology of this disturbing symptom. I begin such consideration by turning to Freud.

EARLY PSYCHOANALYTIC LITERATURE

In *Inhibitions, Symptoms, and Anxiety,* Freud (1926) laid down the groundwork for understanding why and how an ego capacity once available can come to be eclipsed. While not referring specifically to writer's block, Freud's views on ego inhibition are of paramount significance in understanding this phenomenon:

> The ego function of an organ is impaired if its erotogeneticity—its sexual significance—is increased . . . inhibitions obviously represent a relinquishment of a function whose exercise would produce anxiety. . . . There are clearly also inhibitions which serve the purpose of self-punishment. This is often the case in inhibitions of occupational activities. The ego is not allowed to carry on those activities, because they would bring success and gain, and these are things which the severe superego has forbidden. (pp. 89, 90)

In addition to these specific reasons of sexualization, anxiety, and guilt, work inhibitions can also arise out of the overall economic conditions of the ego. Freud noted that

> when the ego is faced with a particularly difficult psychical task, as occurs in mourning or when there is some tremendous suppression of affect or when a continual flood of sexual phantasies is being kept

down, it loses so much of the energy at its disposal that it has to cut
down the expenditure of it at many points at once. (p. 90)[15]

Subsequent analysts (Fenichel 1945, Hendricks 1943) elaborated
on the dynamics of work inhibitions but did not add anything
specific to the understanding of writer's block. Even Greenacre, an
important early contributor to the understanding of creativity,
hardly addressed the topic. However, her work does contain a
blueprint for the potential dynamics of writer's block. For instance,
in a series of papers (1955, 1957, 1958a, 1958b, 1959), she delineated the following four characteristics of the creative mind:

> First, greater sensitivity to sensory stimulation; second, unusual
> capacity for awareness of relations between various stimuli; third,
> predisposition to an empathy of wider range and deeper vibration
> than usual; and fourth, intactness of sufficient sensorimotor equip-
> ment to allow the building up of projective motor discharges for
> expressive functions. (1958a, p. 485)

Impingements on any of these four factors could presumably constitute impediments in the path of creativity. Greenacre also noted

------

15. Difficulties in writing that occur after migration to a linguistically different
environment partly owe their origin to the burdensome task of mourning.
However, there are other factors involved as well. One, for instance, involves the
formal structure of expression. Poetry travels poorly across cultures. Emanating
from a psychic space between music and prose, poetry relies heavily on the prosodic
qualities of language. That, most likely, is the reason why great poetry has never
been written in a later-acquired language. With prose too, matters are far from
simple. That an ordinary immigrant writer might have difficulty expressing himself
in a newly acquired language goes without saying. Those with exceptional skills,
however, circumvent, work-through, or even incorporate areas of relative and
micro-blocks in their use of a second language. For instance, Eugene Ionesco,
Vladimir Nabokov, Samuel Beckett, and Salman Rushdie are four immigrant writers
who show four completely different attitudes in this regard. Ionesco never wrote in
his mother tongue and chose French instead to express his creativity. Nabokov
moved in succession from a mastery of Russian, French, and German to English, in
which he wrote his best-known works. Beckett "migrated" to French and after many
years returned to writing in his native English. Rushdie freely sprinkles his English
text with Urdu/Hindi colloquialisms from India and thus creates a hybrid language
of his own.

that creative work is hardly ever undertaken for self-gratification alone; it has "rather universally the character of a love gift, to be brought as near perfection as possible and to be presented with pride and misgiving" (p. 490). Rich "family romance" (Freud 1909) fantasies, aggressive action upon the environment, and turning personal pain into collective pleasure also contribute to the creative act. The experience of anxiety rather than impeding creativity, at times fuels it. Moreover,

> in some instances the preliminary suffering also is a kind of penance which permits the creative artist, who is guilty for the possession of this superior ability, to claim it and possess it at least for the time being. (Greenacre, 1959, p. 572)

Freud especially is known to have required a certain amount of physical suffering to do his most creative work. He "confessed" this in his personal correspondence to Fliess at least on two separate occasions.

> I returned to a sense of too much well-being and have since then been very lazy because the modicum of misery essential for intensive work will not come back (and) My style has unfortunately been bad because I feel too well physically; I have to feel somewhat miserable to write well. (Freud's letters of April 16, 1896, and September 6, 1899, respectively, in Masson, 1985, pp. 180–181 and p. 370)

Thus states of psychosocial comfort rather than facilitating can paradoxically inhibit creativity and lead to writer's block. Under such circumstances, all a writer can do is to wait for a "modicum of misery" (Freud 1896, in Masson 1985, p. 180) to return. My poem "Full Circle" (Akhtar 1985, p. 31) attempts to capture this very psychic situation.

> And then
> Once without agony
> He chose to write a poem, but words
> Froze on his lips
> Became pebbles. The ink in his pen
> Dried up, and
> His imagination led him to a land without wells.

> So he gave up
> And began
> Waiting for moments of anguish
> In trembling apprehension
> And joyful hope.

Returning to Greenacre's work, it can be safely said that while it offers significant hints about the nature of writer's block, it does not offer a focused elucidation of the phenomenon. The first psychoanalytic contribution of this sort came from Edmund Bergler.

FROM EDMUND BERGLER TO RONALD BRITTON

A prolific contributor to the psychoanalytic literature, Bergler showed a deep interest in the psychology of writers. He saw the writer as struggling with one basic conflict: "undigested masochistic passivity connected with the giant of the nursery—Mother" (1952, p. 81). Bergler asserted that the writer writes to furnish inner alibis to his tormenting inner conscience.

> Unconsciously the writer utilizes a unique defense in the course of his alibiing refutation. The indictment reads: "You want to be masochistically refused (milk, love, tenderness) by the image of the preoedipal mother." The alibi presented reads: "That's impossible, I want to get; Mother does not even exist. Hence she can not refuse." To prove the (rather scurrile) point, the writer acts *both* roles—that of the *giving* mother and the *recipient* child—on his own person. He *gives* to himself, out of himself, beautiful words and ideas, thus establishing an *autarchy* . . . Whereas the typical neurotic needs *two* people (himself and an object) for unconscious reenactment of an infantile fantasy, the writer *combines both roles into one.* (pp. 81–82, italics in the original)

Bergler added that by seeking wide readership and acceptance of his work, the writer enlists the world-at-large to partake of his inner guilt. Other dynamic forces are operative as well. For instance, the writer also struggles with voyeuristic tendencies involved in imagination—"a purified successor to infantile peeping" (Bergler 1952,

p. 91)—and the exhibitionistic defense (having others look at his work) against it. Bergler regarded the writer's chronic exhibitionism as a moral alibi against his deep-seated voyeurism.

Bergler offered some very interesting ideas regarding the phenomenology and etiology of writer's block. He noted that writer's block might be total or partial.

> There exists an interesting intermediary phase observable in many writers between the threatening productive sterility and the last attempts to maintain productivity. This phase may be called defensive trash.[16] The moment the writer begins to produce that brand of trash, the breakdown of his productivity is imminent. (p. 129)

Bergler emphasized that the subjective dread of becoming unable to produce anything meaningful is not necessarily indicative of writer's block; this feeling is a constant companion of all writers. Other indicators of an imminent collapse of literary productivity seem more reliable. The length of written pieces becomes shorter. An insecurity sets in regarding the material, especially about the psychological motivations of characters, if the work under progress is that of fiction. Style becomes tense. Worst, the writer begins to look to others to provide ideas.

> If a writer who previously has done good and original work starts to be influenced by suggestions as to what and how to write, it does not mean that he has changed into a hack; the phenomenon is a precursor of writing block. (p. 132)

Bergler offered significant insights in the realm of etiology as well. According to him, writer's block represents a defeat in the inner moral battle that is the fate of every writer. Four hurdles constitute the foundation of writer's block. The first is "the hurdle of 'oral refusal' as defense" (p. 113). Asserting that productivity thrives only on "autarchic grounds" (p. 114), Bergler portrayed the blocked writer as countering the inner accusation of wanting refusal

---

16. Norman Mailer (1966) has compared forcing oneself to write to making love without desire. "It is hopeless, it desecrates one's furture" (p. 124).

by refusing himself. However, this unwittingly leads him to leave the autarchic situation where he reigned supreme and could give to himself (i.e. create). The second hurdle is that of too little distance between repressed wish and defense. Issues of content (i.e. what one was going to write about) become pertinent in this context. The third hurdle is that of voyeurism. Bergler emphasized that

> it is only when the writer succeeds, unconsciously, in convincing his inner Frankenstein of conscience that his creative imagination does not any longer constitute peeping that his imagination worked. Otherwise, the superego vetoes the procedure, and the result is lack of imagination—or, more precisely *inability* to imagine. (p. 91, italics in the original)

The fourth hurdle is that of "increase of neurosis" (p. 127) especially in its oral regressive manifestations. Thus alcoholism, sexual impotence, deep masochistic depression, and breakthrough of psychopathic impulses can sap the energy of the writer and lead to writer's block. Together these four tributaries lead to writer's block that Bergler wryly termed the *grand block*, as opposed to the *abortive block*, which lasts a few weeks and resolves spontaneously. However, a series of abortive blocks might be a precursor of a grand block. Bergler noted that grand block happens more often in literary writers than in pulp writers. The latter write more from formulas than from inspiration anyway. Moreover, their writing is unconsciously degrading to them and thus satisfies their masochistic strivings.

Bergler's contribution (1947, 1950) to the understanding of writer's block, made in the 1950s, remained peculiarly isolated for a long time. Few subsequent analysts paid attention to the topic. Even Greenacre (1955, 1957), who did address literary creativity, said little about writer's block.

Such silence persisted until Britton (1994) delineated his concept of *publication anxiety*. Viewing it to be ubiquitous, Britton sees such anxiety as leading to writing and publishing inhibition, symptomatic disorders of the text, or simply overt anxiety. The first of these three is of concern here. According to Britton, "a profound fear of rejection by the primary intended listener" (p. 1214) underlies the inability to write.[17] Matters are more complex, however. After all, there is a deep

> conflict inherent in public utterance. The conflict is between the urge to communicate a novel idea to a receptive audience, thus winning their allegiance and the conflicting wish to say something to bind the author to his affiliates and ancestors by the utterance, in a shared language, of shared beliefs—the recital of a creed as a means of unification. This involves the author in a triangular situation which becomes an incarnation of the Oedipus situation. (p. 1215)

Invoking Bion's (1963, 1970) designations of L, H, and K as the three potential links among psychic objects, that is, the desires to love (and be loved), hate (and be hated) and know (and be known), Britton suggests that the oedipal conflict is not restricted to loving and hating but can also involve the desires to love and know. The phantasied consequences of the assertion of knowledge within triangular space, "a space bounded by the three persons of the oedipal situation and all their possible relationships" (Britton 1989, p. 86), can play havoc with creative faculties. In the act of writing, the writer seeks to woo his primary audience and fears retaliation from critics; this replicates the oedipal situation and, if the attendant anxieties are great, leads to writer's block.

> When he writes, the author addresses, in phantasy, an imaginary audience who are the counterpart of the internal parental object whom he hoped to impress or convince. When he publishes, in phantasy, he not only puts this to the test, he invites a *non-participating onlooker*, the other internal parent, to witness his address. I believe that new discoveries of however modest a sort evoke, once-again, the Oedipus situation. Gaining knowledge of an object engenders in the individual a sense of possessing it, and thus it evokes anxiety lest this will provoke retaliation from a third party: publication advertises the possession of the knowledge. (p. 1216)

Anxiety regarding writing and publishing is lesser if it merely refines an established paradigm and greater if it challenges that

---

17. For an elaboration of this dynamic (among other factors) in the case of psychoanalysts who do not write, see Stein (1988a, 1988b).

paradigm. While, at first glance, this seems applicable to scientific fields only, the fact is that a certain iconoclasm is inherent in creativity of any sort. W.H. Auden's mischievous quip that "there is no creativity without audacity" captures the essence of this paradox. Britton (1994) illustrates all this by citing Winnicott's early struggles vis-à-vis Melanie Klein's established position and Darwin's amazing boldness being suppressed, for a long time, by his fears of scientific establishment's harsh reaction to his ideas.[18]

OTHER CONTEMPORARY VIEWS

Following Britton, the subject of writer's block drew the attention of three other psychoanalysts contributing to an edited volume titled *Work and Its Inhibitions* (Socarides and Kramer 1997). These were Maria Bergmann, Lucy Daniels Inman, and Stanley Olinick. Bergmann highlighted the disturbance of narcissism and self-esteem regulation in blocked writers. She noted that such an individual is unable to invest creative work with an adequate amount of healthy narcissism.[19] Based upon detailed clinical material from three analyses, Bergmann offered valuable guidelines for the treatment of such cases. The patient's inner aggression against the creative potential needs to be countered by active therapeutic support of the analyst. Such "extra-analytic activities (might involve) . . . either seeing or hearing something concrete that was in 'creative trouble' or crisis" (p. 204). This can lead to the creative product to be

---

18. Mahler's (Mahler et al. 1975) ideas regarding optimal distance between mother and child are also pertinent here. Creativity requires moving away from a deeply internalized tradition (i.e. the mother of symbiosis) and stretching the *psychic tether* (Akhtar 1992a) to its extreme. Staying close to it keeps one a literary "good boy" or "good girl," while breaking the tether results in utter disaffiliation and Escher-like madness. A creative writer has to avoid both these hazards while accommodating the two poles of his desire i.e. to remain close to the mother tradition and to be himself. Winnicott's (1971) declaration that "there is no originality except on the basis of tradition" best summarizes this situation.

19. This does not preclude a parallel but split-off existence of excessive narcissism and megalomanic self images. An extremely witty, fictional description of a writer giving vent to such fantasies during his analysis is provided by Wheelis (1990, pp. 82–83).

cathected within a shared "narcissistic alliance" (p. 205), which might protect it from the patient's destructive tendencies. At the same time, the analyst must be careful to not monopolize the process and must assure that the patient feels unthreatened in being the sole creator of the product. This is of crucial significance since, as children, many creative individuals have been the caregivers to their parents and have felt used and unconsciously enraged at such exploitation. This last-mentioned theme is also voiced by Inman (1997), herself a therapist and an established writer of novels and short stories. She states that

> a psychological "room of one's own" is a necessity for effective creating. Not only does the creative person need to have autonomy and authority in addressing the medium, he or she also needs to have the confidence that putting one's innermost self out before the world will not result in humiliation due to characteristics clung to unconsciously. For this to be possible, the creative person must feel free to claim his or her inner space and have the courage to sweep it clean (through symbolizations that permit increasingly internal separation and individuation) of characterological hindrances. (p. 131)

With poignant personal details, Inman offers the reader a glimpse of her own inner world of creativity, its blockage, and her painstaking triumph over such inhibition. The theme highlighted by Bergmann (1997), namely the need to free oneself from early parental introjects, is clearly evident in Inman's essay. What is striking, however, is the use of recording various thoughts, feelings, and insights as well as her dreams in her "copy book" (p. 120), which allowed for a transitional space between writing and not writing, between experiencing and understanding, and between her ongoing analysis and her self-analysis. While such transitional measures cannot be prescribed in the course of treatment, a blocked writer's spontaneous "discovery" of them might herald a salutary outcome. Inman's essay thus not only emphasizes the tranformative value of symbolization, it delineates an interesting method of creating a mental space for such symbolization to begin, even if it is inchoate and scattered in the beginning.

The necessity for such psychic freedom in writing was also underscored by Olinick (1997), who noted that conflicts centering

around envy, competitiveness, curiosity, and scopophilia often contribute to the development of writer's block. The process of writing
(both the act itself and the conceptualization of syntax) can itself
become instinctualized and conflict-laden. The most important
factor in both writing and writer's block, however, remains the
nature of one's relationship with one's internal objects. In a
self-disclosing passage, Olinick states that

> during many years, I was at times peripherally aware of writing for
> a vaguely defined, taciturn, critical colleague in some distant city. It
> was necessary for me to keep that fantasy satisfied with the quality
> and nature of my output. This was a projection of superego and
> ego-ideal processes representing a variety of attitudes and control
> over my self-esteem, with a readiness at times to give begrudging
> commendation. (p. 184)

The softening of such introjects and their subsequent loving
approval of one's creativity permits one to produce. In contrast, the
harshness of such internal imagos and their "narcissistic" control of
one's mind leads to conflict-laden, unimaginative, and blocked
writing.

The views of various authors mentioned previously can be brought
together utilizing an object-relations perspective. Thus writer's
block can be seen to result from an inner submission to early
masochistic ties (Bergler 1952), internalization of others' disregard
of one's autonomy and the resulting narcissistic imbalance (Bergmann 1997, Inman 1997), dread of harsh introjects (Olinick 1997),
and oedipally tinged anxieties over charming the reader and being
attacked be the critic (Britton 1994). While emphasizing different
roots of writer's block, most authors seem to gather around the
primacy of aggressivized internal object relations as the cause of
the symptom. This said, I now turn to a recent book-length work
on the subject.

THE RECENT MONOGRAPH BY KOLODNY

Susan Kolodny, a California poet and psychotherapist, has recently
written a well-intentioned, informative, engaging and yet peculiarly

unsatisfying book called *The Captive Muse* (Kolodny 2000) on creativity and its inhibitions. Well versed in psychoanalytic theory, Kolodny devotes focused attention to the phenomenon of writer's block. She views it as arising from multiple conscious and unconscious sources. Prominent among these are anxieties pertaining to the content of the potential topic. Such "resistance to content" (p. 6) tends to develop where what is about to get *mentalized* (Fonagy and Target 1997) is at odds with the creator's sense of self and/or is associated with an unmetabolized traumatic situation.

Inhibitions of creativity arise from other sources as well. Thus the unconscious meanings of creative activity itself can be threatening and block the ego functions pertinent in this regard. This is especially so when developing one's artistic potential comes to represent a fatal outdoing of parents and siblings.

> The sense of danger many feel when we do, or want to do, creative work, often derives from our own fantasies about excluding others, competing with and outdoing them . . . (however) . . . the unconscious belief that creative work is dangerous, comes not only from our own fantasies and wishes. Sometimes it comes, at least in part, from actual experiences with the environment, and what we do with these in our imagination. (Kolodny 2000, p. 21)

Conscious concerns surrounding immersion in a creative endeavor, which almost invariably detaches one from the social surround, can become threatening and might block creativity. Kolodny states

> Writing is a glorious opportunity to leave others out and to live alone in my poem. But the excitement of this had to outweigh the anxiety and to become acceptable to me before I could allow myself to have it. I had to feel that excluding others for hours from my attention or awareness would not necessarily reveal to them my essential disloyalty in preferring my own company to theirs, my thoughts to theirs, my pleasure in writing to their pleasure, real or imagined, in having me always available to them. I had to feel that tuning others out would not necessarily hurt or destroy them, leaving me alone in the universe. Of course, while fears that excluding others is aggressive and will hurt or alienate them can result from our knowledge of their

vulnerability, such fears can also result from our own aggression or competitiveness. (p. 20)

Other inhibitions arise from anxiety regarding the disconcerting effects of the ego regression essential for creative activity, narcissistic resistances to the inevitable task of revising and fine-tuning a product, the nature and/or intensity of affects mobilized by creative work, and threatening transferences to the imagined readers or viewers.[20] In the last-mentioned context, Kolodny makes the following pithy and sophisticated observation:

> Though we are generally unaware of these transferences as we work, the ease of or difficulty with which we proceed, the pleasure or panic we experience, can surely alert us to their presence, perhaps even their shape. Such transferences vary for the same writer or artist with different subject matter and in different emotional states. Several may be present as we work, some helpful, some a hindrance. I suspect they have kinship with muses. (p. 49)

Besides delineating the complex etiology of inhibited creativity, Kolodny elucidates its various manifestations from the most severe to the relatively subtle, almost water-color, types. Thus creative blocks are seen to range from total artistic constipation and tortured procrastination through diffusion of focus and surrender to cliches to reluctance in undertaking necessary revisions and inability to achieve closure by letting go of a piece of creative work.

While focusing upon intrapsychic factors, Kolodny is not unmindful that creativity can, at times, be thwarted by sociopolitical and racial oppression. Such factors, she believes, have

> undoubtedly helped to silence generations of writers and other artists whose life experiences and sensibilities have seemed to them, because of the prevailing literary, artistic, and social climates, as well as because of problems in self-esteem, not legitimate or worthwhile sources of art. (p. 9)

---

20. Here Kolodny's (2000) views come very close to those proposed by Britton (1994) and summarized in the preceding section of this chapter.

Other, less magisterial, external forces (pp. 97–113) that inhibit creativity include parental disinterest, the disparagement of a particular form of creativity by a given culture (e.g. that of poetry in the current North American society), discouraging experiences with school teachers, and even financial constraints that can draw one's attention away from the inner pantheon of muses. Kolodny also discusses the role of gender (p. 42, pp. 109–112). She suggests that men tend to experience greater anxiety vis-à-vis the regression accompanying creative endeavors. Women tend to feel more conflicted in their split allegiance to the (internalized) social dictates of responsibility toward others and to their authentic self-expression. All in all, Kolodny's effort at describing, elucidating, and unmasking the nature of inhibited and blocked creativity seems reasonably successful. And, yet, one is left dissatisfied. There are four reasons for this.

First, it never becomes clear as to who is the audience for this book. Educated laity? Mental health professionals? Both? If the book is intended for the former, then why cite bibliographic references in mid-text and why seek a profession-bound publisher? If the intended audience is professionals, then why adopt a tone that is so informal as to border on being chatty?

Second, Kolodny's manner of writing is rather uninspiring. To be sure, the text contains spicy quotes from this or that poet or artist, but there is little from the author herself that evokes a sigh, scream, sob, or stir. For a poet, the author's language is surprisingly flat and unpoetic.

Third, Kolodny's coverage of psychoanalytic literature leaves much to be desired. Ferenczi's (1911) seminal paper on obscene words is not mined for its riches in the book's discussion (p. 47) of concretization of language, which mixes up the sense and meanings of words. Bergler's (1952) notions about writer's block and Britton's (1994) elucidation of *publication anxiety* are also not mentioned. Balint's (1958) psychic *area of creation* is not invoked in the context of withdrawal necessary for creative work (pp. 22–23). Pollock's (1975, 1977) and Hamilton's (1969, 1976) evocative and metapsycholgically anchored essays on the relationship among object loss, mourning, and creativity, also escape the author's attention. Rose's (1964, 1980) sophisticated, step-by-step delineation of the creative process is also not included. Any and all such omissions, however, pale in the face of the fact that this seemingly psychoanalytically informed book on creativity has not one citation to Freud's work (1907, 1908, 1928) in this realm.

Finally, while Kolodny's book does contain some interesting ideas, these remain ill-developed. Examples include the potentially anxiety-provoking effects of linguistic regression (p. 45), the notion of "distracted states" (p. 40) among writers, the feeling of being shallow that can develop as a result of childhood deprivation (p. 10), rituals associated with beginning creative work (p. 85), and so on. Similarly, while the book discusses too little revising as a form of block, it overlooks too much revising as an impediment to creativity as well.

Such reservations not withstanding, the fact is that Kolodny's book does explore many fascinating details about writer's block in a meaningful and informative way. Even the fact that she devotes extensive attention to this curious, troubling, clinically frequent, and yet understudied problem, is highly welcome.

CONCLUDING REMARKS

Pulling this diverse material together makes it possible to make succinct, even if complex and multilayered, statements about the *phenomenology, etiology,* and *treatment* of writer's block. The *phenomenology* of the disorder can be portrayed along many binary axes. First, writer's block can be primary or secondary; the former is a syndrome unto itself, the latter a consequence of another independent psychiatric disorder, such as depression or alcoholism. Second, writer's block can be partial or total; a writer can plod through distressing inhibitions or become paralyzed and completely unable to write. Third, writer's block can be transient or permanent; most author's experience temporary inhibitions of creativity, others get frozen forever. Fourth, writer's block can be intrinsic or situational; the former is independent of external circumstances, the latter a result of radically changed external realities (e.g. sudden poverty, early phases of immigration and exile). Finally, writer's block can be pervasive or focal; the former precludes the writer from writing anything, the latter eliminates only a certain genre from the writer's ouvere.

The *etiology* of the disorder is similarly complex. Leaving aside the case of "secondary" writer's block emanating from a major psychiatric disorder, one can find many psychodynamic origins of such inhibition. First, writer's block might result from a non-specific, overwhelmed state of the ego as happens, for instance, during mourning. Second, writer's block might result from the inability to create the self-holding function derived from the early holding experiences with the mother. Third, writer's block can follow excessive guilt over the replacement of the object mother by one's own self. Fourth, writer's block might be a manifestation of anxiety over the separation from a tradition that has become unconsciously equated with the symbiotic mother. Finally, writer's block can result from anxiety over desires to please an imaginary audience and fears of one's critics, especially if these two parties come to represent the parental couple in the unconscious; the shadow of unresolved Oedipus complex is clearly discernible under these circumstances.

Treatment of writer's block should take its aforementioned complexities into account. A careful evaluation needs to be made first, whether the block is but one manifestation of an underlying major psychiatric disorder or an independent symptom complex. In the former case, treatment of the primary disorder takes precedence and might itself resolve the symptom. In the latter case, the writer's block needs to be specifically treated. One can then recommend psychoanalysis proper or psychoanalytically informed psychotherapy specifically focused upon the writer's block. The choice depends upon many factors. These include duration and tenacity of the block, presence of other symptoms and inhibitions, the overall level of personality organization, and the nature of the patient's motivation for seeking help. My preference, admittedly based upon only a modest experience in this realm, is to lean toward the more conservative stance of recommending focal psychoanalytic psychotherapy. Such decision is facilitated if the block is of a short duration, is considerably ego-dystonic, is unaccompanied by other symptoms, and occurs in the setting of an otherwise sound personality organization. The existence of a mutually agreed upon goal (i.e. dissolution of the block) should, however, not preclude the exploration of wide-ranging, unconscious factors contributing to the inhibition. Two questions that I have found useful to raise as opening gambits in such clinical work are "Who have you so far written for?" and "Why not be content with what you have already written?" Learning the details of the rituals surrounding the actual writing can also yield clues to deeper issues. Such pointedness of approach does not, however, permit role modeling and advice giving. At the same time, it should be acknowledged that the analyst's demonstration of active interest in the patient's creativity can lead to a "transference cure." Neither entirely avoidable nor utterly undesirable, such dynamics should be tempered by a bit of humor and non-literalness. Through the latter, a transitional quality is imparted to the "transference cure," thus permitting further thought, play, and analytic resolution of it in the due course of time, often after the treatment is long over.

Part II

UNRECOGNIZED PERSONALITIES

3

THE SHY NARCISSIST

Ever since the DSM-III (1980) recognized Narcissistic Personality Disorder as a distinct entity, attempts have been made to refine its phenomenological portrait. An important aspect of these efforts (Akhtar 1989, Akhtar and Thomson 1982, Cooper 1989, Horowitz 1989, Kernberg 1989, Ronningstam 1988, Ronningstam and Gunderson 1989) has been to note that the characteristic manifestations of this disorder—grandiosity, exhibitionism, envy, ambition—are sometimes hidden underneath a superficial facade of modesty and shyness. A detailed clinical description of this variant of narcissistic personality disorder and of its distinctions from the usual flamboyant type have not yet been provided.

In this chapter, I will attempt to delineate the profile of such a *shy narcissist*. I will do so by combining the insights gleaned from (1) revisiting the pertinent material covered in my two earlier reviews (Akhtar 1989, Akhtar and Thomson 1982) of the literature on narcissistic personality, (2) relevant publications by others since my last review of the topic, and (3) my own experience of treating narcissistic patients. I will also highlight the similarities and differences the shy narcissistic personality has with the usual narcissistic personality and certain other personality disorders. I will conclude by commenting upon the implications of recognizing this syndrome.

SURVEY OF THE PSYCHOANALYTIC LITERATURE

Freud introduced the term *narcissism* into psychiatric literature (Freud 1905) and delineated its role in object choices and ego-ideal formation (Freud 1914a). Later, he described the "narcissistic character type" (Freud 1931) and noted its impressive, assertive, and power-seeking attributes. Freud's pioneering description, however, offered little clue regarding the existence of a shy or covert type of narcissistic personality.

The first such hint is found in a paper by Jones (1913), written 18 years before Freud's 1931 description of the narcissistic character. While the term *narcissistic personality* does not appear in Jones' paper, the "God complex" it described is perhaps the first portrayal of the condition. Jones eloquently described the narcissist's grandiosity, exaggerated need for praise, search for glory, and love of language. More significantly, he noted that narcissistic grandiosity is often masked by an "unusually strong series" of opposing tendencies. Prominent among these were undue humility, social reserve, and pretended contempt for money in real life. Unlike the flamboyant, openly acquisitive, and assertive type of narcissistic personality, such individuals are

> characterized by a desire for aloofness, inaccessibility, and mysteriousness, often also by a modesty and self-effacement. They are happiest in their own home, in privacy and seclusion, and like to withdraw to a distance. They surround themselves and their opinions with a cloud of mystery, exert only an indirect influence on external affairs, never join in any common action, and are generally unsocial. They take great interest in psychology . . . phantasies of power are common, especially the idea of possessing great wealth. They believe themselves to be omniscient, and tend to reject all new knowledge. (p. 262)

Following Jones, Reich (1972) also noted that narcissistic personalities either acquire fame and social power or tend toward daydreaming and addiction. Tartakoff's (1966) later distinction between the active fantasy of being the "powerful one" (destined to perform outstanding deeds) and the passive fantasy of being the "special one" (chosen by virtue of inherent uniqueness to receive windfalls) also hinted at two types of narcissistic organizations. Bach (1977) more directly addressed this issue. He noted that narcissistic patients have a divided self in which the hidden part of themselves shows a "mirror complementarity" with their conscious complaints. To the now well-recognized phenomenon of a grandiose individual being secretly afraid of his timidity, Bach added that those who feel weak and powerless on the surface often harbor a dangerously powerful split-off self-image.

Kernberg's (1970, 1975, 1980a, 1984, 1989) extensive writings on narcissism largely dealt with the more overt type of narcissistic personality. However, he too noted that "some patients with narcissistic personalities present strong conscious feelings of insecurity and inferiority" (Kernberg 1975). Their unconscious fantasies of grandiosity and omnipotence emerge only after a sustained contact has been established with them. Unlike the usual narcissistic individuals who are often sexually promiscuous, such persons show much restraint in their erotic lives. With the onset of middle age and its threatening reminders of life's limitations, however, the two types of narcissistic personalities tend to switch places. According to Kernberg (1980):

> The sexually more inhibited narcissistic character of early adulthood may now initiate the road to sexual promiscuity and various sexual deviations which other narcissistic patients are already abandoning in middle age because of their accumulated experience of dissatisfaction with the scant narcissistic gratification in sexual encounters. (p. 145)

Kohut (1971, 1977) too mentioned the less colorful and socially hesitant type of narcissistic personality. Such individuals have a "horizontal split" in the psyche that keeps their grandiosity repressed and, consequently, their reality ego depleted of confidence. They present with symptoms of narcissistic deficiency including low self-esteem, diminished zest for work, and lack of initiative. They also display hypochondriacal preoccupations and a marked propensity toward shame. They feel intense discomfort about their need to display themselves and often suffer from severe stage fright (Kohut and Wolf 1978). Not surprisingly, such individuals keep their distance from others from whom they desire narcissistic sustenance and feel painfully embarrassed upon the exposure of such needs. Alongside this prevailing symptomatology of narcissistic depletion, there are spasmodic breakthroughs of anxious hypomanic-like excitement, which give vent to their suppressed grandiosity.

The tense and conflicted existence of such narcissistic patients also drew Cooper's (1981, 1984, 1989) attention. He noted that the surface manifestations of narcissistic personality might be charm, ambition, and accomplishment, or these might include depression, invitations to humiliation, and feelings of failure. Cooper emphasized that narcissistic and masochistic tendencies frequently co-exist. Indeed, narcissistic tendencies might become unconscious vehicles for attaining masochistic disappointments, and masochistic injuries an affirmation of distorted narcissistic fantasies. More pointedly, Cooper and Ronningstam (1992) described narcissistic patients whose overt presentation is the mirror image of the usual description and who are "too inhibited to expose their fantasies to public view" (p. 94).

In my own two earlier reviews of the literature on narcissistic personality (Akhtar 1989, Akhtar and Thomson 1982), the manifestations of the disorder were divided into *overt* and *covert* categories. These designations did not necessarily imply conscious or unconscious occurrence, although such topographical distribution could certainly exist. The *overt* features included grandiosity, compulsive socialization, intense ambition, uneven morality, uninhibited sexuality, caricatured modesty, and an impressively articulate manner of speech. The *covert* features included morose self-doubts, envy, chronic boredom, materialistic lifestyle, inability to remain in love, and inattentiveness to details. While it was observed that some narcissistic patients initially display the usually covert features while the usually overt ones remain hidden in the first few interviews, the existence of two subtypes of narcissistic personality was not explicitly noted. The current contribution is thus an extension of my earlier work in this area.

Thinking along the same lines, Gabbard (1989) observed that the "official" diagnostic criteria for narcissistic personality characterize only the arrogant and boastful individual who constantly demands attention and fail to identify "the shy, quietly grandiose, narcissistic individual whose extreme sensitivity to slights leads to an assiduous avoidance of the spotlight" (p. 527). Gabbard named the two types as the *oblivious* and the *hyper-vigilant* narcissistic personalities. The former was characterized by persistent attention seeking, lack of empathy for others, and arrogance. The latter was characterized by hypersensitivity to others' reactions and a self-effacing attitude that hid their "secret wish to exhibit themselves in a grandiose manner" (p. 529).

Masterson (1993), too, delineated roughly similar subtypes of narcissistic personality. His *exhibitionistic type* subsumed individuals who flaunt their grandiosity to valued others and his *closet type* subsumed individuals who submit to idealized others and vicariously live out their own grandiose fantasies via such association.

Finally, Hunt (1995) described the *diffident narcissist*, whose grandiosity is hidden and who feels enormous shame at revealing it. His omnipotent strivings are not ego syntonic, and he professes to be egalitarian. Unlike the overt narcissist who frequently throws temper tantrums, the diffident narcissist shows lofty indifference to realistic setbacks. Unaffected by the present hardships, he lives in the future, continually relying on unrealistic hope (Akhtar 1996, Mehler and Argentieri 1989), and waiting for a transforming event without taking much action to achieve it. Hunt further stated that

> Castration anxiety in men, and in women, fear of loss, or loss of love, are prominent. At least in men, there is in both types a sense of a special relationship with the mother, based on her idolisation of him. The overt narcissist feels that he has won the oedipal conflict. The diffident narcissist may feel the same way, but in him this only increases the fear of the jealous, still dangerous, father. (p. 1260)

The inclusion of such "higher level" (Kernberg 1975) conflicts, usually ignored in the descriptions of narcissistic personality, was a superior feature of Hunt's description. However, he made little effort to relate the profile of his *diffident narcissist* to the existing but scattered literature on this topic and to distinguish the syndrome from the phenomenologically akin obsessional and schizoid personality disorders. These deficiencies are rectified in this current chapter. However, before going further, let us take a look at the "official" position of North American psychiatry vis-à-vis the shy narcissist.

DOES THE SYNDROME EXIST IN *DSM-IV*?

The *DSM-IV* (1994, p. 661) offers the following criteria for the diagnosis of narcissistic personality disorder.

A pervasive pattern of grandiosity (in fantasy or behavior), need for admiration, and lack of empathy, beginning by early adulthood and present in a variety of contexts, as indicated by five (or more) of the following:

(1) has a grandiose sense of self-importance (e.g., exaggerates achievements and talents, expects to be recognized as superior without commensurate achievements)

(2) is preoccupied with fantasies of unlimited success, power, brilliance, beauty, or ideal love

(3) believes that he or she is "special" and unique and can only be understood by, or should associate with, other special or high status people (or institutions)

(4) requires excessive admiration

(5) has a sense of entitlement, i.e. unreasonable expectations of especially favorable treatment or automatic compliance with his or her expectations

(6) is interpersonally exploitative, i.e. takes advantage of others to achieve his or her own ends

(7) lacks empathy; is unwilling to recognize or identify with the feelings and needs of others

(8) is often envious of others or believes that others are envious of him or her

(9) shows arrogant, haughty behaviors or attitudes

These criteria seem heavily slanted toward the explicitly arrogant and exhibitionistic type of narcissistic personality. However, the fact that grandiosity "in fantasy *or* behavior" (p. 661, italics added) is mentioned as the main criterion allows for the consideration of a covert type of narcissistic syndrome. Moreover, in descriptive passages that accompany the criteria, it is noted that some narcissistic patients give "an appearance of humility that may mask and protect grandiosity" (p. 659). They might drift toward low social functioning in order to avoid the risk of defeat in competitive situations. The combination of such social retreat and defensive humility stands in sharp contrast to the usually assertive, attention-seeking, and entitled picture of narcissistic individuals.

Finally, certain phrases in the DSM-IV description of narcissistic personality (e.g. "grandiose sense of self-importance," "preoccupied with fantasies of unlimited success," and "lacks empathy") are as applicable to the shy type of narcissistic personality as to its more outgoing counterpart.

A COMPOSITE CLINICAL PROFILE

Synthesizing this literature in the light of related observations made in my psychotherapeutic and psychoanalytic practice (Akhtar 1991, 1992b, 1994, 1996, 1999) yields the following composite profile of the shy narcissist.

Like the ordinary narcissist, the shy narcissist is ambitious, omnipotence-seeking, involved with fantasies of glory and fame, lacking in empathy for others, and defective in his capacity for deep object-relationships. He also yearns for acceptance by everyone, praise, and widespread recognition. Like his better known counterpart, the shy narcissist too believes that he or she is unique and can be understood only by other special or high status people. Finally, like the overt narcissist, the shy narcissist also employs the various "mechanisms of narcissistic repair" (Akhtar 2000) when faced with threat to self-esteem; these include narcissistic withdrawal, contempt for others, omnipotent control, evocation of "transitional fantasies" (Volkan 1973), and "sliding the meanings" (Horowitz 1975) of disturbing external events to cast them in a more agreeable light.

Unlike the usual narcissist, however, the shy narcissist keeps his grandiose beliefs and aspirations tightly under cover. He appears modest and uninterested in social success. Indeed, he might display overt disdain for money and material acquisitions. The "shy narcissist" also possesses a conscience stricter than that of the ordinary narcissist. He holds high moral standards and is less vulnerable to ethical lapses. More than his flamboyant phenomenological sibling, he feels gnawing, dark remorse at his oedipal transgressions as well as at his incapacity to empathize with others. While unable to feel genuine concern for others, he is forever helpful to them. Unlike the ordinary narcissist who discards others after having used them for his purposes, the shy narcissist is capable of feeling grateful and offering reparation to others/The strict conscience responsible for this also pushes his grandiosity and ambition into hiding. Unlike the usual narcissist who feels humiliated upon the exposure of his blemishes, the shy narcissist experiences shame upon the unmasking of his ambition and grandiosity. Indeed, he might live out his own ambition vicariously by playing "second fiddle" to someone whose success he has himself silently engineered.

Keeping a tight rein on his wishes to be noticed, the shy narcissist feels especially uncomfortable upon being photographed; the attention of a camera suddenly floods his ego with primitive exhibitionism and causes him much anxiety. Though yearning to be recognized, he "prefers" to be left alone in social get-togethers. Such reticence gives the shy narcissist yet another quality. His impaired capacity for deep relationships does not become readily visible to others./The difficulties of his sexual and marital life, resulting largely from chronic self-absorption as well as from clandestine and barely disguised transgressions of the incest barrier, also go unnoticed for long periods of time.

Cognitively, the ordinary narcissist comes across as impressively knowledgeable, decisive, and opinionated. The shy narcissist, in contrast, appears dreamy, forgetful, a bit absent-minded, and unable to carry on a sustained intellectual debate with another individual. However, in a circle of close associates, where the availability of soothing admiration is assured, the shy narcissist can shed his reserve and allow his suppressed raconteur self to emerge. Often this requires the help of alcohol. Indeed, the shy narcissist, more than his assertive counterpart, is vulnerable to such dependence. The apparent inconsistency between pervasive reticence on the one hand, and talkativeness with a select few of similar persuasion on the other, is due to the underlying mechanism of splitting, which keeps the two aspects of his personality apart.

DIFFERENTIAL DIAGNOSIS

The particular variety of narcissistic personality disorder described here also needs to be distinguished from obsessional and schizoid personality disorders. Both narcissistic and obsessional personalities display high ego ideals, perfectionism, and great need for control (Akhtar 1989, Akhtar and Thomson 1982, Kernberg 1975). Like the obsessional, the shy narcissist appears modest, careful, emotionally restricted, and interpersonally reticent. Unlike the obsessional, such an individual shows hidden grandiosity, limited empathy with others, an impractical lifestyle, disdain for details, and vulnerability to daydreaming.

Both the narcissistic and schizoid individuals prefer ideas over people and lack wholesome rootedness in their bodily existence (Akhtar 1989, Bach 1977, Kernberg 1975). Like the schizoid individual, the shy narcissist is self-absorbed, timid, socially hesitant, lacking in spontaneity, and driven by his secret, innermost plans. Unlike the schizoid individual, however, the shy narcissist is ambitious, covertly optimistic, and given to an increase in his hidden grandiosity under stress, not withdrawal into objectless states of psychic emptiness. Facing disappointments in others and/or injuries to self-esteem, the shy narcissist resorts to *transitional fantasies* (Volkan 1973), that is, imaginary and rather banal tales of personal glory mentally evoked for the purpose of self-soothing. Schizoid individuals typically lack the ability to soothe themselves under such circumstances.

CONCLUDING REMARKS

While the foregoing demonstrates the existence of the *shy narcissist* syndrome, little seems to be known about its actual prevalence. The use of masculine pronouns throughout this paper is only for literary ease and not meant to suggest that all shy narcissists are men. Indeed, I have encountered the syndrome in both male and female patients; Hunt (1995) has also mentioned such patients of both sexes. Also, while the syndrome can be more readily discerned in the setting of intense psychotherapeutic contact, it is not restricted to individuals undergoing such treatment. Shy narcissists might present with dysthymic complaints, vague inhibitions, and hypochondria to general psychiatrists and might, at times, be brought to clinical attention by their frustrated spouses. Another aspect of the syndrome's epidemiology pertains to culture. Since child-rearing patterns play a crucial role in the manifestation or suppression of an individual's ambitiousness, it is possible that cultures that place a great emphasis upon modesty might have a greater prevalence of the shy type rather than the boastful type of narcissistic personality. My earlier observation that "narcissistic asceticism" (Akhtar 1992b, p. 63) might be a more frequent presentation of narcissistic personality in Asian cultures is pertinent in this context.

Delineating the syndrome of the *shy narcissist* serves to underscore the centrality of splitting mechanisms in narcissistic personalities (Akhtar and Thomson 1982, Bach 1977, Cooper 1989, Cooper and Ronningstam 1992, Kernberg 1970a, 1975, Volkan 1982) and to highlight their divided self. It also brings to attention the fact that diagnostic criteria relying exclusively on manifest symptomatology fail to diagnose narcissistic grandiosity when only the defenses against it are clinically apparent. In contrast, the description of the *shy narcissist* offered here is based upon the inclusion of both the manifest symptomatology and deeper, subsurface constructs. With this broadened vantage point, multiple and even contradictory psychic phenomena can be accomodated in a clinical profile that is closer to human complexity than the grasp offered by behavioral check lists; it is only with such a perspective that one can "understand" the occasional occurrence of a hysterical overlay on a schizoid core (Fairbairn 1952) and the co-existence of expedient mendacity (Tobak 1989) with moralistic self-righteousness in paranoid individuals. This not only gives sounder theoretical underpinnings to the disorder's phenomenology but also prepares the clinician for the *mirror complementarity* of the self that Bach (1977) has noted. The therapist's awareness of the essentially dichotomous self in such individuals will encourage further inquiry and prevent misdiagnosis.

Regarding treatment, the clinician will benefit from the awareness that psychological weakness, hypochondria, undue stoicism, chronic waiting for magical events (Akhtar 1996, Angel 1934, Mehler and Argentieri 1989, Potamianou 1992), and exaggerated humility often mask grandiosity, omnipotence, and masochism. Knowledge of such a defensive constellation will enhance his or her empathy with the patient's underlying, if conflict-ridden, agenda. Interpretive efforts, at first directed at the anxious need for such defense, and later at the covert narcissistic and masochistic fantasies, can then be made.

Finally, the recognition that some narcissistic patients are painfully shy opens up challenging etiological realms for investigation. For instance, does the conflict between exhibitionistic desires and their inhibition emanate from an upbringing in which fame was upheld as desirable and modesty as virtue? Or, does this tension emanate from a battle between a constitutionally given, "hard-wired" propensity toward shyness (Kagan 1984, Thomas and Chess 1977) on the one hand and an environmentally acquired pressure for outstanding recognition on the other hand? Or, does some combination of the two hypotheses, or even explanations hitherto not adequately considered (e.g. involving cultural factors), apply here?

While answers to such questions await further research, it seems that recognizing the syndrome of the *shy narcissist* does have implications for etiological, diagnostic, and therapeutic realms alike.

4

THE OTHER WOMAN

For reasons that remain unclear, little attention has been paid to the specific dilemmas and conflicts of the woman who becomes romantically involved with a married man. The omission is a curious one since professional literature on contemporary marriage deals with almost all other aspects of the extramarital affair in considerable detail. There exist studies of the variety of extramarital involvements (Beltz 1969, Cuber and Harroff 1965), their frequency (Bell and Peltz 1974, Pietropinto and Simenauer 1976), their conscious reasons (Ellis 1969, Whitehurst 1969), their unconscious motivations (Christensen 1958, Neubeck and Schletzer 1969), their effects upon the marriage (Hunt 1969, Spotnitz and Freeman 1964, Ziskin and Ziskin 1973), and the moral and ethical questions that beleaguer such relationships (Ellis 1969, Neubeck 1969). What is not to be found in this literature or in the monographs exclusively dedicated to the study of long-term, extramarital affairs (Block 1978, Strean 1980) is an in-depth account of *the other woman*, that is, the woman who is having an affair with a married man.[21]

---

21. The same can be said of the literature's disregard of the man who repeatedly and exclusively gets involved with married women. Block (1978), in an informal, sociological study of extramarital relationships, does briefly comment upon such men. The somewhat clumsy but insistently non-sexist title of his book *The Other*

The striking paucity of literature on this topic is evident in the fact that a Medlar computer search surveying multiple language resource materials retrieved only two relevant citations. The first of these was a study (Hollander 1976) that compared 10 single women who had been repeatedly involved with married men with 11 women who had never had an affair or a casual sexual encounter with a married man. The instruments used were a personal interview, the Roe-Siegelman Parent-Child Relations Questionnaire II, the MMPI, and the Thematic Apperception Test. The study revealed an excessively close or intense father–daughter relationship and a poorer mother–daughter relationship among "the other women" and no significant differences in hysterical and masochistic character traits between the two groups. The second citation referred to a study (Richardson 1979) of the "management styles" used by 26 single women involved in long-term, intimate relationships with married men and the correlation of these styles with the manner in which the liaison was finally terminated. It was found that women who employed "submissive management styles" felt powerless and emotionally devastated at the end of the affair. They had difficulty letting go of the affair and continued to be distressed for long periods afterward. On the other hand, women "who adopt a dominance management style are more likely to initiate the sudden termination, choose to opt out in a slow, sustained withdrawal, and avoid the drag outs" (Richardson 1979, p. 412). In either case, the study pointed out, such relationships are difficult to mourn and are often not successfully given up by these women.

While both of these studies shed light on important aspects of the lives of "the other women," their data may have limited clinical applicability. The emphasis of these studies is on overt behavior, with relatively little acknowledgment given to the intrapsychic forces at work. Their data are solely based upon conscious recall with little attention paid to the possibility of potential distortion by unconscious factors. Their backdrop is social rather than clinical. The

---

Woman, The Other Man is a testimony to his having paid attention to this matter. My own decision to restrict this chapter to "the other woman" is based upon a simple clinical reality. I have never been consulted by a man who was intimately involved with a married woman and who sought psychiatric help for problems leading to and/or emanating from such involvement.

other women in these studies were volunteer subjects and not patients seeking professional help. All of this tends to restrict the usefulness of these studies for clinical purposes. The same can perhaps be said of the portraits of the other women in literature and movies.[22] One is therefore left with little clinically based information in this area. This is puzzling since such women often seek professional advice and their anguish may be quite familiar to most practicing psychotherapists.

The purpose of this chapter is to highlight the psychodynamic factors that lead a woman to select a married man as her romantic partner. It will also attempt to describe certain specific issues in the psychotherapy of such women. However, before embarking on these topics, let me describe the other women I have seen in my clinical practice and explain their reasons for seeking psychiatric consultation.

DESCRIPTIVE CHARACTERISTICS

My impressions are based upon a clinical sample of eight women seen in brief consultations and upon an additional two such patients treated in psychoanalytic psychotherapy. In developing a descriptive profile of the other woman, I have attempted to stay away from two major sources of distortion: the description of such individuals by

---

22. The portrayal of the mistress and the other woman in Western literature and cinema is a topic worthy of independent study. My own impression (admittedly based on limited knowledge of both fields) is that the topic has constantly fascinated writers and moviemakers. While the classics and even the contemporary, serious literature may fare better, current popular fiction, television, and movies fail to rise above stereotypes in their depiction of the other woman. One frequent stereotype is that of the other woman being a sensually charged, glamorous, and hence primitively idealized, even though dangerous, part-object (e.g. screen movies *Just Tell Me What You Want*, 1979; *Midlife Crazy*, 1983; *Fatal Attraction*, 1987; television movie *His Mistress*, 1984; popular Joy Fielding novel *The Other Woman*, 1983), a deeply conflicted masochist (e.g. screen movie *A Touch of Class*, 1973), and finally, a symbol of the plight of contemporary women in a male-dominated world (e.g. Marilyn French's novel *The Bleeding Heart*, 1980). Obviously these are only individual facets of the same, multidetermined and highly complex phenomenon: a woman's involvement with an unavailable man.

either a male patient who is having an extramarital affair or a female patient whose husband is involved with another woman. Such descriptions—and I have heard plenty of them—tend to be affectively charged, simplistic, and one-sided. Men who are having affairs describe the other woman in unrealistically glowing terms. Among the adjectives and phrases they frequently use are wonderful, kind, warmhearted, unique, deeply human, really compassionate, a beautiful person, and so on. Wives of such men on the other hand portray the other woman as basically a self-centered, immature, and manipulative individual with dubious moral standards. Both husbands and wives may add a few qualifying statements to make their descriptions appear well rounded. However, the depth of perception thus conveyed has never failed to impress me as largely intellectual and not genuinely felt. It is for these reasons that I decided to restrict my phenomenological database to actual and direct clinical contact with women who were repeatedly and/or chronically involved with married men.

Demographic Profile

The age range for the other women in my clinical sample was from 27 to 40, the mean age being 32.5 years. Nine of the 10 other women were white and one was black. Five were divorced and the remaining five had never been married. Being divorced or single did not seem correlated with the age factor. Almost all these individuals had had some education beyond high school, with three of them holding college or postgraduate degrees. All were employed. Their jobs included secretary, school teacher, nurse, air hostess, buyer for a large department store, clinical psychologist, and professional journalist. All these women were financially secure and independent and most lived by themselves.

It is difficult to assess the significance of these demographic features in view of the small size of the clinical sample and in the absence of a reasonable control group. Indeed, it is possible that no difference on numerous demographic variables will be found should a statistical comparison be made between this sample of the other women and the remaining female patients whom I have evaluated or treated over the same period of time. Somewhat impressionistically however, I am struck by the fact that none of these women were currently married, a fact that appears significant when contrasted with the marital status of the other female patients I have seen over the same time period. This finding can have many meanings. For instance, it may be taken as evidence of these women's inherent inability to establish or maintain a deep and full relationship with a man, or it may be interpreted simply as a referral artifact. In other words, it can be argued (Sands 1978) that there are in reality equal numbers of both married and unattached other women, but that only the single and divorced ones seek psychiatric help. This line of thinking would suggest that married other women have better support systems and greater social taboos to contend with and that both of these factors minimize the appearance of these women at the professional's doorstep.

Yet another explanation for the preponderance of unattached women who are chronically involved with married men would invoke the "natural selection" hypothesis; that is, there are more single and divorced other women because married men are more attracted to unattached women since it is logistically easier for these men to have affairs with them than to have affairs with married women (Block 1978). While this explanation has the advantage of appealing to common sense, it does tend to underestimate the complexity of human relationships and the extent to which people will go in order to appease their inner demons. Clearly, these three hypotheses do not exhaust the possibilities. The purpose of this brief digression is therefore not to provide conclusive answers but to point toward a potentially interesting clinical finding and to raise questions about it. Are there really more single and divorced persons among the other woman group? Why?

Clinical Features

The most common presenting clinical feature in this group of patients was depression. The dysthymic complaints, however, were not associated with impairment of job-related abilities or with significant vegetative disturbance. Even the mood disturbance was ill-sustained, with periods of relative relief interspersed with periods of guilt, impotent rage, bleak despondency, and aching loneliness. The depressive feelings were most marked around holidays that these women often had to spend without their lovers. Feelings of anxiety, personal insecurity, and low self-esteem were frequent in the group. Most had sought help following a crisis with their lovers, though only one-third of the patients revealed their involvement with a married man in the very first interview. Others, somewhat better defended individuals, indicated that they were troubled by their relationships with men and only in later sessions elaborated upon the turmoil of being involved with a married man. Sooner or later all of them displayed painful, conflicted, and deeply ambivalent relationships with their lovers, though the mechanisms they employed in dealing with such ambivalence varied considerably. It became apparent that underneath their seemingly well-adapted, poised, and purposive social existences, most of these women were quite distressed and were preoccupied with this particular relationship in their lives.

The way these women described their lovers caught my attention, and I began to suspect that perhaps there were two distinct subgroups in the clinical sample. The first group were women who seemed capable of consciously experiencing deep ambivalence toward their lovers. They described their lovers as unhappily married men who were nonetheless charming, handsome, sophisticated, and efficient in their work. However, at the same time they also felt that these men were weak, childlike, potentially callous, afraid of genuine intimacy, selfish, and unreliable. These women appeared constantly puzzled by what they recognized to be contradictory aspects of their lovers' characters.

They were also disturbed by their own ambivalence toward these men. While the painful ambivalence came readily to the surface in the clinical situation, careful scrutiny revealed that these women had, in their day-to-day lives, handled this ambivalence differently. They compartmentalized their minds, thus keeping the two contradictory attitudes separate from each other. This compartmentalization was akin to what Freud (1927), in one of the many ways he used the term, described as the *splitting* of the ego. In describing this mechanism, Freud specifically referred to the fetishist, whom he saw as simultaneously acknowledging and disavowing the absence of a penis in women by his use of the fetish. Freud saw the ego as effecting a cleavage or division of itself so that it could contain two contradictory psychic configurations. It should be parenthetically noted here that the currently popular use of the term *splitting* occurs in a considerably different context (Akhtar and Byrne 1983). However, the current way in which the term is used has relevance for how the remaining other women viewed their lovers.

While the other women in the second group also had mixed feelings toward their lovers, they seemed unable to experience the two sets of feelings simultaneously. As a result, they failed to hold onto an in-depth, composite picture of him in their minds. At times they experienced him as loving, witty, empathic, and sexually gratifying. At other times, usually following a cancelled date or some other disappointment, they viewed him as petty, cruel, dishonest, and fundamentally untrustworthy. The two descriptions carried comparable conviction, and alternately each appeared to these patients as valid and truly representative of the "real" nature of the men with whom they were involved. The disregard they showed toward the discrepancy in their two accounts was striking. Upon being confronted with this discrepancy during diagnostic or psychotherapeutic sessions, most of these patients intellectually recognized the inconsistency but affectively dismissed it as irrelevant. Some, however, felt anxiety and annoyance at being confronted. In either case it became apparent that the two images of their lovers existed independently of each other in their minds. When one of these internal images—object representations, to be precise—was affectively, cognitively, and behaviorally active, the other was blandly "forgotten," and vice versa.

This propensity toward "forgetting" was obviously a manifestation of defensive splitting. However, unlike the first group of other women, the use of splitting in this group did not seem restricted to the internal image of their lovers. It was pervasive and included almost all their significant object relations. It also affected their view of themselves. Their knowledge of the real objects was, in general, dim as it was determined by the need-satisfying potential of the external objects rather than by the objects' autonomous existence and inherent qualities. In addition, their selves were not solidly established; hence, these patients were vulnerable to extreme oscillations of their self-esteem. All this was reminiscent of the primitive splitting that is associated with a borderline personality organization (Kernberg 1967).

The two groups of other women were distinct, though admittedly with some phenomenological overlap in regard to other clinical features as well. The first group had few overt symptoms besides the occasional dysthymic complaints associated with the relationships with their lovers. They constantly attempted to "figure out" their men and frequently ruminated about the moral correctness of their involvements. Sexually they were reasonably comfortable, though, at times, they did experience anxiety and guilt about having sexual relations with a married man. Romantic love appeared to be of greater significance to them than actual sexual intimacy. They valued friendships of many years' duration.

These women had solid ethnic, vocational, and sociocultural identities; their future plans, though inevitably colored by their troubled relationships with the married men, were reasonably realistic and quite clear to them. Finally, though unconscious masochistic strivings were evident in their involvement with less than optimally available men, these other women did not display overt self-destructive behaviors.

The second group, on the other hand, was composed of women who had many diffuse symptoms besides their involvement with married men. They had had many other frustrating and futile relationships with men in the past, they had fewer friends, and they had experimented with drugs more often than the women in the first group. They were sexually less inhibited; one of them had been quite promiscuous in the past. They drank more and all of them had attempted suicide on one or more occasions in their lives. The other women in this group showed confusion about their identities, experienced feelings of emptiness, and had lived their lives in a fragmented fashion over the years. One of them, for instance, described her life as "floating in the air, wanting to put an anchor somewhere but not knowing where or in what." Another displayed contradictory character traits and *as if* (Deutsch 1942) qualities, in addition to feeling compelled to put on makeup and her business clothes, even on weekends, since she felt empty and directionless without such external manifestations of her identity.

All of this suggested the presence in these women of the *syndrome of identity diffusion* (Akhtar 1984, 1992b, Erikson 1959a, Kernberg 1967). This suspicion was further strengthened by the fact that they also showed many of the cardinal manifestations of primitive splitting (Akhtar and Byrne 1983): inability to experience ambivalence, impaired decision-making, intensification of affects, ego-syntonic impulsivity, and oscillations of self-esteem.

DEVELOPMENTAL BACKGROUNDS

It should be mentioned at the outset that most of the data on the developmental backgrounds of these patients was gathered in brief consultations. Hence, to what extent the recollections of childhood and early family life by these women were defensively altered in the manner of a *personal myth* (Kris 1956) is difficult to determine. One can of course be more certain about the background of the two patients who were seen in psychoanalytic psychotherapy. The brief accounts that follow should therefore be taken as trends in certain directions and not as pathognomonic developmental antecedents of a person becoming an "other woman."

The two groups of other women had both similarities and differences in their developmental backgrounds. With respect to their similarities, both groups seemed to have come from small, nuclear families with few extended relations, a factor that tends to maximize the impact of parental psychopathology on growing children (Modell 1983). Also, women in both groups recalled experiencing feelings of inferiority while growing up. Some related these feelings to rivalry with an older sibling, usually a brother, who they felt had been better treated by the parents. Others more directly related their sense of inferiority to being a girl. Finally, almost all the women in both groups complained about having been unfairly treated, inadequately appreciated, and harshly judged by their fathers.

There were many differences, however, in the developmental backgrounds of the two groups. The three women who recalled themselves as having been happy as children all belonged to the first group. None in the second group remembered herself as having been a happy child. All four women in the second group recalled having been beaten—two rather frequently and badly—by their fathers, while none of the women in the first group were beaten as children. Moreover, while the women in the first group considered their mothers as generally affectionate though a little strict, the women in the second group reported their mothers to be rejecting, critical, and unempathic. Their portrayals of their mothers were regarded as reasonably valid in light of what was learned through the psychotherapy of one of the other women from the first group and another from the second. The mother of the first type of other woman was comfortable with her own femininity but the mother of the more troubled, second type was not at ease with her own womanliness.[23]

Finally, the two groups differed in their accounts of the latency and adolescent phases of their lives. Women in the first group had had reasonably pleasant, energetic school lives, many friends, and painful but not disastrous adolescence. Women in the second group, however, had been chronically unhappy during latency, had daydreamed a lot, and were generally withdrawn and shy. During their adolescence they had had greater difficulties with their parents, indulged in more sexual experimentation, and seemed to have needed tighter external controls over their behavior than the women in the first group.

One curious finding referring to the entire sample was that the fathers of four of the 10 other women had themselves had extramarital affairs about which their daughters had had at least a vague knowledge. Since neither of the two women seen over a protracted length of time had such fathers, it is difficult to hypothesize that the fathers' extramarital affairs played a role in the daughters' subsequent involvement with married men. Clearly, however, factors of continued and prolonged oedipal titillation, identification with the fortunate rival, and identification with the aggressor may all be at work here.

DIAGNOSTIC CATEGORIES

Seven of the 10 other women in this sample belonged to the first group mentioned previously. These women appeared to be deeply

---

23. I. Bernstein (1983) suggests that important among the factors that predispose a girl to future masochistic tendencies is an "early disidentification with a mother who has a negative or depreciatory attitude toward her body, genitals, and femininity" (p. 483). This factor seemed to be one basis for the considerable masochism that was evident in the second group of other women.

feminine, mildly seductive individuals who were prone to affectual-ization of their relationships with older, unavailable men. They had solidly established ego identities and fairly strict and internalized superego systems. Their capabilities for experiencing genuine guilt, sadness, mourning, empathy, and concern, though somewhat com-promised in the specific area of their romantic involvement, were generally intact. They were also capable of peaceful aloneness. Almost all of them displayed intact *autonomous functions of the ego* (Hartmann 1958). Despite frequent emotional crises in their ro-mantic affairs, they were remarkably stable and appropriate at their jobs. Their object relations appeared to be of the "total" type insofar as these permitted ambivalence, separateness, and the ability to maintain libidinal ties despite temporary frustrations (Altman 1977, Kernberg 1974). Their intrapsychic conflicts were of the "structural" type (Arlow and Brenner 1964), and their defenses centered around repression. These patients therefore displayed evidence of a "higher level" (Kernberg 1970b) character organi-zation. The descriptive nosological label appropriate for most of them was "hysterical personality disorder," though obsessional, depressive, and masochistic features existed in them as well. Within the hysterical personality range (Zetzel 1968) itself, there was some variation regarding the level of integration and functioning, though none of these women appeared to be what Lazare (1971) has labeled the "sick hysteric."[24]

The second group, comprising three other women, displayed considerably different characteristics. Self-destructiveness was pro-nounced in these women. Their emotional lability was generalized and diffuse. There were few, if any, conflict-free areas in their lives. They experienced much confusion about their identities. "Non-specific manifestations of ego weakness" (Kernberg 1967, p. 660) were evident in some of them. These included lack of anxiety tolerance, lack of impulse control, and lack of developed sublima-tory channels. These women had limited capacity for empathy, concern, and mourning. This was most evident in their response to disappointments with their lovers. Under such circumstances they

---

24. For a detailed discussion of the differences between *hysterical* and *histrionic* personalities, see Akhtar (1992b) and Kernberg (1985).

either used flat denial or were filled with consciously experienced impotent rage. Thus, not only was their capacity for mourning and sadness limited, but their ability to experience inner guilt was also compromised. Their superego functions, though archaic and sadistic, were vulnerable to reprojections and externalizations. They frequently experienced fear and shame rather than genuine guilt. Their intrapsychic dilemmas were of the nature of "object-relations conflicts" (Dorpat 1976), rather than intersystemic, structural conflicts, and their defensive operations revolved around splitting, denial, and projective identification. These patients therefore seemed to display from "intermediate level" to "lower level" (Kernberg 1970b) character pathology. The nosological labels that seemed most appropriate to this group included "narcissistic" and "schizoid personality disorders." A borderline personality organization (Kernberg 1967) was clearly discernable beneath these women's overt narcissistic level of functioning. One other woman in this group, however, was more overtly borderline and seemed to have experienced occasional psychotic breaks of brief duration in the past.

PSYCHODYNAMICS

Why does a woman who is unattached and has other options open to her get involved with a man who is married to someone else? What internal forces compel her to have a relationship so encumbered by societal taboos, logistical nightmares, and personal torment? What anxieties prevent her from making a different choice? What profound joy helps her to overlook the deep frustrations of such an entanglement? Where is the wellspring of her adamant hope, and what pain makes it unspeakably difficult for her to let go of this relationship? These and many other similar questions demand answers when one encounters an other woman in the course of clinical work. Clearly, there are no simple answers. Being or becoming an other woman seems, like any other neurotic symptom or character trait, overdetermined and subject to the "principle of multiple function" (Waelder 1936).

The involvement with a married man may have many different meanings, some of which may exist simultaneously. Such a relationship may thus be an enactment of certain infantile instinctual wishes and at the same time an execution of superego-induced punishments over these wishes. It may have its ontogenetic origins in the oedipal and/or the preoedipal period of development, and its multifaceted phenomenology may contain important unconscious fantasies about oneself, others, or both (Kernberg 1980b). It should also be pointed out that while many different psychodynamic explanations underlie the syndrome of the other woman, some constellations were more frequent in the first group mentioned previously, while others were seen more often in the second group. Which constellations were present seemed predominantly determined by the level of character organization. In general, the "higher" (Kernberg 1970b) the level of character organization, the more being an other woman seemed to have oedipal underpinnings. Similarly, in the other woman with an overt or covert borderline personality organization, the more frequent mechanism appeared to be the search for an "all-good" object as a defense against a paranoid and cynical distortion of all other relationships. These are, however, generalizations and should be taken as such.

Caution is also required in consideration of the psychodynamic explanations of a woman's involvement with a married man since the categories that follow are neither intended to be exhaustive nor are the various factors necessarily mutually exclusive. Only certain themes, repeatedly encountered either clinically or in the literature, are highlighted with a tacit acknowledgment of etiological heterogenerity and hitherto undetected mechanisms. Needless to add that the focus here is on the intrapsychic, since the external realities can only facilitate and not cause such involvement.[25]

Unresolved Oedipal Longings

In one of his papers on the psychology of love, Freud (1910) described a special type of love object chosen by certain men. This

---

25. This is not to deny that most lay writers (e.g. Sands 1978), as well as certain professionals (e.g. Ellis 1969), hold the contemporary social realities (e.g. relaxed sexual mores) responsible for involvement between married men and single women. In my view external reality can merely facilitate the expression of intrapsychic tendencies. Its etiological role in extramarital liaisons is contributory, not causative.

object is characterized by two "necessary conditions for loving." The
first of these preconditions is

> that there should be an "injured third party"; it stipulates that the
> person in question shall never choose as his love-object a woman who
> is disengaged—that is, an unmarried girl or an unattached married
> woman—but only to whom another man can claim right of posses-
> sion as a husband, fiance, or friend . . . The second precondition
> is . . . that a woman who is chaste and whose reputation is irre-
> proachable never exercises an attraction . . . but only a woman who
> is in some way or other of bad repute sexually, whose fidelity and
> reliability are open to some doubt. (p. 166)

In addition to these two preconditions, Freud described two
characteristics of the man's behavior toward his love object: (1) the
consuming nature of this involvement, and (2) the powerful urge to
rescue the woman he loves. Freud suggested that these four features,
present to a variable extent in each individual case, emanated from
a growing boy's sensuous longings toward his mother and were
defensively disguised expressions of those longings. The precondition of the woman belonging to someone else and the attitude of
overvaluation seem quite directly derived from the mother image.
The "injured third party" of course is none other than the father.
Freud saw the precondition of sexual ill-repute as a cynical exag-
geration by a child of his newly acquired knowledge of his mother's
sexual activity with his father. Finally, the rescue motif, consciously
rationalized as an attempt to protect the supposedly weak woman,
has a meaning and history of its own that is related to certain other
aspects of the Oedipus complex.

The reason for mentioning all this in some detail is that the other
women reported here showed a similar proclivity when it came to
choosing a love object.[26] They fell in love with men who were
already attached and whose sexual reputation carried at least a
"faint breath of scandal" (Freud 1910); a few of these men were

---

26. It was almost 10 years after his description of such object choices in men that
Freud (1929) demonstrated the occurrence of precisely the same type of object
choice in women. However, the case was one of a homosexual girl and not of an
"other woman."

openly promiscuous. All these other women were deeply and intensely involved with their lovers. Their erotic lives became consciously idealized but unconsciously masochistic enactments of their repressed sexual excitement toward their fathers. My poem "Surrender" (Akhtar 1993, p. 23) portrays this very state of affairs (pun intended!) from a subjective viewpoint:

> A mysterious hand
> Caresses me, leading
> Me to unknown paths of fantasy,
> With gentleness and passion,
> Tenderly yet strongly numbing
> The senses of reality.
> Leaving me weak in delirium.
> I find myself drowning in the sea of forbidden desires.
> (Akhtar 1993, p. 23)

Most such "other women" thought that they were giving these men the love and understanding that their allegedly cold and unempathic wives had failed to give them. This appeared to be a variant of the rescue fantasy described by Freud. There was thus considerable phenomenological evidence of oedipal underpinnings to these women's involvements with married men.

In the case of one such woman seen in psychoanalytic psychotherapy this was amply confirmed. Intense, romantic, and guilt-ridden attachment to the father and hostile rivalry with the mother, frequently appearing in the patient's associations as the current lover's wife, emerged as the main dynamic theme in this particular case. Interestingly, this woman's initial description of the father as harsh and critical came to be understood in different terms during her treatment. He had appeared harsher to her than perhaps he was in reality because he had failed to appreciate the depth of her love for him. Also, viewing her father in this manner served a defensive purpose vis-à-vis her erotic longings for him, in addition to assuaging her guilt over such longings.

Masochism

Almost all the other women complained of the chronic suffering that resulted from being involved with married men. They felt constantly deprived of their lovers' affections. They felt treated as second-class citizens every time they were excluded from an important social function, a religious festival, an anniversary, and so on in which they would have participated had they been married to their lovers. They experienced sadness, humiliation, and resentment at having to keep their romances secret. The assertions of some other women that a secret liaison was somehow more romantic than one publicly acknowledged often proved to be a defensive rationalization. Despite all this torment these women clung to their married lovers. Or was it *because* of this torment? Instances where consultations went beyond one or two interviews and especially in the two cases seen in psychoanalytic psychotherapy, it did appear that one of the many needs being gratified by such a relationship was that of suffering.

The sources of masochism[27] were, however, quite varied. In the case briefly mentioned previously, a prominent motive for seeking pain and suffering was an "unconscious sense of guilt" (Freud 1924a, p. 166) related to unresolved oedipal longings. This woman felt that she was not allowed a painless relationship. For her, the involvement with a married man was both a near actualization of an oedipal wish and a punishment for having this desire. In the other case seen in-depth, however, there existed additional and perhaps more significant origins of the need to suffer. This particular woman had had a very traumatic childhood. She was the fourth and youngest daughter of her parents and she felt that she had been a burden to them. She remembered frequently being ridiculed by her parents for her large build and for her "unfeminine" behavior, which *they* perhaps unconsciously encouraged. At the same time, her mother constantly bemoaned the plight of women and repeatedly told the patient that she was unfortunate to have been born a girl in this male-dominated world. The patient had grown up feeling unworthy of making demands, secretly ashamed of being a woman, and with a self-representation of being a burden to others. The progression from such an internal state of affairs to masochism is

---

27. The term *masochism*, frequently employed "with little consistency and at varied levels of abstraction" (Maleson 1984), is being used here in its purely descriptive sense.

expectable (D. Bernstein 1983, Blum 1976, Reich 1954), though it may take varying routes. A degraded and ugly self-representation may lower what one may confidently seek and result in a phenomenological masochism. Such a self-representation may itself result from the turning inward of the anger directed at frustrating objects of childhood, a "secondary masochism" (Freud 1924). This particular kind of interpersonal relationship may be unconsciously recreated again and again (Bergler 1969) in order to achieve belated mastery and/or to maintain a semblance of object relationships, since it has now become seemingly the only way of object contact (Berliner 1958).

In view of all of this, it was not surprising that for this patient her lover not only stood for the prohibited oedipal father but more importantly for the disappointing father who failed to help her extricate herself from the mother during the separation–individuation process (Mahler et al. 1975). Beyond that, of course, her lover represented the deeply conflicted and frustrating image(s) of her preoedipal mother from whom a satisfactory separation had not been achieved. The involvement with a married man and the associated masochism here were more a result of preoedipal than of oedipal conflicts. Seemingly genital strivings for the father were being used as a substitute gratification of the oral-dependent needs that were frustrated by the mother. However, the traumatic experiences—I prefer the term *experiences* since it encompasses both the actual events and their internal processings by the child—of childhood mentioned previously may result in additional dynamics that underlie such object choices.

The Continued Need for an Omnipotent External Object

Individuals who have successfully resolved the separation–individuation process (Mahler 1974, Mahler et al. 1975) no longer demand absolute perfection from their love objects. They come to accept the reality that "all-good" external objects—derivatives of the mother of the symbiotic phase—do not exist. Hence, these individuals can accept limitations in others and experience ambivalence toward them. Individuals who have failed in resolving the separation–individuation process, however, continue to demand perfection from themselves and from others. They keep searching for blissful union with bountiful others, a sort of "symbiotic omnipotence" (Khan 1969) in which all aggression is split off and denied.

The three other women with a borderline personality organization displayed a tendency to use such primitive idealization toward others. This mechanism, according to Kernberg (1967) refers to

> the tendency to see external objects as totally good, in order to make sure that they can protect one against the "bad" objects, that they cannot be contaminated, spoiled, or destroyed by one's own aggression or by that projected onto other objects . . . One other function of such an ideal object is to serve as a recipient for omnipotent identification, for sharing in the greatness of the idealized object as a protection against aggression, and as a direct gratification of narcissistic needs. (p. 668)

The use of primitive idealization, generally alongside the defensive mechanism of splitting, creates powerful, unrealistic, and "all-good" objects. Reliance upon such objects is badly needed by individuals with borderline personality organization since they lack a sustained, internal feeling of safety and optimism. In the absence of such "emotional object constancy" (Mahler et al. 1975, p. 166) they are vulnerable to the dreadful, subjective experience of inner emptiness (Kernberg 1975, Singer 1977a,b), as well as to the lure of potentially ecstatic encounters. Their need and search for all-good objects is further heightened by their weak ego's inability to contain ambivalence, a necessary condition of all deep human relationships. All these features of borderline personality organization, along with the deficient superego integration, predispose such individuals to a peculiar kind of interpersonal relationship. This relationship invites idealization, limits actual knowledge of the love object, discourages genuine intimacy, and conspires to discharge aggression exclusively outside the boundaries of the relationship. Obviously, however "loving" such a relationship may overtly appear, its internal psychological structure runs counter to the prerequisites of mature love (Bergman 1971, Kernberg 1974, 1995a). Although devotion to cult leaders more graphically illustrates a relationship born out of primitive idealization, the attachment of the three other women with borderline character organization to their lovers was not much different. These women knew little about their lovers. Especially striking was their lack of curiosity about how their men came to be married to such allegedly cold wives in the first place. It is this aspect that most clearly distinguishes primitive idealization from mature forms of idealization. In the latter, the knowledge of the external object is deep, and despite idealization some ambivalence is permissible.

Other Psychodynamic Factors

The three dynamic factors commented upon so far—oedipal strivings, masochism, and a continued need for omnipotent external objects—are neither totally mutually exclusive nor do they exhaust the list. I do, however, regard them as the more frequent and thus the more important psychodynamics to consider. Among other factors is the formation of a *negative identity* (Erikson 1959a) with the resultant desire to live in a drastically different fashion from the one dictated by parental mores. Often, however, the need for such deviation emanates from the deep-seated awareness of one's lack of internal separation from the parental introjects of childhood. Another factor that may facilitate such relationships among women with low self-esteem is the manner in which their lovers treat them, especially in the beginning phases of their relationship. These men pour out their complicated and often tragic life histories during hours and hours of intense conversation with these women. They seek warmth, empathy, and understanding. While this kind of self-disclosure seems phenomenologically real, what these men are often seeking is absolution for guilt, mutual denial of their aggression, and encouragement to further project and split off their hostile introjects.

All this leads to a sort of transference idealization of the other woman in which she is viewed as a savior, friend, mother, therapist, and lover: in essence, someone badly needed to depend upon. It is this feeling of being needed that may be intoxicatingly pleasurable to women with low self-esteem and cause them to get more and more deeply involved in such relationships. Yet another common factor that may facilitate such relationships is a fear of intimacy (Berdy 1984). This fear is frequently an outgrowth of childhood disappointments in parental responses to one's needs and is especially true in the case of schizoid individuals. The self of such an individual, having felt unsupported in its once vigorous needs for attachment and interaction, has undergone a split between a superficially compliant, social, false self, and an inwardly withdrawn, trapped, inexperienced true self (Guntrip 1968, Winnicott 1960a). To such individuals, the semi-relationship with a man who is already attached and hence is not available for a fuller relationship may offer a desirable compromise between their deep longings to love and their reflexive but powerful tendency to retreat into interpersonal indifference.

Finally, it should be kept in mind that the manifest content of a character trait or a symptom is not a very reliable guide to its childhood origins or its current psychodynamic meanings. In order to understand the nature of a symptom—in this case involvement of women with married men—it is necessary to take a deeper look at the entire character organization. This would mean taking into account the developmental history, the nature of intrapsychic conflicts, the defensive organization, the state of the ego and its identity, the degree of superego integration, and the depth of internal object relationships. The initial formulations about a patient may thus serve only as guidelines since a deeper understanding of this sort is often not possible unless the patient is involved in ongoing, in-depth psychotherapeutic work.

TREATMENT

One may treat an other woman with supportive psychotherapy, psychoanalytic psychotherapy, or psychoanalysis. The choice of treatment modality would depend upon the treatment goals,[28] the

---

28. It should not be automatically assumed that the other woman seeks psychotherapy to become able to relinquish her painful romantic involvement. Though this is frequently the case, there are other conscious and unconscious motives for entering treatment. Prominent among these are seeking moral absolution and searching for more adaptive skills in the face of a puzzling relationship. All these have to be taken into account while deciding upon therapeutic strategies and goals. One especially difficult situation is when the other woman is quite schizoid. Therapeutic zeal based upon naïve theoretical purity may dissolve this "pathological" relationship only to leave her in a bleak and potentially

nature of presenting complaints, the urgency with which symptomatic relief is required, the level of character organization, the degree of analyzability, the reality situations as these affect the overall quality of the patient's life, and the feasibility of an ongoing treatment process. Before such a choice can be made, a careful diagnostic assessment is required. In addition to the conventional aspects of anamnesis, a detailed description of the affair should be obtained. Attention should be paid not only to what is being said but also to how it is being said, as well as to what is not being said and why it is being withheld. Most important, however, is the assessment of the level of character organization.

In general, if the other woman presents with a higher level character organization, displays other evidences of analyzability (e.g. Glover 1954, Joseph 1967, Lower et al. 1972, Tyson and Sandler 1971), and the affair is not presenting acute and dramatic distress but is a source of mild albeit lingering and chronic difficulty, the treatment of choice should be psychoanalysis. If, however, there are more pressing needs to resolve matters relating to the affair and/or there is doubt about the level of character organization and analyzability, then face-to-face psychoanalytic psychotherapy on a twice- or thrice-weekly basis should be recommended. Finally, if the affair is at the end and/or the patient shows marked ego weakness and/or presents in a crisis situation, a more reality-oriented, supportive approach should be undertaken.

Since it is my impression that the majority of other women seeking psychotherapeutic help belong to the second of the three categories outlined previously, I will restrict my comments to this group. Even in this realm of psychoanalytic psychotherapy I am aware that each individual other woman will pose unique dilemmas and challenges. It is therefore not possible to generalize regarding

---

dangerous, object-less despair. Yet another unusual clinical situation (A. Goldman 1984, personal communication) is when the other woman becomes overtly symptomatic and seeks help only after learning that her married lover has finally decided to leave his wife and to marry her. She thus acts in a manner reminiscent of "those wrecked by success" (Freud 1926, p. 316). All this suggests that there is considerable variation in clinical phenomenology, psychodynamics, character organization, and the realistic situations of various other women, a variation that affects the objectives of her treatment.

the problems one might expect and the therapeutic strategies one might choose. One can only say that like any other psychoanalytic psychotherapy, such treatment will not involve the development of a full-blown, transference neurosis nor will it lead to the resolution of transference by interpretation alone. Also, there will be only an incomplete genetic reconstruction of various transference developments and the treatment will include supportive and ego-strengthening elements. While these comments are valid in a general way, there are three specific aspects of psychoanalytic psychotherapy with the other woman that need further comment. These are (1) the patient's use of external reality, in this case the involvement with a married man as a massive resistance to revealing, experiencing, learning, and changing; (2) the effect of carrying a secret upon the patient's overall life and specifically upon her engagement in the psychotherapeutic work; and (3) the potential countertransference difficulties in the treatment of a woman involved with a married man.

Reality as a Resistance

One major problem in doing psychoanalytic psychotherapy with the other woman is the continued presence of a painful external reality in her life. To a much greater extent than women with more conventional relationships, she has to contend with social taboos, logistical difficulties, broken promises, and lonely holidays in the context of a romantic relationship. Not only does she have to constantly mourn her own unmet yearnings, but she also has to repeatedly digest and "metabolize" the more than usually traumatic aspects of this relationship. Moreover, she is not the only one who has mixed feelings about the relationship. Her married lover too has conflicting and contradictory stances toward their liaison. He is usually a troubled, narcissistic individual who idealizes her but cannot provide her with sustained empathy and concern. All this leads the other woman to seek help with dysthymic suffering that has both intrapsychic and interpersonal determinants.

It is this interpersonal component that causes difficulties in an insight-oriented work. The patient tends to focus on it and to avoid exploring potential intrapsychic contributions to her malady. She yields to the temptation to view her distress as largely related to and at times even as being caused by her lover's attitude. She presents "evidences" of *his* indecision, *his* ambivalence, *his* cruelty in some sessions, and of *his* kindness and *his* wanting a deeper relationship during other sessions. She sees the "push and pull" of their relationship as largely coming from him and not as representing two sides of her own intrapsychic conflict. This externalization is a major resistance in the therapy of the other woman.

Three things need to be kept in mind about this matter. First, a head-on confrontation with this externalization propensity is generally not very productive. Such an approach may enhance resistance, causing the psychotherapeutic sessions to become quasi-legal battles where the patient and the therapist both present contrary "evidences" to prove their points. Indeed, the patient may soon drop out of the treatment. It is therefore more tactful and productive (and perhaps even more truthful) to acknowledge in a straightforward manner the real difficulties of the relationship and not to dismiss the patient's elaboration of the affair as "only a resistance." Indeed, it is through listening to the detailed description of this relationship that the therapist can begin to discern the unfulfilled needs and hence various potential transference paradigms of the patient. Paradoxically, it is paying attention to the affair (though clearly more at the beginning of the treatment than during its more advanced stages) that leads to a minimalization of the resistance use of this material. On the other hand, it should be emphasized that this listening should not be *too* focused merely on the reality of the affair; rather, it should use the affair as important, but only one manifestation of the patient's unresolved intrapsychic conflicts.[29]

Second, it should be remembered that patients who have a marked tendency toward the use of primitive defenses of projection, splitting, denial, and externalization will sooner or later bring these up in their relationship to the therapist. Thus, the push and pull and the contradictory expectations attributed by the patient to her lover may soon become the characteristics of the therapist in the patient's mind. Despite its seemingly chaotic effects on the treatment situa-

---

29. In a similar vein though different context, the eminent British photographer Lord Snowdown said, "A background has to be just this side of being something, and just the other side of being nothing" (Lacayo 1984).

tion, this is a welcome development since it provides the therapist with an opportunity to clarify and interpret the distorting effects of these mechanisms in the here and now of their relationship (Kernberg 1975).

Third, it is also useful to keep in mind that patients whose use of externalization borders on what Klein (1940) labeled *manic defence,* that is, almost complete negation of their inner reality as a result of the emphasis on external reality may not be suited for psychoanalytic psychotherapy and may have to be treated with only a supportive approach.

Secret Aspects of Being "The Other Woman"

A secret is an intrapsychic cul-de-sac. It not only disrupts life's experiential continuity but it also sets in motion defensive processes to guard its own existence. It may defensively contain significant contemporary and/or past experiences and fantasies that are symbolic stand-ins for each other. Or the very fact of a secret may itself serve symbolic purposes irrespective of its contents. Thus hidden omnipotent, obstinate, retentive, teasing, seductive needs (and associated fantasies) from different levels of psychosexual development may all find expression in an individual's keeping a secret. On the other hand, a "secret life" may imply the existence of a defensively split-off sector of psychic organization with quasi-independent self and object representations. Keeping a secret may also serve narcissistic purposes and help to allay fears of humiliation and shame. All these matters clearly have significant effects upon the day-to-day life of the individual. Moreover, by getting surrounded by more and more material, rather like a gallstone, a secret effects a psychotherapeutic dialogue adversely.

The other woman is brought to the psychotherapist by her secret agony. The immediate temptation for the therapist, therefore, is to assume the role of sympathetic confidante and to overlook the foregoing issues, as well as the possibility that concerns that led to the birth of a secret pocket of social and psychic existence may be active in the here and now of the treatment situation. It is important to keep in mind that the patient's bringing in a secret story as the centerpiece of her suffering may serve as both a major impetus for psychological inquiry as well as a built-in resistance that can be easily overlooked.

Countertransference Difficulties

The other woman's therapist encounters two sets of countertransference difficulties. The first of these involves the countertransference hatred characteristically generated by patients with self-destructive tendencies and self-defeating behaviors (Kernberg 1976b, Maltsberger and Buie 1974, Winnicott 1949). As a rule, the greater the self-destructiveness in the patient, the stronger is the intensity with which these countertransference feelings are experienced by the therapist. Thus, the group two other woman induces more such feelings than the group one other woman. These patients' therapist finds his efforts repeatedly thwarted, his professional self-esteem chronically lowered, and his interventions invariably falling as if on deaf ears. The patient's contradictory versions of her lover make it difficult for the therapist to develop a composite picture of him or of their relationship. He feels pulled in one direction by the patient during some sessions and in a totally opposite direction in other sessions. He may feel confused and impotent. All this in and of itself may not be a source of any difficulty in the therapy. Indeed, such feelings in the therapist if carefully "diagnosed" by him may lead to a deeper understanding of the disowned, dissociated, and externalized aspects of the patient's psychic structure (Kernberg 1992). The situation is thus one of "concordant identification" (Racker 1957) with the patient's sadistic parental introjects. However, such understanding and its potential technical usefulness depends upon the therapist's ability to recognize in himself the existence of such strong feelings without acting upon them. The therapist's anxiety about his own aggression on the other hand may lead to a premature defensive warding off of such affects in him. This would necessitate defensive operations such as reaction formation (e.g. being excessively concerned and worried about the patient), turning against the self (e.g. excessively doubting one's therapeutic abilities), displacement (e.g. irritability with others), and may predispose the therapist to subtly act out his hostility toward the patient (e.g. forgetting an appointment or being late for sessions). Therefore, it is the "absence" of the negative feelings in the therapist that are more problematic than in the situation where such feelings and accompanying hostile fantasies can be permitted conscious awareness. In the latter situation a therapist can derive hypotheses from such fantasies regarding the aspects of the patient that have undergone projective identification.

The second set of countertransference difficulties involves the stirring up in the therapist of a moralistic stance that insists that a woman *not* be romantically or sexually involved with someone who is married. This may propel the therapist to subtly or overtly disparage the woman's lover and to overlook the depth and complexity of the patient's need for such a relationship. Very often, however, such a moralistic stance is an unconscious disguise for strong oedipal wishes that are being stirred up in the therapist. The patient has put herself in between a couple (her lover and his wife) and has put the therapist in a *complimentary identification* (Racker 1957); that is, an identification with the infantile in the patient that compels him to put himself in between another couple (the patient and her lover). The wish to rescue a woman from an unsatisfactory lover (Freud 1910) and the attraction of the other woman (Feldman 1964) get powerfully mobilized in the therapist and may impinge upon his work ego.

In view of the foregoing, it is obvious that the therapist of the other woman should be prepared to handle in himself the development of strong aggressive and libidinal wishes toward his patient. His knowledge of his own childhood wishes and conflicts, gained from personal analysis, whether therapeutic, didactic, or self-conducted, should help him in this regard.

CONCLUDING REMARKS

Women who have sustained intimate relationships with married men are generally of two types. The first type is a deeply feminine, affectualized, and histrionic one whose involvement with a married man represents unresolved oedipal wishes as well as punishment over those wishes. This type of other woman led a relatively peaceful life until her entanglement with a married man began. She is socially well adapted and is capable of mourning, sadness, empathy, love, and concern. Her superego is strict and well internalized; she experiences guilt regarding her sexuality and intimacy with a married man. The second type had a troubled childhood, a searing adolescence, and an adult life characterized by overt self-destructive acts, inner uncertainty, cynicism, and chronic boredom. Her object relations are shallow and she displays a continued need for omnipotent external objects. This need finds expression in her relationship with a married man. A pseudorelationship of occasional intoxicating pleasure is established at the cost of sacrificing knowledge and ambivalence, two prerequisites for genuine intimacy.

Both types of the other women present to the mental health professional with dysthymic complaints centering around their romantic entanglements. They are distressed and puzzled by these relationships. The first type of other woman feels this anguish on a more sustained basis than the second type, who at most times splits off and denies such concerns only to suffer libidinally unmitigated agony and doubt at other times. However, some defensive splitting and denial of the painfully ambivalent nature of the relationship are seen in both types of women. These mechanisms either cause (in the first type) or result from (in the second type) a cleavage of the ego, which has its own deleterious effects upon affect integration and decision-making processes. It is with these problems and a generalized, low-grade dysthymia that the other women seek psychotherapy.

One can help the other woman by recommending psychoanalysis, psychoanalytic psychotherapy, or supportive psychotherapy. The choice of treatment modality depends upon the nature of conflicts, the level of character organization, the degree of analyzability, the realistic feasibility of establishing and maintaining a treatment situation, the urgency with which symptom relief is required, and the degree to which one suspects that involvement with the married man will continue to foster externalization and negation of intrapsychic conflict. In most instances, however, psychoanalytic psychotherapy seems to be the treatment of choice. This treatment, while following the general rules and expected developments of any psychoanalytic psychotherapy, may pose certain specific dilemmas. These include a built-in reality resistance, exploring the effect of keeping a secret upon an overall life situation and the treatment alliance, and a greater than usual risk of countertransference difficulties. With careful attention, however, these problems should generally be manageable.

Finally, it should be remembered that these descriptions, hypotheses, and recommendations regarding the other women are based upon a relatively modest clinical experience. Methodologically sounder studies with larger samples of women who are involved with married men on the one hand, and deeper, more detailed psychoanalytic data on the other, are required to shed further light on the nature of the various phenomena involved. Meanwhile, I can conclude this basically clinical contribution by saying to the inquisitive reader what Freud (1933) said to his audience at the end of his lecture on femininity: "If you want to know more . . . enquire from your own experiences of life, or turn to the poets, or wait until science can give you deeper and more coherent information" (p. 135).

Part III

UNCELEBRATED PARTNERS

5

ANIMALS

While the celebrated case histories of Rat man, Little Hans, and Wolf man (Freud 1909a,b, 1918 respectively) have immortalized the role of animals in human psychopathology, the fact is that animals have long roamed the terrain of diagnostic categories in clinical psychiatry. In the disrupted mind, the zookeeper leaves the cage doors ajar and lets the animals assume power over man by invading his thoughts and his body. Appearing as psychic hints and guesses, they wink at him mischeviously in dreams. Becoming cuddly maternal substitutes, they relieve his loneliness and isolation. Turning cold blooded and vicious, they terrify him by vague or explicit persecutory dreads. Becoming receptacles of his erotic emissions, they soothe his bodily tensions. Crawling under his skin and infesting his guts, they torture him from within. If the resulting chaos is intense, human identity becomes so fragmented that man comes to believe or act as if he is transforming into an animal.

This chapter will offer a guided tour of this anguished, puzzling, scary, and, at times, darkly erotic mental zoo. It will cover a large terrain of psychiatric symptomatology involving animals, stopping at the scenic spots of delusions and hallucinations, confusional states, lycanthropy, culture-bound psychiatric syndromes, obsessions and phobias, personality disorders, sexual perversions, and childhood psychiatric disorders. The emphasis of this discourse will be descriptive and its overall stance biopsychosocial with occasional forays into deeper psychodynamic issues involved in these symptoms.[30]

DELUSIONS AND HALLUCINATIONS

Psychotic symptomatology often involves animals. In 1977, the famous case of "Son of Sam," the New York serial killer who felt commanded to commit murder by his neighbor's dog Sam, brought the link between human madness and animals to public awareness. Less dramatic delusions involving animals are, however, more common. The belief of having had sexual contact with them, for instance, is not rare among schizophrenics (Kraepelin 1919); two in a sample of 75 schizophrenics studied in narcoanalysis (Norman 1948) expressed such a delusion. However, the amytal-induced drowsiness is not a precondition for such delusions to surface, as was evident in the following case (Akhtar and Thomson 1980).

- Case 1

A middle-aged chronic schizophrenic woman, relatively stable for two years, suddenly exhibited symptoms of frank psychosis after receiving a letter from her sister, who stated that their father, a very regressed schizophrenic, had been indulging in sexual acts with a family dog named after the patient. On admission to the hospital, the patient had the delusional belief that she herself had had sexual activity with a dog named after her daughter. The fact that no such dog existed became clear only much later.

More frequent than such delusion is the syndrome in which the individual believes to be infested with parasites. While generally this *parasitosis* (Berrios 1985, DeLeon 1992) involves ideas about alimentary infestation, sensations and fantasies about skin involvement are

---

30. The clinical material presented here is disguised to protect confidentiality of these patients. Cases 1, 2, 6, 8, 9, and 11 come from Dr. Akhtar's practice and cases 4, 5, 7, 10, 13, 14, 15, and 16 are from Dr. Brown's practice. Cases 3 and 12 have been kindly provided by Drs. Irene Dadson and Saif Abdullah respectively.

not infrequent. Worms, ticks, mites, and scabies thus enter the human psyche as delusions and hallucinations. The nosology, which varies from *Magnan's sign* (Magnan and Saury 1889), and *Cocaine bugs* (Siegel 1978), to *Ekbom's Syndrome* (Ekbom 1938), and Munro's (1982) *monosymptomatic hypochondriacal psychosis*, offers both a historical perspective and confusion. Terms like *acaraphobia* (Myerson 1921) and *zoophobia* (Eller 1929) are misnomers and have been replaced by "delusions of parasitosis." The latter term correctly depicts the syndrome not as a "fear" but as a tenacious belief that insects are on or under the skin. Indeed, some patients carry "proofs" of such insects with them in a phenomenon called the *matchbox sign* of infestation (Morris 1991). This is a good indicator of a primary psychiatric illness: either a delusional disorder (if confined to the single false belief system) or part of a depressive, manic, or schizophrenic psychosis (Berrios 1985, DeLeon et al. 1992, Jibiki 1992, Mitchell and Vierkant 1991, Morris 1991, Podoll et al. 1993, Trabert 1991). Scratching behavior may also indicate the induced psychosis of folie a deux or folie partagee, for a significant percentage of patients do have a close relative with a similar delusional disorder (Bourgeous et al. 1992, DeLeon et al. 1992, Gieler 1990, Gonsalez et al. 1993, Maier 1987, Mester 1975, Morris 1991, Siegel 1978). The literature debates whether the delusion of parasitosis is primary or secondary to real or hallucinated tactile sensations.[31] Moreover, the etiology of these conditions is viewed as multifactorial. While impaired vision, social isolation, and history of actual parasitic infestation in past (Jibiki 1992, May 1991) might act as predisposing factors, deeper intrapsychic issues are invariably associated with such psychotic symptomatology. Thus the literature is replete with references to "psychological precipitants" and "symbolic meanings" of insects (Freinhar 1984, Hopkinson 1973, Reilly 1988, Skott 1975).

Psychosexual conflicts heavily contribute to the onset of such a delusional state where the delusion functions to keep sexual and aggressive conflicts repressed (Horstein et al. 1989, May 1991,

---

31. Using neuroimaging, Musalek (1989) and DeLeon (1992) have explored anatomic location (limbic cortex verses prefrontal and associative areas) to understand further the etiology and pathogenesis of the delusions and hallucinations of animals under the skin.

Paulson and Petrus 1969). Obsessive-compulsive personality traits (Berrios 1985, Reilly 1988, Skott 1975), paranoid defenses (Sizaret and Simon 1976), and the *symbolic recuperation of loss* often lurk in the background (Horstein et al. 1989, Sizaret and Simon 1976). Dynamic theories also offer reasons for the prevalence and significance of the insect in fantasies and delusions (Ostapzeff 1975, Roux 1988). "The insects' ephemericality, ubiquity, and ability to penetrate give it the ability to cross barriers of time and space, and are thought to be the reason for its special place in the subconscious of humans" (Roux 1988). Ferenczi (1926) connects vermin to the unconscious phantasy of being pregnant, "of sheltering little things in and on the body," and notes that the German word for *worm* is applied to children as "an affectionate diminutive" (p. 361). Family dynamics have also been applied to delusions involving parasites (Macaskill 1987, Reilly 1988, Verbeek 1959). In folie a deux involving animals, passive and dependent characteristics are commonly associated with the originally healthy partner (usually child or spouse) in which the delusion is induced. While this occurs in the setting of clear consciousness, some other symptoms involving animals depend upon a clouding of the sensorium.

CONFUSIONAL STATES

First and foremost, the delusions and hallucinations of parasitosis (either in the form of alimentary infestation or bugs crawling on or under the skin) often occur in association with a clouded sensorium. Cocaine or amphetamine intoxication, alcohol withdrawal, and certain states associated with vitamin B_{12} deficiency are especially associated with tactile hallucinations referred to as *formications* (DeLeon 1992, May and Terpenning 1991, Mitchell and Vierkant 1991, Reilly 1988). Differential diagnosis of such cases should also include organic causes such as medications, occult neoplasms, renal dysfunction, diabetes, and neurologic conditions like Alzheimer's disease or cerebral infarction or tumor (Berrios 1985, DeLeon 1992, Flynn 1989, Kanazawa 1992, Marneros et al. 1988, Morris 1991, Reilly 1988, Trabert 1991). Second, the declining cognitive functions associated with dementia often lead to the neglect of pets. Hitherto loved animals go uncared for and become a source of concern to the family and neighbors. Finally, incomprehensible acts of violence toward pets can also result from a paroxysm of brain dysfunction during which the individual is completely confused. The following case reported by Akhtar and Brenner (1979) depicts one such occurrence.

Case 2

A young man was hospitalized after he bizarrely choked his dog to death and could not recall doing it. He did, however, remember leaving home to walk his dog and a few hours later discovered himself on an unfamiliar road, his dog lying dead at his feet. Witnesses called the police and he was admitted for evaluation. Despite thorough interviewing, he did not reveal significant psychopathology and little symbolic significance to his act of violence could be detected. He was very perplexed and quite concerned about it also. There was no history of head trauma or seizures, but a nasopharyngeal EEG was consistent with temporal lobe epilepsy.

The dramatic quality of such epileptic fugue states is surpassed only by a syndrome in which the individual begins to claim or act like he has turned into an animal.

LYCANTHROPY

When disruption of the mind is so severe that projection can no longer prevent the dissolution of identity, man and animal merge in the syndrome known as *lycanthropy* (Campbell 1989). Lycanthropy is the belief that one can change into a wolf and the display of behavior suggesting such a belief. Those affected do not sleep, go out at night, and wander till morning. They perceive themselves as evil and disgusting, ruminate, and dream about wolves and believe themselves to possess satanic powers (Fahy 1989). They yearn for raw flesh and might even hunt and devour small prey. At times, they seek sexual intercourse with cats and talk to animals (Kulick 1990). When they look in the mirror, they see the head of a wolf (Verdoux and Bourgeouis 1993).

This syndrome has historic and mythic roots that are universal.

Known also as *zoophilic metamorphosis* (Fahy 1989) and *insania zooanthropia* (Fahy 1989), lycanthropy derives its name from the Greek *Lycaon*, who was turned into a wolf by Zeus for having deceitfully fed him human flesh. In the Middle Ages, hundreds were condemned to death in France for demonic possession in the form of lycanthropy. Among South American Indian tribes, animal metamorphosis was commonly recorded (Kulick et al. 1990). In the last two decades, there have been almost 20 case reports of lycanthropy in the medical literature (Benezech et al. 1989, Coll et al. 1985, Dening 1989, Keck 1988, Koehler et al. 1990, Kulick et al. 1990, Malliaras et al. 1978, Mellor 1988, Rajna et al. 1990, Rojo-Morenno, et al. 1990, Surawicz 1975, Verdoux and Bourgeouis 1993). From Spain, Canada, France, England, and the United States, patients present imitating and/or believing themselves to be wolves (as well as tigers, cats, dogs, rabbits, and birds). Today, lycanthropy is recognized as a non-specific delusion that can be understood through the varying perspectives of individual psychodynamics, disease state, and cultural and religious predisposition.

Intense frustrations and sadomasochistic object relations during early infancy and childhood at times lead to the internalization of a pet rather than a parent as the ideal self-object (Kulick et al. 1990). Projection of oral rage creates cannibalistic fears and intensifies castration anxiety. Thus there are elements of identification with aggressor as well in these instances. In cases where the onset follows sexual intercourse, lycanthropy serves as a defense against violent sexual urges (Jackson 1978, Rosenstock and Bincent 1977). Lycanthropic behaviors may represent the splitting off of primitive drives and thus might be a bizarre escape mechanism from guilt (Keck et al. 1988, Surawicz and Banta 1975). The wolf might also represent an archetypal symbol of sadistic behavior and an expression of primitive identity (Eisler 1978, Jung 1954). Dreams of werewolves may signify oral-sadistic or cannibalistic impulses condensed with oedipal conflicts (Fahy 1989 on Jones 1937). Unlike the sphynx, the centaur, or the mermaid, in which the amalgam of a man and animal leaves the nether regions to the animal half of the hybrid creature (Stone 1992), the werewolf is the metamorphosis of identity as a whole. In the former, man simply conceals his animal-like sexual and aggressive drives, while in the latter he becomes them.

Interestingly, lycanthropy has been seen in association with many medical and psychiatric disorders including drug-induced psychoses (Keck 1988), temporal lobe epilepsy (Keck 1988, Kulick et al. 1990), porphyria (Illis 1964), schizophrenia (Coll 1985, Keck et al. 1988, Surawicz and Banta 1975), affective psychosis (Coll 1985, Dening 1989, Keck 1988, Mellor 1988, Verdoux and Bourgeouis 1993), borderline personality (Deutsch 1942, Keck 1988), antisocial personality (Benezech 1989), and even factitious disorder (Keck 1988). Removing themselves from the medical model, several authors (Fahy 1989, Kulick et al. 1990, Merkur 1981, Yellowlees 1989) emphasize the effects of religion and culture on the lycanthropy. The "culturally syntonic" animal-like behaviors that led to increased tribal power for the shaman were commonly ascribed to demonic possession and punished by death in the Middle Ages (Kulick et al. 1990). Navajo Indians religiously enact the behavior of the coyote in a tribal ceremony before the hunt. When "the psycho-hygienic function of the ritualism fails, hunting neurosis develops" (Merkur 1981, p. 243), in which the guilt and horror of the hunt leads to delusional transformation of man into coyote. Such culturally facilitated symptomatology involving animals is, however, not restricted to the syndrome of lycanthropy.

CULTURE-BOUND PSYCHIATRIC SYNDROMES

Psychotic symptoms involving animals cross not only the boundaries of skin and reality but also those of culture. In societies where animals are in close contact with humans, they are perhaps more readily drawn into the psyche as projective containers for unacceptable sexual impulses, sadomasochism, guilt, fear, and shame. Three such culture-bound syndromes that involve animals are amafufanyane, *latah*, and piblokto. *Amafufanyane* (Kaplan and Sadock 1989, Robertson and Kottler 1993) is a psychosis of delusions and hallucinations seen in African men and women. One particular presentation is of a woman who awakens acting bizarrely and reporting that she is pregnant by a baboon. The belief surrounding the psychosis is that an evil spirit is sent to the patient through an animal like a baboon or a bird. Symptoms also include sleep paralysis, abdominal pain, paralysis, blindness, shouting, sobbing, hysterical seizures, and amnesia. Thinly veiled symbolic enactments of sexual themes are invariably associated with these fits. *Latah* (Kaplan 1989, Tseng and McDermott 1981) is a Malaysian or Indonesian cultural psychosis with symptoms of a startle response, echolalia, and echopraxia. Patients make inappropriate verbal and motor behaviors frequently mimicking animals. Most accounts describe a frightened woman who begins to threaten and curse following a mild stimulus such as a sudden noise or some physical contact such as a slap on the back or tickling. Interestingly, the attack may follow a snake bite, seeing a snake, or dreaming of a snake. There is often erotic character to many of the latah manifestations. *Piblokto* (Kaplan 1989), also called "arctic hysteria," is an episode of psychosis or dissociation affecting arctic Eskimos. Mutism may precede an attack in which a woman tears off her clothes and runs through the snow imitating the cry of some animal or bird. Periods of melancholic brooding may also herald an attack, which typically lasts for one to two hours. The afflicted person is believed to be possessed by evil spirits and observers remain at a distance. After the attack, the person gradually resumes normalcy while suffering amnesia for the episode.

Today, despite the prevalence of mental illness and drug abuse, animal metamorphosis is a rare syndrome most commonly observed in a subcultural context.[32] Thankfully, the modern werewolf stalks mainly the cinema and the literary imagination. While saved from this uncanny horror, the modern man, however, cannot escape the more common fear of being victimized by animals invisible to the naked eye, that is, parasites and germs.

OBSESSIONS AND PHOBIAS

Although fleeting concerns involving animals may appear in all types of anxiety reactions, the anxiety disorder par excellence involving animals is simple phobia. In fact, animals have been

---

32. With the progress of civilization, computers and other electrical devices have forged their way between man and the animal world. As cultural determinants influence mental life (Akhtar 1983, Yellowlees 1989), we are more likely to see delusions of being wired by the CIA through silver-plated fillings than of lycanthropy.

identified as four of the five most common objects of phobias
(Boudon et al. 1988). Snakes, spiders, mice, bugs, birds, and dogs
(Boudon 1988, Marks 1987) are perhaps the most commonly feared
animals. Strikingly, while the "choice" of the dreaded animal varies
from individual to individual and region to region, these animal
phobias occur with stability over culture and time (Arieti 1974). In
an attempt to understand the etiology of such fears, psychodynamic,
learning, and biological perspectives have been evoked in the
psychiatric literature.[33]

Animals also figure in the symptomatology of other anxiety
disorders. Unlike childhood phobias, adult-onset phobias are usually precipitated by a relevant trauma such as a dog bite or a bee
sting (Friedman 1966, Marks 1987, Solyom 1974). Symptoms of fearful preoccupation and recurrent nightmares lead to merging diag-
noses of phobia and post-traumatic stress disorder (Marks 1987).
Similarly, individuals with obsessional neurosis might display behaviors such as compulsively searching for the feared animal or
refusing to touch the feared animal or anything the animal may
have touched (Marks 1987). "Intrusive repetive visual images involv-

---

33. Modeling, vicarious learning, and observational conditioning have been
discussed as alternative means by which animals have acquired their evocative
potential (Cook and Mineca 1987, Emde 1984, Eysenck 1965, Marks 1987, Mineka
et al. 1984, Solyom et al. 1974, Wolpe and Rachman 1960). This perspective reports
cases of phobias arising after a child observes a parent responding fearfully to an
animal (Solyom et al. 1974) or, as in Mineka et al.'s (1984) experiments, after
lab-reared rhesus monkeys view wild-caught monkeys reacting fearfully to snakes.
More recently, learning theory has been challenged and broadened by biological
research in animal phobias (Bennett-Levy 1984, Davey et al. 1992, 1993, Marks
1987, McNally and Steketee 1985, Mineka et al. 1984). This view suggests that
learning is "biologically prepared" in that there are anatomic portions of the brain
preprogrammed to perceive specific fear-evoking animal movements much like the
nondominant parietal lobe perceives faces. Sudden movement and speed are
animal qualities of "stimulus configurations" that may cause certain animals to be
"chosen" as fearful. Some of these authors have pointed to the fact that most animal
phobias involve harmless (spider, cockroach, maggot, snake, and rat) rather than
predatory animals (lions, tigers, sharks): They postulate that animal phobias
correlate more with contamination and disgust rather than with fear. Together,
these three etiological perspectives, namely modeling, vicarious learning, and
observational conditioning, might explain why specific animals have remained
both "chosen" phobic objects and symbols in mythology in almost every culture.

ing sex with animals" that are ego dystonic occur and may require psychopharmacological interventions (Hollander 1995, p. 10). They might also suffer from hand-washing rituals enacted to relieve intrusive ruminations of contamination by the feared animal. Here the overlap between a specific animal phobia and obsessive compulsive disorder becomes evident (Marks 1987). Thus, through a mixture of unconscious fantasy, cultural learning, and biological evolution of the mind, the long-enduring association between man and animal becomes endowed with fear-inducing potential of a highly personal nature. Given a symbolically significant trigger from the external environment, this might become manifest as a recurrent nightmare, simple phobia, or obsessive-compulsive symptomatology.

Case 3

A 23-year-old single woman presented with a recent intensification of her obsessive-compulsive symptomatology. While she had always been detail oriented and orderly, it was only at age 16 that she had developed distressing ruminations regarding germs and contamination. Treatment with psychopharmacological means relieved her symptoms to a certain extent, though she continued to lead a socially inhibited and asexual life. She lived with her mother, took occasional courses at a community college, and had few friends. Two months prior to her seeking consultation, she had developed a new concern. If she saw a housefly going into her bedroom, she would not be able to sleep there. She would spend that night in the living room, even if she had witnessed the fly exit her bedroom. She feared that the fly might have brought dirt from outside and deposited it on her bed.

The patient's parents were divorced when she was five years old and she had visibly suffered at the resultant distance from her father, who left the marital home. He died when she was 12 and she was heartbroken. Passage through puberty and adolescence was difficult, with much hostility toward the mother. She responded adversely to mother's dating, fearing that the mother might catch a venereal disease. She hated it when the mother had the lover stay overnight, especially because the mother asked her to clean the bathroom after the boyfriend had finished taking a shower there.

For the past few months, the boyfriend had been staying over more often and it is around this time that the preoccupation with the fly entering her bedroom had started.

The potential links between the loss of father, inhibition of sexuality, anger at mother's psychosexual freedom, concern about mother's catching a venereal disease, exposure to the mother's boyfriend, and her own fears of contamination together hinted at a complex unconscious fantasy with prominent regressive, anal elements. The fly, and the associated contamination fear, most likely represented the return of the repudiated wish for the father's (mother's boyfriend's) penis and his semen.

Just like the ordinary housefly, the phallic snake, the sperm-like worm, and the free-flying bird acquire unconscious significance from the myths and totems of the past (Freud 1913, Abraham 1927) as well as from the unconcious conflicts of the present. As such, they serve as ready symbols for the displacement of internal anxiety onto relatively harmless external objects (Abraham 1927, Domangue 1985). In addition to a generalized or cultural meaning, the psychodynamic perspective also attributes phobic object choice to idiosyncrasies of both individual experience and the associative process of unconscious mental life; thus, hens, millipedes, spiders, flies, cats, horses, frogs, butterflies, and locusts enter the phobic menagerie (Arieti 1974, Abraham 1927, Domangue 1985, English 1945, Fenichel 1945, Ferenczi 1926, Freud 1895b, 1909, Jones 1948, Kolansky 1960, Searles 1960, Sperling 1971, Sterba 1935, Tyson 1978, van der Hart 1981, Volkan 1972).

While both the descriptive and psychoanalytic literatures have focused upon symptomatic phobias, the fact remains that diffuse phobic tendencies that are assimilated in an individual's character are perhaps more common. Such a "phobic character" (Akhtar and Byrne 1983, Fenichel 1945, MacKinnon and Michaels 1971, Stone 1980) is organized around the defenses of repression and displacement. The fearfulness of such an individual centers upon specific situations and objects. While resembling the dread experienced by a paranoid individual, the phobic constellation is actually quite different. Wurmser (1981) points out three differences between phobic and paranoid characters. In the phobic, the feeling is "It is a danger, but I do not know why. It may be for this or that reason," while in the paranoid it is "It is a danger *and I know why*, namely, such and such is his or her intention" (p. 314, author's emphasis). In other words, the phobic character does not display the personalization and intentionality of the outside menace. Second, the leading affective reactions in the two conditions are different. In the paranoid personality, it is rage, hatred, contempt, and grudge, while in the phobic character it is anxiety, guilty fears, and their somatic counterparts. Third, the paranoid reacts by attack or provocation of attack, while the phobic reacts by avoidance and flight. The phobic organization is essentially a neurotic one while the paranoid leans toward the use of psychotic mechanisms. The phobic says that he is afraid of dogs while the paranoid maintains that dogs are out to get him!

THE SYNDROME OF ANIMAL HOARDING

While striking accounts of it periodically appear in newspapers and popular magazines, animal hoarding was only recently delineated as a specific psychiatric syndrome. Worth and Beck (1981) noted that this syndrome consists of a socially isolated individual relentlessly "collecting" animals, seemingly out of concern and pity for them. A large number of stray cats or dogs (often up to 50–60) are brought home to be cared for. Preoccupation with them is great and physical contact constant. Self-care and attention to the living quarters suffer in the process. There is often no telephone or adequate plumbing in the house. Monetary resources, usually meager, are all spent on these animals. A deep sense of belonging toward them prevails and can preclude proper disposal in case of their death. More recently, Patronek (1999) reported on 54 cases of animal hoarding. Most were female and a large proportion were 60 years of age or older. The most common animals involved were cats and dogs. Dead or sick animals were discovered in 80 percent of the cases, yet the hoarder did not acknowledge this as a problem.

Several etiological models have been suggested (Lockwood 1994) including delusional beliefs, dementia, addiction, sexual perversion, attachment disorder, and obsessive-compulsive neurosis. How-

ever, these etiological models are not exclusive of each other. Some
(e.g. sexual perversion and obsessive-compulsive disorder) might be
independent but others (e.g. delusional and attachment) can easily
coexist. Moreover, the models are not on the same level of abstraction. Some (e.g. delusional, obsessive-compulsive disorder) are at a
phenomenological level while others (e.g. attachment) are on an
etiological level. The linkage between obsessive-compulsive disorder
and animal hoarding is also not as clear as it is portrayed by Frost.
To be sure, the defense of reaction formation is operative in both
obsessive-compulsive disorder and animal hoarding. However, a key
component of obsessive-compulsive disorder is missing in the latter.
The symptoms in obsessive-compulsive disorder are ego dystonic
and distressing to the patient while animal hoarding is ego syntonic.
In this connection, it is important to remember what the great
descriptive psychiatrist (the late) Sir Aubrey Lewis has explicitly
stated: "The more enjoyable the act, the less likely it is to be
obsessional" (1936).

The syndrome of animal hoarding is actually more likely to
be associated with schizotypal personality disorder. Dynamically,
it represents a desperate rescue effort in which the inwardly
endangered remnants of the positive self-representation are pro-
jected onto stray animals. They come to represent the individual's
lost, fragile, and retrospectively idealized child self. This projection buttresses the individual's own identification with an imagined
bountiful mother who can take care of any number of children
(standing for any amount of hunger in a child). All aggression
is split off and deflected away from this mother–self and the
child–animal dyad. However, this is true only of the conscious
experience. At a deeper level, neither the self (mother) nor the
animal (child) can find adequate psychophysical nourishment. The
dilapidated housing and filthy circumstances testify to the under-
currents of masochism and the frequently marasmic animals to the
unconscious sadism.

PERSONALITY DISORDERS

Psychiatric symptomatology involving animals is also found in
association with personality disorders. Though rarely included in

standard interviewing techniques, questions regarding an individual's involvement with animals frequently reveal inflexible and maladaptive attitudes. Individuals with some personality disorders display intense involvement with animals. Those with a hidden psychotic core (e.g. schizotypal personalities) might develop split-off identifications with animals and might even behaviorally enact these identifications in private or in public; Volkan (1995) has reported the case of a young man whose clowning and dramatic identification with a dog brought him social acclaim underneath which a cauldron of anguish simmered. For less disturbed individuals, animals become narcissistic or exhibitionistic extensions (Mouren et al. 1980) and they draw intense satisfaction from flattering comments about their pets. Schizoid patients often feel more comfortable with animals than with fellow humans and might carry on an intense imaginary dialogue with them. Yet another group of patients intensely involved with animals are those with borderline personality. They often use animals as transitional objects (Akhtar 1992b, Mouren et al. 1980) to ease the pain of separateness and aloneness. Such attachments can be striking.

Case 4

A middle-aged man with borderline personality disorder celebrated his birthday with a cake and candles shared only with his two dogs. He expressed a yearning to be valued by others and not used by them for his money or his willingness to do them special favors. At the same time, he felt unable to join in social activities and, feeling misfit, would become silent and withdrawn. With his dogs, he felt needed and loved and did not experience the anxious detachment he felt with people. The company of his pets during his birthday celebration thus saved him from complete isolation.

Such reliance on the company of pets is usually characterological. However, this behavior is not uncommon in the elderly who, either missing their grown-up and alienated children or having been childless to begin with, refer to their pets as their "babies." At other times, it arises as a response to the disturbed equilibrium of a dependent transference during the course of psychotherapy.

Case 5

A 42-year-old woman with borderline personality disorder was in twice-a-week psychoanalytic psychotherapy. Whenever our work was interrupted by my leaving, we would discuss how her anger toward me was directed at herself and how it was triggered by painful feelings of abandonment. Nevertheless, during my absence, she would threaten to take an overdose of her medication and require crisis intervention. She would experience me as "the best and only" doctor who could help her. All other doctors were "bad and cold." In the session preceding an interruption in the second year of treatment, the patient expressed a wish to hold onto me and keep me from leaving her. On my return, she came to my office and proudly told me she had not tried to hurt herself. She then described how she had purchased, cuddled with, and cared for "a little brown" guinea pig. This transitional object provided her with comfort at the same time as it allowed her to express her rage by devaluing her doctor "a little."

In view of the borderline individual's use of splitting and the propensity toward intense idealization and devaluation of others, relationships with animals provide a relatively peaceful avenue of connectedness. However, under states of stress, their pets might also become the targets of their intense rage (Akhtar 1994).

Case 6

A severely borderline young man with an exquisite sensitivity to rejection was seen in thrice-weekly, face-to-face, psychoanalytic psychotherapy. Once, early in his treatment, I informed him of an upcoming interruption in schedule. He responded with a pained silence, gaze avoidance, and a noticeable drop in his voice. My empathic affirmation of this and encouragement of him to put his feelings into words met with little success. Later that evening (he told me amid sobs during the next session), the patient saw on his front yard a little frog that appeared sad and lonely to him. He picked up the frog, took it inside, and made a "home" for it in a little box. He tried to cheer up the frog by talking to it and giving it bread crumbs. The frog, however, jumped out of the box and soon was nowhere to be found. He looked for it all over his place. He repeatedly called for it, and with the absence of any response began to feel rejected and angry. This grew into rage. Then, suddenly, he saw the frog. Cursing loudly, he chased it around the room, damaging many of his belongings in the process. In a fury, he caught the frog and repeatedly smashed it against the wall with all his might. Later, a dawning awareness that he was "committing murder" stopped him. He let the now badly injured frog out of a window.

The good frog–bad frog split, the shift from caretaker to murderer, the incapacity for ambivalence and the flooding of the ego with raw aggression are as explicit in this enactment as are the transference themes of feeling abandoned by the analyst (the bad frog), and the consequent loneliness and rage. Blum (1981) notes that in such cases because of the blurring of the self-object boundaries the object's wish for independence is experienced as an agonizing, hence unforgivable, betrayal. Such anxious attachment to objects may even be maintained at the cost of mistreatment from them. This is especially characteristic of individuals with dependent personality disorder.

Case 7

A young woman struggled without insight in a relationship with a man who treated her quite cruelly until he threatened to leave her unless she gave away her cat. Identified with the cat, who she viewed as "friendly, affectionate, and vulnerable," she began to be able to see that the way her boyfriend treated the cat was not dissimilar from the way he treated her. Her insight resulted in her telling her boyfriend that she should not move with him to another state. Yet, after the move, when the boyfriend agreed to her bringing her cat, the patient found herself more and more anxious to engage in the treatment. She expressed feeling as if the treatment might result in her leaving her boyfriend. Within several weeks, she opted to move with her cat to live with her boyfriend, rationalizing how she knew that the way he would now treat both of them would be different.

Such struggles over autonomy often go back further and involve the primary objects of childhood while still manifesting within the matrix of neurotic symptomatology involving animals. The initially puzzling clinical picture turns out to be a phenomenological screen for the rapprochement subphase (Mahler et al. 1975) type push–pull for independent selfhood.

Case 8

A 27-year-old legal intern sought consultation with depressive complaints. For about a quarter of his first interview with me, he elaborated upon his apathy, anhedonia, and diminished sexual desire, relating their onset to the birth of his six-month-old son. Then he abruptly stopped and said that while all he had said so far was true, there was something else that was troubling him even more. This "something" had been with him for many years and he had never revealed it to anyone. I responded by gently encouraging him to say more both about what this hidden problem was and also about the concerns that had led him to keep it a secret. After some hesitation, the patient revealed that he liked to chew upon cats' nails. He would frequent friends, acquaintances, and, at times, scout the neighborhood to find a cat. Holding the animal up in his arms, he would bite off a chip of its nails. He kept these bits and pieces in a little glass jar and chewed upon them at his leisure. As the interview progressed, a second interaction with cats emerged. He also liked to bring the cat's face very close to his own face and breathe in the air that came out of the cat's nostrils. Both these acts gave him deep gratification, though he also worried about their apparent oddity and did not quite know what to make of them.

In the second interview, while describing his family background, the patient came upon the topic of his mother. He sighed, saying, "You don't want to know about her. She is so controlling, so intrusive that I can't describe. She lives about a thousand miles from here but I constantly feel her claws on my arms." As he said this he grabbed the upper part of his left arm with his right hand, making the latter appear like a claw, and dug his nails into the skin. Seeing the connection between the biting off of a cat's nails and the alleged claw of his mother on his arm, I said, "Did you notice what you just said?" He was puzzled. "What?" he responded. I said, "What do you make of your saying, 'claws'? And, how do you connect them with 'nails'?" He was at first dumbfounded and then became somber and began to talk about his chronic difficulty of maintaining an optimal distance from his mother. To my mind, the biting off of the cat's nails and breathing the air of the cat's nostrils were two sides of his distance–closeness conflict. Why a cat was chosen to symbolize his mother was to come up much later in the course of his treatment.

A relatively less noticeable psychopathological use of animals is the practice of grotesquely decorative exhibitionism involving pets (Mouren et al. 1980). Such behaviors are thinly disguised forms of self-aggrandization in less sophisticated, often rural, narcissistic, and histrionic patients. On the more severe end of psychopathology are two other forms of involvement with animals. The first refers to animal sacrifice in satanic rituals. Though subcultural factors might play a role here too, such animal abuse should raise the suspicion of a sadistically tinged paranoid personality disorder. The second form of involvement with animals is sexual contact with them.

SEXUAL PERVERSIONS INVOLVING ANIMALS

Bestiality, or sexual contact with animals, usually occurs in association with subcultural predisposing factors[34] (Kinsey 1948, Schneck 1974), lower levels of education (Kinsey 1948), and schizoid tendencies. However, the use of animals for sexual purposes is not restricted to direct tactile contact with them.[35] Indeed, Krafft-Ebing (1938), the pioneer in the descriptive classification of sexual perversions, distinguished two syndromes of erotic interest in animals: *zoerastia* and *zoophilia*. The former involves sexual acts with

---

34. The sprinkling of "sheep jokes" in the usual repertoire of obscene humor nearly always reflects such subcultural distribution of bestiality.

35. At times the erotic element of physical contact with animals remains unconscious. In certain tribes of central Australia, for instance, one may observe a woman with a baby feeding at one breast and a puppy at the other. Similarly, in New Guinea, till a few decades ago, it was not uncommon to come across a woman suckling a pig (Roheim 1943). Such practices, while culturally sanctioned, do contain an inhibited zoophilia at their base.

animals in lieu of human partners. The latter involves the use of an animal (e.g. via petting and stroking) to enhance sexual desire for human partners. Stolorow and Grand's (1973) description of an individual who used little bugs to terrify women as an erotic precondition for masturbation belongs in this latter category, though it may at times be difficult to separate the conditions of zoerastia and zoophilia. Psychoanalytic literature generally does not make this distinction and employs bestiality as an overarching concept. In any case, the reports pertaining to this matter are few and far between. Greenacre (1951) described the case of a girl who became very attached to her dog during puberty and engaged in sexual play with it. The dog represented the transitional object of her early childhood. Shengold (1967) found many instances of sexual contact with dogs in his "rat people." Rappaport (1968) reported on two analytic cases with significant sexual contact with animals. One was that of a young man who had been adopted as a child and had had many other losses while growing up. Upon becoming an adult, he slept with a cat, encouraging the animal to lick his hand or to engage in a sham fight with him. This gave him an erection and subsequently led to masturbation. His perversion was, however, not limited to cats. Habitually, he broke into stables and would try to squeeze the neck of a horse between his legs, at the same time masturbating the horse's penis. The second case involved a man whose zoerastic abuse of a cat was a reenactment of primal scene memories and fantasies generated in him by witnessing his mother's adultery. Most recently, Daniel Traub-Werner (1986), using the term *bestophilia*, described a case in which a young man had sexual intercourse with a dog as well as with a variety of farm animals. Strikingly, the patient had trained the dog to reverse the active-passive positions, and, on occasion, practiced bestial fellatio as well. This activity subsided in late adolescence when he became aware of, and frightened by, a powerful homosexual fantasy. The patient had a history of torturing little animals during his child-hood and his central masturbatory fantasy of adolescence revolved around his father's dog. This animal stood for the primal parental figure imbued with cannibalistic powers with whom the wish for and dread of reunion was repeatedly enacted in a libidinized manner. The animal also served as a fetish and sustained the fantasy of the phallic mother. Viewed from either perspective, the element of sadomasochism was prominent in this patient's symptomatology. This element, while always lurking in the background of such perversions, at times comes to occupy the center stage.

Case 9

Once every two or three months, a tall, handsome, highly affluent, middle-aged, married businessman had his sadomasochistic, erotic encounter with the family pet. All dressed up to go to work, he would suddenly announce to his wife—herself a lawyer and ready to leave for the office—that he was not feeling well and would perhaps go to work a bit late. Deftly overcoming her protests, he would convince his wife that she need not delay her departure. With her gone, he would find himself alone with their cat in a large sprawling and now suddenly very quiet, suburban house. Their game would begin.

He would retrieve a ball of yarn, hidden in the metallic underside of his bed. One by one, he would tie each of the cat's legs to four different chairs. Pouring himself a scotch in a short stubby glass, snugly fitting in his large confident hand, he would put on some classical music. Sipping his drink, he would begin to walk around the four chairs gently pushing the chairs a bit farther apart. Soon the cat was stretched, making noises of pain. Its anguished shrieks gave the man an erection and he would now circle the chairs more rapidly and push them even farther apart from each other. The cat would scream. The man would get more aroused. Soon, he would masturbate with an intense orgasmic release. Exhausted, he would then take a brief nap. By evening, his wife would come back and things would return to the routine hum drum of an affluent suburban life. This serenity would last for two or three months until the macabre dance would be staged again.

Not surprisingly, this patient had a background of severe frustrations in childhood. He grew up in a small one-family dwelling in an ethnic neighborhood. His father was an alcoholic and his mother a hypochondriacal, chronically sighing housewife. There was much primal scene exposure as well as inappropriate physical closeness between the mother and the child. Growing up, he felt idealized for his academic talents but neglected as a person in his own right. He hated his home but felt trapped there. The sexual perversion of his adulthood reflected the continuation of this hatred, symbolic enactment of primal scene fantasies, as well as a profuse libidinization of the sadomasochistic object relations of his early childhood.

CHILDHOOD PSYCHIATRIC DISORDERS

The "average expectable environment" (Hartmann 1958) necessary for a harmonious psychological growth consists not only of reliable parents and siblings but also of a consistent inanimate world. Animals thus enter and exit the evolving psychological structure of a child. Emotions and fantasies not verbalized with the human figures in the environment are often mastered through enactments with animals (Searles 1960). In societies where the man–animal separation is less pronounced than in the West, such a growth-facilitating role of animals may be greater. In any case, children "have no scruples in allowing animals to rank as their full equals. Uninhibited as they are in the avowal of their bodily needs, they no doubt feel themselves more akin to animals than to their elders, who may well be a puzzle to them" (Freud 1913, p. 127). In the child's eye, animals are less able to fit into the rules of adult life (Schowalter 1983). Animals may also represent power and courage for the child. That they bite, bark, sting, claw, and devour makes animals ready recipients for conflict-ridden aggressive drives (Fenichel 1945, Freud 1909a,b, Schowalter 1983). Because their sexual organs and reproductive lives are often more visible to children (Jelliffe and Brink 1917), animals may also become the objects of libidinal derivatives. Because many animals are warm, soft, and available on an as-needed basis, they come to be substitutes for emotionally absent parents.

While a child's use of an animal may be part of normal development, at times the bars of normality bend a little too far or are broken right through. Unleashed into the unconscious, the animal may now transform into a hallucination or a delusional representation of self. It may creep into the patient's current life as either a captive object of the compulsion to repeat cruelty or as a feared one.

Case 10

A four-year-old girl was hospitalized for one week after awakening one night with the sensation and belief that spiders were crawling over her legs and stomach. She tried to scratch and brush them off of her. Complete medical work-up was negative. Later it was learned that the mother's boyfriend had frightened the girl with a fake spider on the day prior to the onset of her psychosis. Further inquiry revealed that the nature of this boyfriend's play with this oedipal-age child was often overstimulating and involved frightening the child. Intervention included parental guidance regarding the differences between types of play that help children work toward mastery and those that may result in symptomatology by overwhelming the child's ego. The hallucinations recurred at nap and bedtimes for the next month. Whenever the hallucinations occurred, the mother learned to comfort the child by verbal reassurance and to allow the child to talk about feeling frightened. Following these interventions, the symptoms resolved in one month. It is interesting that the child's hallucination of sensations of crawling were restricted to the lower half of the body. The original scare by the boyfriend was only visual and did not involve touching. Since no further treatment was requested by the patient or her family, the exact meaning of the hallucination remained unknown, and, with its resolution, sank into the depths of the unconscious.

The hidden presence of animals in such recesses of the mind may not be revealed until the child grows up and enters analysis as an adult. An apt transference stimulus might then evoke pertinent memories of childhood enactments with animals.

Case 11

A 42-year-old, well-mannered but explosive attorney, who had grown up from age five onward with a bedridden mother, tyrannical father, and four other siblings, got extremely enraged when I told him that I had to take a week off from our analytic work on relatively short notice. Feeling a bit remorseful the next day, he rambled on until he stumbled upon a disturbing episode of his childhood.

He came from an affluent family that lived in a rural area and had many animals. As a child, the patient was extremely fond of the pigeons the family owned. Once when he was 10, a stray cat killed one of the pigeons. The patient got so furious that he picked up the cat, carried it some distance in the fields, and threw it in a dry well on the property. With the cat pacing on the well's floor, he returned to the main house, played with his siblings, ate supper, and went to sleep. However, at midnight, he woke up in anxiety. What was the cat doing right now? Was it still alive? Had he killed the cat? Nauseated with remorse, he woke up his 16-year-old brother and pleaded with him to help rescue the cat. The brother said that he would go out with him but would not get into the well itself. An agreement was struck between them whereby the patient put on his raincoat, galoshes, gloves, and a hat and was lowered into the dark well by a rope by the older brother. There he picked up the now furious cat in his arms and then released it upon being pulled up to the ground. Only after the rescue could he peacefully sleep. The patient sobbed bitterly as he told me this anecdote. The transference implications of this recall (my "killing" a week, his angry attack, his subsequent remorse) were explicated only later.

The fact that this deliberate act of hurting an animal was followed by intense remorse suggests the existence of intrapsychic conflict. The two sides of this conflict (hurting the cat—rescuing the cat), however, took control of the consciousness alternately in a fashion reminiscent of borderline splitting (Kernberg 1975). In children whose psychic structures are organized at a higher level, aspects of such intrapsychic conflict remain deeply unconscious. As a result, unintended acts of neglect of a pet happen more or less accidentally with a concomittant (not subsequent) sense of horror and guilt.

Case 12

A 13-year-old girl, in psychotherapy for depression and delicate self-cutting, would frequently complain that there was "no food in my house." Her affluent background and specific questioning regarding the contents of the family refrigerator suggested that this was not factually true. The complaint seemed to represent her sense of inner depletion that, in turn, emanated from her not feeling loved and supported by her mother. The patient described her mother as not having "a life" of her own, as being "no fun," always duty-bound, self-absorbed, hypochondriacal, miserly, and unempathic. She could not recall a single attempt by her mother to instruct her about bodily care, make-up, sexuality, or what boys were about or how to handle them. She had a better relationship with her father, who took note of her talents, encouraged her, and regarded her with warmth. However, she could not utilize him for the maternal support she needed at this crucial transition from childhood into adolescence.

As psychotherapy proceeded, the patient obtained a pet rabbit. She wanted the rabbit to stay in her room but the mother, citing its "bad smell," sternly objected to this. Father's gentle protests in support of his daughter's position went unheeded and the mother quickly bought a cage for the rabbit to be placed in the backyard. Each afternoon after school, the patient had to go out of the house to play with the rabbit and feed it.

A few weeks later, the patient came in very, very upset, The rabbit had died. Apparently, busy in track running after school hours, the patient had forgotten to feed the rabbit for four or five days. Her father had been away for a professional conference and her mother, too, had failed to feed the pet. Indeed, the mother sarcastically said that this is why she was always opposed to pets since she would end up with all the responsibility of taking care of them. As the patient told all this in the midst of much crying and sobbing, I asked her, "What do you think the rabbit would be saying again and again in his last few days to himself?" She looked at me, eyes filled with tears, pleading me to continue. I said, "The rabbit must be saying, 'There is no food in my house. There is no food in my house.'"

Unlike such conflicted and guilt-ridden enactments, remorse-free cruelty toward animals almost always suggests a serious conduct disorder of childhood. Indeed, such "cruelty to animals" is the only other time, besides the description of simple phobias, that the *DSM-IV* (1994) refers to human involvement with animals. This symptom usually represents an identification with the aggressor as the ego's way of discharging hostile impulses toward parents. Difficulties of metabolizing parental introjects are clearly evident here with the consequent disturbances of superego formation. Not surprisingly then, children who are cruel to animals are at a higher risk for developing antisocial personality disorder in adulthood; they have not internalized those "Jimminy-Cricket"-like aspects of the superego that help to "always let your conscience be your guide." By hurting a helpless animal, the child gives vent to his sadism, turns passivity into activity, and replaces narcissistic mortification by manic triumph.

Case 13

In a psychiatric residential treatment center for 9- to 12-year-old boys, six boys caught a fish. They brought the fish into their facility and proceeded to torture it for close to an hour. They kicked it, threw it into the air, and laughed at it before flushing it down the toilet. They reported how they enjoyed watching the fish squirm and thrash against the toilet bowl before disappearing.

The boy who was most active in this fish torture and who thought of using the toilet as the final sadistic chamber was often "the butt" of his peers' jokes. His early life was a history of repeated acts of neglect by his mother, who was addicted to drugs, and physical attacks by her boyfriends. He as well as the other boys in the facility had a tortured past. In days prior to the fish torture, his "friends" had been particularly cruel to him, teasing him about his mother dying of AIDS. When asked his feelings about his mother and her illness, he had remained silent as tears rolled down his face. He was unable to express the hurt and shame she had caused him or the anger he felt regarding multiple abandonments, including her dying. When asked what made him want to torture the fish, he again was silent and tearful and re-experienced the affect he felt in relation to his mother. Like the fish, he felt abused by his peers, his parents, and life circumstances. Earlier in his life, he had attempted to commit suicide. The episode of fish torture was a shift in the direction of expressed hostility from self to other.

When the humiliation and helplessness felt by a child is less intense, its externalization upon an animal does not lead to deliberate cruelty but unintended neglect of a pet. In such cases, the interpretation of the underlying dynamics usually leads to the resolution of the problematic behavior.

Case 14

A 16-year-old girl with symptoms of post-traumatic stress disorder and feelings of intense anger was dissuaded from running away from home when her parents agreed to buy her a puppy. In this case, the animal walked literally into the treatment as the child insisted on bringing her to sessions. Along with the new arrival came a revival of early childhood memories of having been laughed at for an episode of "wetting" herself in front of her family. Though responsible for training the dog, the girl found it difficult to wake up with enough time to walk the dog; frequently, the dog would whimper and then wet itself. She stopped bringing the pet to sessions saying that she was afraid it might wet itself.

The dog then became aggressive and the veterinarian told the patient that unless she spent extra time with her pet, the dog's aggression might become so severe that it would have to be put to sleep. Interestingly, the girl began struggling with sleepiness during sessions and had requested to come to therapy less often. An interpretation identified the puppy with the patient and further stated how the patient was shaming and neglecting her puppy as she herself felt she had been shamed and neglected by her family. Her sleepiness was discussed as a way she tried not to feel the shame, hurt, and anger of her situation. She was able to verbalize her feelings and started taking better care of her dog and herself.

Children's symptomatic involvement with animals can at times be a way station to healthier adjustment. In such instances neurotic symptoms and seemingly provocative acting out serve to ameliorate a developmental crisis, putting the child ahead in the game of psychosocial mastery.

Case 15

A 12-year-old boy's unremitting daily pleading with his parents to allow him to take his uncle's German Shepherd to school with him resulted in his coming for treatment. He described how he wanted to bring the dog because he could not defend himself against the aggressive teasing of his peers. Despite his age-appropriate physical build, he was frightened and uncomfortable with healthy aggressive impulses. While avoidant of other children due to feeling unable to defend himself, the boy was quite comfortable with animals. He began to use animals to display his fearlessness to other kids and also to frighten them with snakes, iguanas, and large attack dogs. Eventually, however, he began to use dogs as a metaphor for talking about his feelings of vulnerability and passivity, which were associated with a discomfort with the seductive behavior of his mother. He recalled how his father had a little dog when he was a boy and how little dogs can protect themselves by strategic biting. As he developed internal confidence, the insistence on bringing a dog and other various creatures to school diminished. After animals had been used to overcome inhibition with normal aggressive drives, the boy came to the office, seated himself, and suddenly unzipped his coat to flash me with a now barking Chihuahua. Animals had finally come into the transference and had begun to serve as a means of expressing sexual impulses!

The dog-penis equation here was unmistakable. This use of animals to represent body parts might extend to an overall identification with them (Kupferman 1977). At times, such transient identifications are the child's way of sorting out inner conflicts of identity while passing through a stormy developmental phase.

Case 16

A 15-year-old girl, who was born with a mild facial palsy, sought treatment for depression. All of her life she had felt painfully different from others. Through latency and preadolescence, she was teased by peers. She coped by withdrawing into a menagerie of pets including exotic birds, lizards, mice, snakes, and a very special rat. Absorbed in playing with her pets, she escaped ridicule and feelings of alienation. In weekly sessions, she began first to talk about her rat. She explained that people were always frightened of rats and that rats were very misunderstood. They were not animals of attack but gentle creatures with the powerful attribute of being survivors. She talked about not wanting to be seen and having a wish to be nocturnal like her rat. With continuing psychotherapy, she began to recognize that she too was a survivor and how this was an attractive quality to her adolescent peers. Gradually she shifted her sense of self-esteem by making a virtue of her difference.

All in all, animals hover on the border between psychically savage and civilized in the lives of children. They might facilitate normal development or press against the bars of the ego and break through them into neurotic or borderline symptomatology. Such symptoms might be transient and serve as developmental bridges. Or, they might be fixed and hence harbingers of problematic outcome in adulthood. Deliberate and ruthless cruelty toward animals is the example par excellence of such childhood psychic pathology.

THE EFFECT OF IMMIGRATION
UPON THE MAN–ANIMAL RELATIONSHIP

Immigration can also alter man's relationship to animals. This is especially true of migration from predominantly agrarian societies to industrialized nations, but it is also valid for migrations from rural areas to large cities within the same country (Akhtar 1999). In the rurally based societies, the psychosocial distance between man and animals is significantly lesser than it is in the industrialized nations. Animals of all varieties—cows, buffaloes, horses, donkeys, cats, dogs, camels, monkeys, snakes, spiders, butterflies, and even elephants, bears, and tigers—form a part of man's everyday existence. They become receptacles of mythic projections, containers of unexpressed personal emotions, careers of phallic exhibitionism, providers of maternal soothing, targets of dark eroticism, and brotherly companions in the journey of life (Akhtar and Volkan 2003a,b, Freeman 2003). When an individual thus raised moves to a country where contact with animals is limited to the possession of pets or visits to the local zoo, something subtle but of paramount importance is lost from his subjective experience. While I am referring to a more pervasive loss of contact with animals here, the fact that individual pets often get left behind at the time of migration should not be overlooked.[36] The resulting environmental discontinuity

---

36. Of course, this does not have to be the case. Freud's dogs traveled with him when he had to migrate from Vienna to London in his old age (Gay 1988). A more powerful testimony to retaining relationships with pets while migrating is evident in the instance of the psychoanalyst, Dominic Mazza. Born and raised in the rural

taxes the ego's capacity for temporal continuity and the pain, unknown to the natives of the adopted country, goes unnoticed.[37] The frequent use of animal metaphors by immigrant poets from the so-called Third World countries testifies to the subterrainean existence of such pain. Walking through the aisles of a grocery store, the Indian–North American poet Panna Naik asks:

> Milk is fortified, homogenized,
> pasturized, and vitamins added.
> How do the cows feel, I wonder?

Portraying the anguish of poor and unemployed migrants, the Colombian–North American poet Carlos Castro Saavedra (1986, p. 94) evokes a deeply cynical image:

> Out of work
> Just like those dogs
> Who silently urinate on the corners of the world.

And, Indran Amirthanayagam (1995, p. 37), a North American immigrant poet from Sri Lanka, wistfully laments the loss of her childhood playmates:

> What happened to the elephants?
> The conversation goes on and on
> What happened to the elephants
> and Rangoon, where does the rhino roam?

The different ways in which a particular animal is viewed in the immigrant's two different cultures (for instance, the owl is regarded

---

community of Scranton, Pennsylvania, Mazza entered psychoanalytic training in the cosmopolitan Washington, D.C. Throughout his 15-year stay there he had a sense of being an immigrant. When he decided to move back to Scranton, he dug up the grave of his dog, a Doberman named Damien, and re-interred the remains in the backyard of his house in Scranton.

37. Alexander Solzhenitsyn (1969), until recently himself an exile, has put it this way: "Nowadays, we don't think much of a man's love for an animal, we laugh at people who are attached to cats. But if we stop loving animals, aren't we bound to stop loving humans too?"

as stupid in India and wise in the United States) also burdens the ego. This shifts the nature of projections contained by the animal. As a result, the linguistic ploys of curses and endearments involving it suffer the fate of confusion, contradiction, and atrophy.

It should also be acknowledged, however, that animals can play a helpful role in the process of migration. The accompaniment of pets during migration can indeed be quite soothing. Also, in circumstances when one suddenly becomes an exile within one's own country—*emigration without leaving home* (Kahn, 1997, p. 255)—animals can play a highly significant symbolic role in stabilizing the psyche. Volkan (1976), for instance, notes that when Cypriot Turks were confined in enclaves surrounded by their enemies between 1963 and 1968, they created a symbol, a parakeet in a cage, that represented their imprisoned selves. Thousands of such birds were taken as pets by them. It was as if as long as the birds sang happily, the Cypriot Turks maintained hope that they would one day regain their freedom.

CONCLUDING REMARKS

Psychiatric symptomatology involves animals in myriad ways. These range from frank delusions and hallucinations through sequestered sexual perversions to subtle obsessions and phobias. Some animals seem to occur with a greater frequency than others in the terrain of psychopathology. Our own cases, while certainly involving other animals, largely focus upon dogs, cats, and spiders. Such distribution might be due to the inherent capacities of these creatures to evoke and/or contain intrapsychic projections, as well as to cultural factors. Thus, in societies where man–animal contact extends widely, other animals might figure more often in psychiatric symptoms. Another thing to be noted is that animals appear in the psychiatric symptoms of both children and adults. Their involvement in adult psychopathology has, however, remained less recognized. Underscoring it serves to remind clinicians to include a question or two about animals in their diagnostic interviews. A simple inquiry like "Tell me something about the role of animals in your imagination or actual life" might lead to important clinical data that could otherwise be withheld.

Animals also make their appearance in the course of psychotherapy and psychoanalysis. The most readily noticeable, and perhaps the most frequent, manner in which they enter the treatment situation is by way of language and metaphor. Projecting their own deviousness, patients refer to the analyst as a sly fox. Angrily, they call him a son of a bitch. Wanting to accompany the analyst on vacations, they evoke the image of a baby kangaroo in its mother's pouch. Yearning for his penis, they dream of snakes. Fearing entrapment, they suffer dark visions of spiders. Celebrating the mending of their hitherto split-off libidinal and aggressive self-representations, they refer to themselves as zebras (see the case of Ms. H. in Akhtar 1994). And so on.

At times, however, matters go beyond metaphor. Actual pets are talked about in great detail during treatment sessions. These might be current pets or those from the patient's childhood. In either case, the pet often signifies an unassimilated self-representation of the patient as well as aspects of an unacknowledged transference configuration. The border between allusion and reality is narrow here. The resulting "animal transferences" might contain reactivation of early object relations with animals (containers of still deeper layers of parent–child relations), as well as metaphorical molding of the analyst into a "new" animal, rather like a "new object." Countertransference experience might also involve complementary (Racker 1957) phenomena whereby the analyst comes to feel toward a regressed patient feelings he might have had toward pets of his own. The analyst might also develop feelings of envy and jealousy vis-à-vis the patient's real or imaginary, past or current, relationships with a pet.

Pets might also be acquired for the first time during the course of treatment. This can serve as a resistance to further exploration of the internal world in the here and now of the transference–countertransference axis. More often, it is a developmentally progressive step in a patient's moving on to greater capacities for commitment, tolerance of ambivalence, and identification with the (maternally) caring aspects of the analyst. The pets might be actually brought into the office. While child patients more frequently do so, this practice is not restricted to them.[38] This is not entirely surprising. After all, relationships with real and imagined animals play a big role in hiding and expressing childhood concerns and curiosities, matters that persist well beyond the beginning years of life, and give shape to adult psychopathology. Wishes, dreams, fantasies, and fears of childhood are what underlie the grown-up psychiatric patients' sense of foreboding and misery anyway. If animals are the internal objects of the child, then they are the internal objects of the adult. Indeed it might only slightly stretch matters to paraphrase Freud here and conclude by saying that "The mind is first and foremost an animal mind!"

---

38. This is different from a deliberate use of animals by the therapist in "pet therapy" (Hoffman 1991, Jenkins 1986, Redefer and Goodman 1989), which might provide companionship, solace, and psychic relief to the elderly and terminally ill patients. In this connection, it is interesting to note that many state hospitals have a dog, usually a pet of a senior staff member, that is friendly to (hence psychically used by) its patients. More striking is the fact that the founder of psychoanalysis himself had his dogs present while conducting sessions with his patients. Perhaps, they diminished his loneliness and distress while encountering his patient's psychic suffering!

6

THINGS

It is my impression that psychoanalysis has paid inadequate attention to the constructive, sustaining, and symbolic significance of the inanimate surround in which the human mind evolves and functions. With the notable exception of Searles' 1960 monograph *The Non-Human Environment*, the profession has largely ignored the fact that from birth until death a human being is constantly involved with inanimate objects, many of which come to acquire profound psychological meanings for him. To be sure, Hartmann's (1939) notion of *average expectable environment* can be seen to have a geophysical dimension, and there are a few scattered papers devoted to certain specific uses of physical objects. However, there does not exist a concerted effort to pull this material together into an up-to-date and harmonious gestalt. This is what I will attempt to accomplish in this chapter.

I will start with a step-by-step delineation of the role of inanimate surround and physical objects in personality development as it unfolds over the lifespan. Following this, I will describe the various ways in which inanimate objects become involved in psychopathology. Finally, I will highlight the technical implications of paying attention to the non-human aspects—both real and imaginary—of the therapeutic situation. In elucidating such developmental, psychopathological, and technical aspects of the inanimate world around us, I am not merely paying homage to this uncelebrated partner of our emotional existence. My aim is to broaden the reach of psychoanalytic theory and to enhance the clinician's empathy with matters that are frequently overlooked.

THE ROLE OF INANIMATE OBJECTS IN PERSONALITY DEVELOPMENT

The inanimate world plays a crucial role in the development and sustenance of the human personality throughout its lifespan. From the very beginning of life until death, physical objects impact upon the human mind which, in turn, utilizes them to express, consolidate, and enhance itself. Such *ecological self* (Spitzform 2000), or more accurately, the *ecological dimension of the self* (Akhtar 2001a), can be considered under the following ten categories: (1) learning to distinguish between animate and inanimate objects, (2) development of reality constancy, (3) use of transitional objects, (4) physical objects enlisted for mastering separation–individuation conflicts, (5) use of physical objects to enhance self-esteem during oedipal phase, (6) the role of collections, hobbies, and board games during latency, (7) neo-generational objects of adolescence, (8) conventional acquisitions of young adulthood, (9) changing attitude toward material objects in middle age, and (10) attachment to the health-care accouterments and preparation for the final separation from the world of things in old age.

Distinction between animate and inanimate objects

The distinction between animate and inanimate develops along many axes ranging from the simple perceptual one to the most complex one of conceptual interpretation. From very early on, infants appear to react selectively to human and non-human objects (Lichtenberg 1983). In response to the mother, the infant gives a social response, while in response to a toy, the infant gives an acquisitive response. Stern (1977) suggests that infants' differentiated responses to animate and inanimate follow separate paths. The interaction with people leads to internalized object relations while reactions to inanimate objects result in consolidation of sensorimotor schemata of reality.

The timing of such developments remains unclear. Spitz (1963) observed that it was around the sixth month of life that

> the child will no longer accept the inanimate object in place of the living partner, however briefly. Endowing the inanimate with the privileged gestalt (of human face) and with movement is of no avail. Indeed, it would seem that, the more the inanimate artifact approaches the living prototype, the more anxiety provoking it becomes. (p. 149)

Spitz added that around eight months of age, when *stranger anxiety* appears, many infants show "anxiety reactions in response to toys and other inanimate objects" (p. 150) as well. Indeed, he held that the *second organizer of the psyche* is not only the capacity to distinguish the primary love object (mother) from strangers but also animate from inanimate. Failure to achieve this discrimination is one of the factors leading to misinterpretation of reality and the resulting developmental maladaptation.

While Hoffer's (1950) empirical observations and Searles' (1960) clinical reconstructions support Spitz's ideas, the fact is that such early degrees of differentiation between animate and inanimate are partial and superficial. Piaget (1936) asserts that the capacity for making such distinctions evolves over a long time. Childish animism continues to endow spontaneity of movement with life far beyond infancy. The movement of heavenly bodies (e.g. sun, moon) especially is regarded as a manifestation of their will, that is, of their being alive. *De-animation* of the inanimate world develops over a long period of time during which anthropomorphic explanations of external reality continue to predominate.[39]

Reality Constancy

With increasing awareness of the distinction between animate and inanimate, the capacity for *object permanence* (Piaget 1936) evolves.

---

39. The converse prevails in the body-image development of individuals who have had to use mechanical devices (e.g. metallic leg splints) from very earliest parts of their lives. Here an inanimate part of external reality becomes incorporated in the core body image and therefore becomes integral to the individual's mental make-up.

The child begins to know that an object's removal from his field of vision does not mean its actual disappearance. Such stability of representation, initially restricted to what is at hand, gradually spreads to cover larger terrain. Frosch's (1964) concept of *reality constancy* is important in this context. According to him,

> Reality constancy evolves out of a concatenation of environmental experiences, memories, perceptions, ideas, etc. deriving from cathectic relationships with the human and non-human environment . . . It . . . enables the individual to preserve his identity and tolerate alterations and changes in environment with psychic disruptions and adaptational dysfunctions. (p. 350)

While not using the term *reality constancy* itself, Goldfarb (1963) had earlier alluded to its development as follows:

> In the process of evolving a clear differentiation of the whole self from the whole environment, it is clear that there must be a consciousness of the environment as a constant source of stimulation, shifting and yet permanent and continuous in time and space. (p. 51)

This forms the background of perceptual experience of the physical aspects of external reality throughout life from this point onward. Pacella's (1980) concept of *waking screen* is an elaboration of this very notion.[40] Also called *primal matrix configuration* by Pacella, it plays "an active role in scanning, integrating, rejecting, or modifying all the new precepts of object representations throughout life" (p. 130). The *waking screen* at the deepest level, the capacity for *reality constancy* at the intermediate level, and the need for *average expectable environment* at the surface form the basis of self's relation with the external reality. When these three are intact, the use of

---

40. The deleterious consequences of early object loss are not only due to the departure of a supportive person but due to the ruptures of the child's reality constancy as well. In adults, the same sort of laceration happens in the context of immigration. It is as if a movie is being shown and someone has caused a gash in the screen with a knife. The drama goes on but its seeing (and, therefore experiencing) is disrupted. It is my impression that inanimate objects, rather than human contact, act as a better glue for mending such psychic ruptures. This is because physical objects are more controllable than human relationship.

external objects is largely for drive, fantasy, or ego-related aims. When these are disturbed, the use of external objects is largely for psychic structuralization and stability.

Transitional Objects

Winnicott introduced the term *transitional object* in 1953. Since then a considerable body of literature (see, for instance, the volume by Grolnick et al. 1978) has evolved pertaining to this concept. Leaving room for wide variations, Winnicott placed the appearance of such an object at "about 4-6-8-12 months" (p. 232) of a child's age. He proposed that this first "not-me" possession has the following seven characteristics

> 1. The infant assumes rights over the object, and we agree to this assumption. . . . 2. The object is affectionately cuddled as well as excitedly loved and mutilated. 3. It must never change, unless changed by the infant. 4. It must survive instinctual loving, and also hating. . . . 5. Yet it must seem to the infant to give warmth, or to move, or to have texture, or to do something that seems to show it has vitality or reality of its own. 6. It comes from without from our point of view, but not from the point of view of the baby. Neither does it come from within; it is not an hallucination. 7. Its fate is to be gradually allowed to be decathected, so that in the course of years it becomes not so much forgotten as relegated to limbo. (p. 233)

Winnicott emphasized that the transitional object, which is vitally important to the child (especially at the time of going to sleep), is neither repressed nor mourned over the course of later life. It loses meaning since this "intermediate area of experience" (p. 30), that is, that which lies between the inner reality and the external world, spreads over the cultural field at large. Thus capacity to play and enjoy poetry, music, fiction, and movies (all being neither real nor not real) develops.

Physical Objects and Separation–Individuation

While the basic core (Weil 1970) of the infant awakens in a state of enmeshment with the mother's reverie in the symbiotic phase, it is

126   NEW CLINICAL REALMS

only in the *differentiation subphase* (from about 4–5 to 8–9 months),
which is the first subphase of separation–individuation (Mahler
1958, Mahler and Furer 1968, Mahler et al. 1975), that the child,
inwardly propelled by autonomy strivings, starts to discern his
psychic separateness through rudimentary exploration of the self,
mother, and the inanimate world around them. There may be
engagement in peek-a-boo games, using mother's hands or other
physical objects (e.g. a book, a piece of cardboard) in which child
still plays a passive role (Kleeman 1967). This phase is followed by
the *practicing subphase* (from 9 to 16 months or so) in which the
crawling child, and later, the walking toddler, is elated by asserting
his newfound psychic and motoric freedom. Buoyed by pervasive
secondary narcissism and impervious to external challenges, the
child seems involved in a conquest of the world. Exploration of
physical objects is his prime and elated concern. And, he constantly
brings them (e.g. a leaf, a piece of paper) to his mother. Indeed,
physical objects are recruited in the entire course of the separation–
individuation phase. Winnicott (1960b) and Fischer (1991) have
referred to the older child's use of strings and the fantasy of a
transatlantic cable respectively, to overcome separation traumas.
Much more impressive is Freud's (1920b) observation (1920) of his
18-month-old grandson, who employed an inanimate object to
master such concerns.

> The child had a wooden reel with a piece of string tied around it. It
> never occurred to him to pull it along the floor behind him, for
> instance, and play at its being a carriage. What he did was to hold the
> reel by the string and very skillfully throw it over the edge of his
> curtained cot, so that it disappeared into it, at the same time uttering
> his expressive "o-o-o-o." He then pulled the reel out of the cot again
> by the string and hailed its reappearance with a joyful "da" ("there").
> This, then, was the complete game—disappearance and return . . .
> It was related to the child's great cultural achievement—the instinc-
> tual renunciation (that is, the renunciation of instinctual satisfaction)
> which he had made in allowing his mother to go away without pro-
> testing. He compensated himself for this, as it were, by himself staging
> the disappearance and return of the objects within his reach. (p. 15)

Gradually, however, the practicing phase child senses that his
autonomy has limits and the external world is more complex than

he imagined. Narcissistically wounded, the child regresses in the hope of refinding symbiotic oneness with mother. However, this *rapproachement* (from about 16 to about 24 months) is ambivalent since the drive of individuation is at work and the child has tasted the ego pleasure of freedom. The resulting vacillations in distance from mother, if resiliently responded to by the mother, gradually settle down. A more realistic and less shifting view of the self and a deeper and more sustained internal representation of mother— *object constancy*—develops.

Physical Objects and Oedipus Complex

During the oedipal period, the growing child has to negotiate his or her way through many challenging tasks. All sorts of questions seem to need answers (Freud 1908b). What is the relationship between Mommy and Daddy? Why do they sleep with each other and I am barred from their bed? Where do babies come from? Why do people cover up their genitals? Does Mommy have a penis? Why does Daddy have such a big one? What is this thing called "fucking"? And so on.

The sense of mystery is exciting but also helplessness producing. Feelings of inferiority and exclusion, especially if left uncompensated by other forms of parental support, can be quite painful (Freud 1924b). To mitigate this anguish, the child strives to identify with the rival parent and court the opposite-sex parent. Physical objects come to his aid. The little girl puts on mother's necklace and uses her lipstick in her coquettish efforts to woo the father. The little boy wears father's raincoat and his large shoes; he stands on stairs and claims to be taller than his father. Both use keyholes to peep and pretend to fall asleep in closets in efforts at spying on parental sexuality. Gradually, however, the tension diminishes. Some rudimentary understanding, parental admonition, superego formation, diminution of drive pressures, and compensatory affections from parent lead to a reduction in oedipal curiosity and rivalry. The stolen pleasure of using adult physical objects also diminishes.

Hobbies, Collections, and Board Games of Latency

The latency-age child gets vigorously involved in mastering external reality. The games he plays, and the innumerable rules he makes for them, help him rework both phallic-oedipal as well as separation-related concerns in an aim-inhibited and ego-dominated way (Glenn 1991, Waelder 1933, Winnicott 1971). Most such games (and their board game and video counterparts) involve leaving a zone of safety, courting danger, more or less voluntarily, and returning to a secure *home base*. They permit the player (rather like the rapprochment-phase toddler and the curious oedipal child) the vicarious enjoyment of distance and closeness, peeking into mysterious places, rivalry and competitiveness, and a counterphobic management of castration anxiety.

A similar "mixture of fear, pleasure, and confident hope in face of an external danger is what constitutes the fundamental nature of all thrills" (Balint 1959, p. 23). This is nowhere more evident than at amusement parks. The rides offered there involve high speeds, exposed situations, tunnels, darkness, giddiness and vertigo, and unfamiliar angles. By exposing the thrill seeker to physical danger and then returning him unhurt, such rides serve as counterphobic reassurances against castration anxiety. However, by removing an individual from familiar and safe ground (home, mother) and then returning him to it, these rides also capitalize on libidinization of separation-related fears.

Ego pleasures of mastery and narcissistic investment of cognitive and motor skills during this phase (Erikson 1950) also manifest in the child's love of collections and fondness of hobbies.

Neo-Generational Objects of Adolescence

The peaceful period of latency ends with the advent of puberty. A turmoil now begins.

> All sameness and continuities relied on earlier are more or less questioned again, because of a rapidity of body growth which equals that of early childhood and because of the new addition of genital maturity. . . . In their search for a new sense of continuity and sameness, adolescents have to re-fight many of the battles of earlier years, even though to do so they must artificially appoint perfectly well-meaning people to play the role of adversaries, and they are ever ready to install lasting idols and ideals as guardians of a final identity. (Erikson 1950, p. 261)

The forging of identity under such circumstances uses inanimate objects in two different ways. One is for the purpose of disengaging from parental mores and the other is for creating new ego ideals. The former include cut-out jeans, nose and tongue rings, T-shirts with outrageous declarations, painting the room's furniture over with flowers and Eastern motifs, and so on. The latter include the ever-growing CD collection, the inevitable guitar, and the posters of various athletes or musicians that adorn the walls of the adolescent's room. Together, these *neo-generational objects* help in disengagement from the earlier parental dictates internalized in the form of a strict superego and express the parallel reliance on the value of one's peers. Trial identifications and role experimentations, using such physical objects, gradually broaden ego autonomy and help consolidate a resilient and mature self-represatation. With progressive trends beginning to dominate, the capacity for object-relations, especially of romantic type, deepens.

Conventional Acquisitions of Young Adulthood

With the developmental tasks of adolescence (e.g. reworking of internal ties with parents, consolidation of identity, beginning sense of life's direction) under the belt, the individual enters young adulthood. In contrast to the adolescent, who insisted upon being different, the young adult is ready for intimacy, joining in, and conventionality (Erikson 1950). The *ideal spouse representation* (Colarusso 1997) developed in adolescence now meets reality and, if the resultant mourning process goes well, leads to the capacity to enter marriage. Still later, the desire for producing children gets mobilized. The individual now has to provide formal structure for these functional ego achievements.

This is manifested via the conventional acquisitions of young adulthood, that is, a house, car, furniture, and so on. To be sure, socioeconomic and cultural variables impact upon the precise nature and magnitude of such physical possessions. Regardless of this, the *consolidation of adulthood* (Valliant 1977) invariably carries a material dimension to it. Stereo systems, televisions, dining tables, and liquor cabinets now populate the psychic space. Moreover, raising children forces the young adult to come in contact with his childhood objects again (e.g. stroller, highchair, tricycle, board games), an encounter that can have significant replenishing effects on his ego.

Changing Attitude Toward Material Objects in Middle Age

Midlife brings new developmental tasks. Prominent among them is the encounter with limits. The individual begins to sense the limits of his achievements, acquisitions, creativity, and most importantly, of his life itself. Time now enters the psychic domain in a powerful way (Erikson 1950, Kernberg 1980a). Less of life appears to be left, more spent. Death no longer remains merely a topic for courses in a community college. Bodily changes, children's moving on, and parents' passing away cause further ego strain (Colarusso 1997).

At this point, an existential fork appears in life. One side tempts with *greed*, the other with *asceticism*. Both choices affect man's relationship with material possessions. In the greed-determined outcome, grotesque changes in wardrobe and purchase of a flashy car are seen as offering solace. In the ascetic outcome, growing disinterest in lovingly acquired possessions leads to their neglect and the emergence of a cynical world view. Such extremes, however, happen only in those individuals who were quite narcissistic to begin with and cathected external over internal objects in their lives (Kernberg 1980a). Healthier individuals are able to achieve a synthesis of the two extreme options. They enter into a gradual *downsizing* of material life, buy less but enjoy what they have more, and start considering the fate of their possessions after they are gone. They write wills and think privately about their graves[41] and the fate of their ashes, if they are to be cremated. Life begins to be suddenly lighter and yet more anchored. Grandchildren appear on the psychic horizon and offer hope that one might outlive life after all, as it were, through identification with them (Colarusso and Nemiroff 1979). This stability lasts for some time but then is challenged by the arrival of old age.

---

41. The graves of one's parents often play an important role in the ongoing elaboration of internal relation with them. Elsewhere, I, along with Smolar (1998), have elaborated on this matter in some detail.

Old Age and Things

Old age further alters the individual's relationship with physical objects. This is an inevitable accompaniment of the profound psychic and biological changes in life at this time.

> As we enter the waning years of life, we become more and more infantile, both biologically and psychologically . . . We become more incapacitated, we lose our ability to walk and talk, incontinence returns, and we require diapers. We become edentulous and our diet consists of soft foods. We become more sensitive to temperature changes, as is the infant. (Madow 1997, p. 165)

All this leads to a great dependence upon, even anxious attachment to, health-care accoutrements (e.g. walking cane, wheelchair, diapers, dentures, pill boxes), which assure one's psychophysical safety. Madow (1997) notes that "The elderly become more and more dependent, increasingly helpless, and, to conclude metaphorically, end up with an I.V. drip as an umbilical cord and ultimately are reunited with Mother Earth" (p. 166). He thus turns Freud's dark reminder that "the aim of all life is death" (1920, p. 38) into a more reassuring aphorism that "the aim of all life is a return to symbiosis" (p. 166).

Nonetheless, death awaits all and this forces everyone to say goodbye to the world of things. The individual makes one last effort to deny his separation from his possessions by giving things to his grandchildren, who offer him the promise of *genetic immortality* (Colarusso 1997). But in the end, everything has to go. Or, is it that we go away while things remain as they were? The great Argentinian poet Jorge Luis Borges (1899–1986) makes a solemn statement to this effect in his poem titled "Things."

> My cane, my pocket change, the rings of keys,
> The obedient lock, the belated notes
> The few days left to me will not find time
> To read, the deck of cards, the tabletop,
> A book and crushed in its pages the withered
> Violet, monument to an afternoon
> Undoubtedly unforgettable, now forgotten,
> The mirror in the west where a red sunrise

Blazes its illusion. How many things,
Files, doorsills, atlases, wine glasses, nails,
Serve us like slaves who never say a word,
Blind and so mysteriously reserved.
They will endure beyond our vanishing;
And they will never know that we have gone.

INCORPORATION OF PHYSICAL OBJECTS
IN THE SYMPTOMS OF PSYCHOPATHOLOGY

Manifestations of psychopathology involving the inanimate world include (1) loss of animate-inanimate distinction in psychosis, (2) delusions of control by physical objects, (3) the schizophrenic's magical objects, (4) autistic objects, (5) sexual perversions, (6) addictions, (7) the linking objects associated with pathological grief reactions, (8) obsessions and phobias, (9) hysterical and narcissistic objects of adornment, and (10) the nostalgic objects of the immigrant. In the following sections, I will comment upon these.

Loss of Animate-Inanimate Distinction in Psychosis

True to the well-regarded psychiatric aphorism, the psychotic has lost what the infant is yet to achieve. One manifestation of this is the schizophrenic's confusion about what is alive and what is not. Feelings that one is dead, made of cardboard, or has turned into stone arise with violent intensity, lose metaphorical quality, and become literal. In severe catatonia, such beliefs render mobility difficult, if not impossible (Cameron 1963). The patient, regarding himself to be inanimate, sits vacantly staring into space for hours. Like a piece of furniture, he can be moved, but only in response to another's volition, not from his own agency (Slater and Roth 1969). Less dramatic manifestation of the loss of animate-inanimate distinction include partial distortions of body image whereby a particular bodily part is regarded dead, alien, or machine-like and hence something that might need removal. Many self-amputations by schizophrenics emanate from such delusions. On the other hand, the blurring of the animate-inanimate distinction in schizophrenia

can also result in experiences of merger with nature accompanied
by feelings of bliss and awe (Searles 1960).

Delusions of Control by Physical Objects

The confusion between animate and inanimate is not restricted to
the self-experience. Significant individuals in one's environment
(e.g. parents, spouse, children, employers) can be felt to have
undergone a transformation and become automatons or robots. On
the contrary, inanimate objects can be experienced to have become
alive and menacing. Projection of the violently destroyed links and
the accompanying fragmentation of the ego into the external world
results in the emergence of *bizarre objects* (Bion 1967). The radio
smells awful, the chair smiles wickedly, and the shoe seems to sing
ballads. Less strangely, television delivers threatening messages, the
oven says stick your head in, and the doorbell keeps ringing
endlessly though no one seems to hear it. Machines start to interfere
with one's thoughts and, at times, even with one's bodily functions.

Case 1

A middle-aged schizophrenic man was brought to the emergency
room one night after being arrested for disorderly conduct. Apparently he had been cursing loudly at a renowned local institution and
throwing stones at its building. During the intake interview, he
revealed that he had vowed to lead a celibate life but was finding it
difficult since there was a machine in the basement of this particular
building that was giving him erections. The lever of this machine
had to be broken for him to lead a peaceful life, he insisted.

While this was clearly delusional, self-object confusion along
animate-inanimate lives can also have milder forms.

Case 2

A schizoid librarian sat in his little cubicle after having had an
encounter with his supervisor during which he felt severely mis-
treated. Deep in mental pain and barely holding on to his fragment-
ing self, he found himself looking intently at the corner of his desk.

"Wood," he thought, "interesting thing, this wood . . . can be tough . . . can hurt . . . baseball bats are made of it." And so went his associations. Rapt in such thoughts, he found himself wondering what would happen if his desk jumped up and its corner hit him in the face. He contemplated the welt that might result, its shape, its raised aching margins. He sat there deeply absorbed in his thoughts; the desk had become his beloved nemesis, the container of his hostile projective identification.

The Schizophrenic's Magical Objects

Schizophrenic regression rekindles the magical qualities of the inanimate world. Physical objects appear to possess all sorts of powers. They seem to offer protection from imagined dangers, maintenance of psychic boundaries, enhancement of dwindling narcissism, and a pathway to evaporating object ties. For *self-protection*, the psychotic might carry physical objects felt to be acting as talismans. Staercke (1920), for instance, described a patient who carried corks with him to alleviate a variety of risks in external reality. Volkan and Luttrel (1971) described a "mechanical boy" who used a tape recorder with many auxiliary gadgets to relate to other people, recording their heartbeats and then playing them back to help him fall asleep. For *boundary maintenance*, the psychotic might utilize physical objects (e.g. sunglasses, masks, multiple layers of clothing) as defensive buffers between what can enter the internal world and what must be kept outside. For *self-decoration* (even if overtly grotesque seeming to others), all sorts of objects can be used.

> Pieces of paper and rags are cut into several bands, and bracelets, rings, necklaces, and belts are made with them. Many, predominantly female, patients paint their faces in a conspicuous, ridiculous manner. Many patients of both sexes adorn themselves by placing buttons, stamps, small boxes, corks, or coins on their chests. (Arieti 1974, p. 421)

In more advanced stages of schizophrenia, less often seen than some decades ago, one notices the *hoarding of physical objects*. According to Arieti (1974), the range of objects thus accumulated is indeed wide and includes

papers of any kind—old letters, toilet paper, pages of newspapers,
and so on—pieces of wood, stones, leaves, sticks, soap, spoons,
strings, rags, hairpins, old toothbrushes, wires, cups, feathers, cores of
fruit, stale food, feces, hair, pencils, pens, combs, small boxes,
cardboards, and other things. (p. 416)

Arieti also noted that the hoarding habit seems to evolve in three
steps: collecting and wrapping objects of the same kind in separate
bundles, putting them all together, and using one's body cavities for
depositing objects. The purpose of hoarding lies in its serving as a
"substitute for objects" (Fenichel 1945). In other words,

the regressed patient has lost so many object relations that he is now
in the position of making the last effort to maintain some of these
relations, no matter how concrete, inadequate, and inappropriate
they are. The useless objects that the patient collects are very useful
to him: they represent the last vestiges of his object relations; they
replace the important relations he once had; they maintain some ties
with the external world. (Arieti 1974, p. 419)

My poem "Bag Ladies" seeks to capture this very sentiment

> Daughters of unknown mothers
>   and shy fathers,
> They roam the streets and alleys.
> Weaving the fabric of one final dream of refuge.
> Their dirty fingers busy.
> Their brown bags full of fragments.
> Embarrassing pieces of a broken toy, as it were.
> In search of coherence,
> They wearily look into trash cans.
> The homes of their wasted childhood.
>   (Akhtar 1985, p. 49)

Autistic Objects

The concept of *autistic objects* was introduced by Tustin (1980), who
observed that psychotic children often use physical objects (e.g.
keys, little metallic cars) in sensation-dominated ways that impede
mental development. An outstanding characteristic of such objects

is that they are not used for the purpose for which they are intended. Instead they are deployed as scaffolds that seem absolutely essential for the stability of mind. According to Tustin,

> They have a bizarre and ritualistic quality and the child has a rigidly intense preoccupation with them, which is not a feature of fantasy play. . . . They may have no fantasy whatsoever associated with them, or they may be associated with extremely crude fantasies which are very close to bodily sensation. . . . (They) are sensation dominated objects. . . . They are static and do not have the open-ended qualities which would lead to the development of new networks of association. (pp. 27–28)

Tustin further noted that there is a sort of promiscuity in their use that exists alongside intense preoccupation with the object. Its loss is felt as a loss of a body part. Therefore, it is immediately replaced. The main idea is to continue experiencing the sensation they provide. Significantly, most *autistic objects* are hard and seem to add a hard bit to the child's self. "These objects are not experienced by him as *substitutes* for longed-for people. For him, they *are* that person because they give him the sensations he desires" (p. 29, italics in the original).

The pseudo-protection provided by autistic objects or *sensation-objects* (Tustin 1980, p. 30) unfortunately prevents the child from using and developing more realistic means of ego protection. Most importantly, it prevents him from getting involved with caring human beings around him who could help to modify his inner dread of annihilation.

Sexual Perversion and Inanimate Objects

Essentially, there are five formulations of perversion in psychoanalysis. The first views it as a sequestered dominance of a pregenital drive that defies genital primacy (Freud 1905). The second proposes that the pervert's ego is split and continues to attribute a penis to the female on the one hand and acknowledges anatomical differences between the sexes on the other hand (Freud 1927). The third view emphasizes the pervert's desperate inability to establish genuine connection with others (Khan 1980). According to this formulation, "The pervert puts an impersonal object between his desire and his accomplice: this object can be a stereotype fantasy, a gadget or pornographic image. All three alienate the pervert from himself, as, alas, from the object of his desire" (Khan 1979, p. 9). The fourth view, implicit in the writings of Fairbairn (1952) and Kohut (1977), regards perversion as a frustrated response to inoptimal support from needed self-objects; in this formulation, pleasure principle emerges only when reality principle fails to offer the required gratification. The fifth view regards the denial of generational boundaries and the associated irreverence of equating the childish "anal universe" (Chassageut-Smirgel 1984) with parental sexuality as the source of all perversions.

All five views leave space for inanimate objects to be recruited in the service of perverse erotic pleasure. Phenomenologically speaking, *fetishism* is the perversion par excellence in this context since it mandates the use of a physical object (e.g. shoe, corset, dangling earrings) to deny castration anxiety and achieve sexual pleasure. The fact, however, is that the list of perversions in which physical objects are utilized is endless. *Sadomasochistic acts* alone involve the use of physical objects including "whipping, paddling, spanking, fisting, piercing, tattooing, cutting, hanging, stretching on racks, imprisonment, mumification, altered consciousness by suffocation or drugs, hair pulling, head shaving, burning, dripping hot wax, branding, ankle and wrist slashing, diaper cuddling, boot licking, etc." (Stoller, quoted in Akhtar 1991a, p. 742). Besides being directly used, physical objects may play a silent part in deviant sexual practices, as did chairs and a ball of yarn in the case of a man who used them to tie up and torture a cat (case 9 in Chapter Five).

Dynamically, physical objects directly used in perversions help deny the disturbing fantasy of female castration, enhance omnipotent control, keep the hazards of intimacy at a minimum, forestall the breakthrough of hostility, or help discharge it in a dramatized and false manner. Concrete illustrations of such object usage include the high-heel shoes that excite the fetishist, the handcuffs and whips that fuel the sadist's passion, and the dildo that helps the angry young woman deny that neither does she possess a penis to please her mother nor has her seductive father delivered on his promise to marry her. In addition, there are the two vestimentary perversions. The better-known one is *transvestism* in which putting on the clothes of the opposite sex facilitates the denial of genital differences (Stoller 1976) and creates sexual excitement. The other is of *homovestism* (Zavitzianos 1972) in which the wearing of slightly oversized or overdecorous clothes of the same gender provides homosexual gratification on an unconscious level. Needless to add that these peculiarities of dress[42] not only offer hidden drive gratifications but also become a salve for the lacerated gender identity of such individuals.

The Addict's Paraphernalia

The range of inanimate objects involved with addictions is wide. It includes the alcoholic's bottles, shot glasses, beer mugs, martini shakers, corkscrew openers, pocket flasks, and a large variety of bar-related accoutrements. It also includes the pot smoker's pipes, the heroin addict's needles, the cocaine snorter's "cutting" devices, and so on. And, it includes all sorts of plebian as well as dramatic objects used to hide addictive substances from others. Dynamically, physical objects involved in addiction provide three kinds of psychological gratification. First, they come to symbolize the human contact lacking from the addict's life. The longed-after breast takes the shape of a bottle and the wished-for homosexual penetration arrives at the horizon of the skin in the form of a needle, for instance. Second, being subject to greater control than human beings, physical objects enhance the addict's regressive narcissism. Finally, by being idealized,[43] the physical surround of addiction helps suppress the desperate anguish of loneliness, lovelessness, and compensatory *pharmacothymia* (Rado 1933). Addiction makes psychic pain bearable. Beautiful objects make the addiction bearable.

---

42. There also exist neurotic forms of dress peculiarities. Individuals can dress sloppily owing to low self-esteem and gaudily for exhibitionistic purposes. They can attempt to make themselves look younger or older by dressing in a particular way. The early monograph by Flugel (1930) elucidates such matters in great detail. See also Taylor's (1980) interesting paper on mask wearing in this context.

43. Alcohol, a not-infrequent cause of biopsychosocial suffering, is almost always stylishly packaged and places where it is served compete with each other in charm and elegance.

Linking Objects

An important role is also played by physical objects in the process of mourning. Faced by a deep laceration of the ego (Weiss 1934) and the associated *seelenschmerz* (Akhtar 2000, Freud 1926), the mourner clings to the physical possessions left behind by the deceased. If love predominated over hate in their relationship, mourning proceeds along the usual track of denial, idealization, rage, de-idealization, sadness, acceptance, and substitute formation (Freud 1917, Kubler-Ross 1979). Under such circumstances, the physical objects of the deceased gradually get divided into three categories: things that are thrown away, things that are given to poor people and institutions of charity, and things that are kept as family heirlooms. The last mentioned provide a sense of continuity amid change and prevent a rupture of identity following grief. They are proudly displayed, placed at prominent places in one's residence, and only gradually lose their magic. In the long run, such objects come to be increasingly personally owned by the bereaved. Their connection to the departed one dims and is relegated to the topographic preconscious. The physical object is used for its realistic purposes, with little arousal of affect.

In complicated grief, however, such is not the fate of the deceased's physical possessions. Volkan (1981), who has studied pathological grief reactions extensively, posits the important concept of *linking objects* in this context.

> A linking object is something actually present in the environment that is psychologically contaminated with various aspects of the dead and the self . . . the significance of this object does not fade as it does in uncomplicated mourning. Rather, it increasingly commands attention with its aura of mystery, fascination, and terror. (p. 101)

A noticeable feature is that the linking object can come from the category of physical objects that ordinarily would have been discarded (e.g. a toothbrush, a glass eye, a half-used bottle of cold cream). However, many things can be used as linking objects. These include:

(1) a personal possession of the deceased, often something he used routinely or wore on his person, like a watch; (2) a gift to the

mourner from the deceased before his death, such as something
a husband gave his wife before perishing in an accident; (3) something the deceased used to extend his senses or bodily functions,
such as a camera (an extension of seeing); (4) a realistic representation of the deceased, the simplest example being a photograph—
or a symbolic representation such as an identification bracelet;
(5) something at hand when the mourner first learned of the death
or saw the dead body—what could be considered a "last minute
object." (Volkan 1981, p. 104)

Such objects can neither be rationally used nor discarded. They
are usually hidden away in the house and might remain so for years.
Looking at them stirs up pain as well as a vague sense of fear. Pain
is caused by the physical object's reminding one of the original loss.
Fear results from the mechanism of projective identification that
endows the physical object with menacing and accusatory qualities.
In other words, when one looks at the much ambivalently held dead
grandmother's toaster, the toaster also looks at one and brutally
unmasks the hostility one had toward her.

These phenomena, are, however, not restricted to complicated
mourning related to death. Other forms of loss (e.g. divorce,
desertion, break up of an affair) can also utilize physical objects to
freeze the mourning processes in a similar fashion. Indeed, decathe-
xis of the departed person's possessions often characterizes progress
in the treatment of such individuals.

Obsessions and Phobias

The obsessional character is organized around a regressive replacement of oedipal conflicts by anal struggles that are, in turn,
defended by processes of reaction formation, displacement, and
repeated efforts at undoing (Fenichel 1945, Freud 1918, Nemiah
1967). Unconscious incestuous wishes are thus turned into impulses
to cause disorder, which are then held in abeyance by rigid devotion
to the sterile pleasure of routine. Physical objects come to occupy a
prominent role in this scheme. The obsessional loves control of his
possessions. His inability to get rid of useless things (e.g. clothes that
will never be worn, records of obsolete transactions) results in an

unwittingly cluttered life.[44] In addition, he is prone to actively gather physical possessions. The specific nature of such collections (e.g. books, maps, coins, animal replicas, matchbooks, and so on) has its own meanings, but of concern here is the profusion of things in the obsessional's life. They bring him mental peace.

Everything goes well till some oedipal threat sets in further regression. Now the world of physical objects threatens to get out of the obsessional's control. Doubts begin to haunt him. Has the oven been really turned off? Is the door actually locked? Has the mailbox properly swallowed the morsel of that envelope? And so on. Helpless, he checks and checks, and checks again, pleading his things to bring him peace. If they behave, he is fine. In contrast, the phobic feels a more direct and focused fear of physical objects. The sliding door of the cavernous elevator threatens to castrate him. Riding in an airplane stirs up scenes of a thunderous crash, the condyne punishment for his repressed transgressive wishes. Buttons scare him, for they symbolize links (between parents) that he unconsciously wishes to break. The sudden and winding movement of the roller coaster excites him with somatic pleasure and threatens him with castration.

While the obsessional and phobic are both deeply affected by their physical surround, their defensive styles differ. The obsessional struggles to control the inanimate world and is relieved when he is successful in this effort. The phobic fears the power of physical objects and finds peace in avoiding them. Unlike both of them, the hysteric and the narcissist continually celebrate their relationship with the world of physical possessions.

The Aesthetic Adornments of the Hysteric and the Narcissist

Physical objects occupy a very important place in the world of the hysteric and the narcissist. The hysteric, graceful of posture (Reich

---

44. There is a developmentally earlier dimension to this as well. Love of objects (manifested in carrying too many things around, overpacking for travel, clutter at home) and love for empty spaces (manifested in traveling light, preferring contemporary houses), designated *ocnophilia* and *philobatism* respectively (Balint 1959), derive from the differential cathexis of closeness and distance from primary love objects, especially the mother.

1933) and diligent about the body's amorous potential, uses physical adornments in an exquisitely sophisticated manner. A provocative necklace, the just slightly higher slit in the dress, the stylishly cut blouse covering that breath-stopping bosom, are partners of the female hysteric's everyday life. The male hysteric adorns himself with a rugged wristwatch, parades in leather boots, and drives around in an unmistakably phallic car. Both the female and male hysteric feel helped by such physical objects in their agenda of competition, seduction, and transgression. There is nonetheless a quality of childlike innocence about all this since the incestuous and hostile aspects of this psychic manifesto are largely unconscious.

In contrast, the aesthetic objects of the narcissist have an exaggerated and affected quality (Chassageut-Smirgel 1984, Kenberg 1984, 1989). Interest in art and antiques is used as ointment for the wounded self. The painting bought must bring accolades and the rare book raise the self-esteem of its owner regardless of whether he has read the book or not. However, with passage of time and changing climate in the marketplace of art, the treasured possessions tend to lose their sustaining power. At this point, the narcissist might discard them, often rationalizing the shift of attitude with a pretended disinterest in material culture (see Jones 1913 in this regard). Or, the manic hunger for possessions might grow, leading to an insatiable quest for more and more things. The cycle of idealization, acquisition, and devaluation might continue endlessly and consume the narcissist's inner world of already feeble good objects entirely.[45] The contrast with the masochist and the *moral narcissist* (Green 1986), who pride themselves in self-deprivation and needlessness for physical possessions respectively, is indeed great under these circumstances.

Nostalgic Objects

The nostalgic potential of physical objects is ubiquitous since each generation has its own emblems of youth, beauty, eroticism, and

---

45. A dramatized version of this is evident in the 1941 movie *Citizen Kane*. Loosely based upon the life of the publishing magnate Randolph Hearst, it depicts the insatiable drive to amass material possessions and its origin in inner emptiness.

power. The glimpse of a soda fountain creates for a current 80-year-old the same bittersweet affective turbulence as does the sight of a jukebox for a 50-year-old. Encounter with such *mnemic objects* (Bollas 1992), in which affect-laden self-states have been deposited, mobilizes the pain of loss as well as the pleasure of reunion with an idealized version of the lost object (Werman 1977). Such experiences acquire a greater poignancy in the case of immigrants (Akhtar 1999a). Leaving a culturally and topographi-cally distinct region for another involves not only the disruption of identity and relationships but also a fracture of *reality constancy* (Frosch 1964). There is a loss of familiar landscape and common-place physical objects. Denford (1981) notes that

> going away leads to different consequences for a man's human and non-human experience. He can reproduce the old life with people in the new place, because people do not differ greatly from one to the other. He eventually finds new friends. But places can differ so profoundly that it is no longer possible to have certain sorts of experiences of place at all. Such deprivations and losses inevitably increase awareness of the non-human world, both the old and the new. (p. 325)

The immigrant remains acutely aware that he is living in a foreign land. He searches for places that look like his original home and have similar ecology and climate. He collects cultural homoethnic artifacts, often turning his home into a shrine of attempted conti-nuity (Akhtar 1999a). This is in sharp contrast to the exile who, like an individual suffering from a post-traumatic stress disorder, avoids reminders of past and abhors nostalgia (Akhtar 1999c).

TECHINCAL IMPLICATIONS
OF THE REAL AND IMAGINARY ECOLOGICAL
ASPECTS OF CLINICAL WORK

The foregoing discussion of the role inanimate objects play in development and psychopathology lays the groundwork for consid-ering the implications of such ideas to the conduct of psychotherapy and psychoanalysis. For didactic ease, I will elucidate such technical implications under seven subheadings: (1) treatment of children, (2) treatment of psychotics, (3) things in the analyst's office, (4) things that the patient brings with them, (5) exchange of gifts between the patient and analyst, (6) deliberate use of physical objects in the course of treatment of adult patients, and (7) non-human experiences in the transference-countertransference axis. With the caveat that each topic is complex and my comments will fall short of being exhaustive, let me turn to these areas of clinical concern.

Treatment of Children

Child psychotherapy and psychoanalysis rely heavily upon the use of physical objects (especially toys and board games) to facilitate the expression of feelings and fantasies by the child who lacks verbal facility. To be sure, child analysts differ in the frequency with which they use such devices and even in the nature of things used.[46] They also differ in the readiness with which they interpret the meanings of a child's use of inanimate objects in their offices. Yet almost all agree that such objects play an important evocative role in the treatment process. Common among the objects used by children for symbolic purposes are trains (phallic); doll houses (home, bodily cavities); puppets (self, parents, analyst); and so on. Playing board games (e.g. chess, *Monopoly*) allows for the expression of competitive desires. Bringing a *transitional object* (Winnicott 1953) along acts as a stop-gap measure before deeper attachment with the analyst is allowed to develop. Bringing an *autistic object* (Tustin 1980), in contrast, tenaciously thwarts interpretation and requires greater patience from the analyst.

Treatment of Psychotics

Treatment of psychotic individuals, especially in hospital settings, also requires attention to the inanimate environment. This is especially so since the terror of self-fragmentation lies

---

46. Melanie Klein is known to have used very small toys, believing that they allowed for more *phantasies* to be expressed by children (Grosskurth 1986).

not merely in that it brings with it bizarre and frightening and confusing experiences (hallucinations, delusional distortions in perceptions of self and other persons, and so on), but also in that it means the *loss* of familiar relationships with [an]other person (family members at home, co-workers, and so on) *and of the familiar non-human environment.* (Searles 1960, pp. 19–20; italics in the original)

To ameliorate this psychic disaster, at least partially, the therapist should ascertain that there is as much continuity as possible in the inanimate accompaniments of the patient. Ideally, the patient should be allowed to wear his or her clothes in the hospital or, at least, should be allowed to resume wearing them as soon as possible. Even the seemingly inconsequential and odd physical possessions of the patient must be left with him. They might symbolize (or be) the patient's only link left with his sane self. Interestingly, as noted by Searles (1960), improvement in a psychotic patient's condition often first becomes manifest in the manner he treats his non-human environment (e.g. making the bed after getting up, more organized manner of dressing).

Another area of pertinence here is that of occupational therapy. Such institutionally facilitated contact with wood, paint, paper, metal, yarn, and so on not only keeps the patient physically active and mentally distracted but, at a deeper level, assures continuity of relatedness to external reality, at least, in its non-human aspects. Searles (1960) has most emphatically underscored the need to further explore the theoretical "common ground in which the psychoanalyst and the recreational therapist are working" (p. 15).

The Analyst's Office

Scarce literature exists about the psychological significance of the analyst's office and the physical objects in it. This is surprising since most analysts recognize that their patients are fascinated by things in their offices.[47] Indeed, analysands might develop transferences both because of and to various artifacts, especially the couch, in the

---

47. The publication of the photographs of various analysts' offices in recent issues of the IPA newsletter showed how curious *we* are about such things!

analyst's office.[48] This concern leads some analysts to have rather spartan offices, though certainly bare walls can evoke as much projection as a shelf overflowing with books. Pertinent in this context is Kurtz's (1989) observation that Freud had filled up every conceivable space in his office with things of beauty and value to compensate for the loneliness he felt in sitting behind the patient. Talking of Freud's ecological self-care, Kurtz (1989) states that

> the visual and tactile plenum he created left no vacancy for the eye, no opening devoid of stimulus. Beyond the stimulation of the room, the demands of the role he created required highly focused attention to the stimuli provided by his patients. At least for the well-defined space of a session, the effort of work facilitated the coalescence of his dispersed self. Between hours, this task was accomplished principally through writing, and secondarily through the constant availability of his cigars, his dog, and his family attending in the rooms next door. (p. 28)

I too have wondered about the profusion of books, paintings, and sculptures in analysts' offices and have concluded that four factors are responsible for this. First, most analysts are cultured individuals, knowledgeable in humanities and aesthetically inclined; the cultural artifacts represent their authentic existence. Second, most analysts identify with Freud and thus carry some attributes of his office to theirs. Third, spending long hours behind closed doors listening to conflict and pain mobilizes the necessity (both as a healthy adaptation and manic defense) to surround oneself with objects d'art. Finally, the presence of such things in the office betrays an unconscious reliance, on the analyst's part, of their evocative and containing power in the course of treatment. In this way, the

---

48. It is sobering to hear during the course of an analysis that one was chosen by the patient to be his or her analyst because of the way one's office looked or even because of a particular physical object in it. Yet another inoptimally discussed matter is that of the location of the analyst's office. Besides the obvious issues of having a home office versus one in a professional building, the nature of the building matters as well. I, at least, am convinced that having an office on the ground floor makes a real, however subtle, enhancement of one's relatedness not only to the non-human environment but also to one's self and one's patients.

analyst's physical possessions come to acquire *totemic* (Freud 1913) and *shamanic* (Kakar 1997) attributes.

The technical handling of changes in the analyst's office (or the change of office itself) is also an issue. Some patients, especially those lacking object constancy, find such alterations quite destabilizing. While interpretative handling of such distress is ideal, in some instances it is not altogether a bad idea to inform the patient of an anticipated change in the office.

Case 3

A very fragile borderline patient was in treatment with me. She would get extremely pained (and, therefore, angry) at the slightest change in schedule or if I moved something in my office from one place to another. Once during her treatment, I ordered a set of bookshelves for my office. Knowing that she would be deeply distressed by their arrival on Monday, I decided to tell her about them during the session on the preceding Thursday, thus giving her one additional day (I saw her Friday, too) to get used to the idea and mourn, as it were, the loss of an empty wall before encountering the new bookshelves. Clearly, some will see the intervention as my attempting to bypass her hostile reaction. And, certainly, there is an element of that here. However, my experience with her had taught me that deeply pained states did not add to the progress of her treatment and an ego-stabilizing measure better armed us for investigating her reasons for getting upset at changes in the environment.

That countertransference enactments might contribute to such decisions goes without saying. Here is an example:

Case 4

Another patient, less fragile than the one mentioned in case 3 but certainly given to distress upon encountering change, was in analysis with me. We had recently moved to a new office and though she was off and on quite distressed and angry, the turmoil seemed manageable by usual analytic means. On the sixth or seventh day in the new office, while I was still in the process of setting it up, I brought a small Oriental rug to place on the floor near the couch. I put it there and liked the way it looked. As I walked toward the door to open it and welcome her in (she was my first patient on that day), I suddenly got anxious. I felt afraid of her rage at noticing the rug, could hear her interrogating me sarcastically about it, and felt an impulse to roll up the rug and take it back home. A moment's self-scrutiny reassured me that what I was doing was not inappropriate and her reaction, even if hostile, would have to be handled analytically. I opened the door. The patient came in, saw the rug, and exploded into rage. However, by this time, I was prepared to contain and analyze this transference manifestation.

An entirely different sort of situation vis-à-vis a physical object in my office developed in the following case.

Case 5

An extremely ascetic, depressed, and socially isolated woman with a childhood of profound neglect and abuse made a request of me in the third year of her psychotherapy. I had moved into a new office and the changed seating arrangement forced her to face a certain painting that she disliked. She requested that I put it elsewhere in the office. While curious about the potential meaning of the request, I sensed something different at work here. The patient had begun experiencing entitlement! I therefore responded by saying, "It is encouraging that you can allow yourself to demand something of me. Now, as it happens I rather like the painting and its location so I would not remove it altogether. However, in keeping with your desire, I will take it off the wall before each of your sessions so that you will not have to look at it." I reliably did so for about three or four months, after which she said that it was fine with her if I stopped the practice. (Deeper understanding of the meanings of this request came much later.)

Such *developmental interventions* (Abrams 1978) provide the patient a greater access to the silent progressive trends activated by the treatment. They underscore the dialectical relationship between the interpretive resolution of psychopathology and the resumption of psychic growth. With each undoing of some aspect of pathology there is the opportunity for resumed development in that area, and with each such developmental advance there is an enhancement of the patient's tolerance for the exposure of unacceptable, anxiety-provoking wishes and fantasies (Settlage 1994).

Things That Patients Bring with Them

From the first encounter until the last session of their treatment, patients often arrive at the analyst's office carrying various things. "The observation that the patient arrives carrying too many things should be silently registered. It may lead to something or it may not, but it cannot simply be ignored" (Akhtar 1992b, p. 283). Quantity is, however, not the only issue here. The nature of things patients bring with them, especially when they arrive for the very first interview, can be quite revealing.

Case 6

As a young man entered my office for his first interview, I noticed that he was carrying a popular magazine in his hand. As he sat down, he put the magazine on a little table near him. The session proceeded along conventional lines while, in a corner of my mind, I kept wondering about the magazine. Oblivious to my concern, he went to describe the interpersonal difficulties that had forced him to seek this consultation. He said that while finding women was not difficult for him, keeping them involved certainly seemed a problem. One after another, they left him. Most complained of his aloofness and one who left him most recently specifically protested about his self-sufficiency. Quietly, I looked at the magazine he had brought but decided to wait before saying anything about it.

Moving on to his family background, he revealed that his parents had divorced when he was four and for the next three years his mother toiled hard to raise him and his two older sisters. She worked long hours and the children were expected to be well behaved. He grew up to be a courteous man who was repeatedly left by women who found him nice but unengaged. He suffered greatly since he wanted involvement and mutuality in his life. At this point, I asked him about the magazine. He seemed surprised and said that he had bought it for reading in the waiting room. I asked him if he did not expect to find any reading material there and if he could see how this seemingly innocuous behavior betrayed his anxiety about dependence and attachment. He was taken aback but could readily see the dynamics in action. His eyes filled up with tears.

I can offer many other examples of this sort but will suffice to say that the analyst must note, and if possible, make use of the messages contained in the physical possessions patients bring with them. This applies to the entire course of treatment. One particular matter that awaits systematic exploration is why some patients bring the photographs of their relatives for their analysts to see while others do not. Interestingly, these photographs are usually of parents and much less frequently of siblings and children. Few, if any, in my experience, bring the photographs of a spouse. What does it all mean? Are the meanings idiosyncratic? Do they vary from patient to patient? Or, are there patterns waiting to discerned here?

Exchange of Gifts

In contrast to the things unwittingly brought to the office, gifts are special offerings by the patient to the analyst. The literature on this topic is vast and has recently been summarized by Smolar (2002). He notes that while some analysts (Langs 1973, Talan 1989) regard accepting gifts from patients as almost always wrong, others (Blanck and Blanck 1974, Wolberg 1954) argue that, at times, it is alright to do so. Both groups have attempted to isolate variables that can help the analyst decide whether or not to accept a gift. Such a list includes the value of the gift, its nature and degree of "instinctual" quality, the phase of treatment when it is offered, the type of patient who makes the offer, and, above all, the dynamic meaning and purposes of giving the gift. While no consensus exists, the prevailing sense is gifts might be accepted if they are (1) modest in value, (2) given at holidays or termination, (3) offered by fragile patients, and (4) represent a developmental advance in ego-capacities and not resistance or major enactment in the transference. (See Smolar 2002, for a comprehensive bibliography on this topic.) Needless to say, discerning all this is not easy. Matters are even more difficult if there has been no previous indication that the patient is about to give a gift and the analyst is caught off guard.

Case 7

At the end of a session in the third month of her analysis, an otherwise psychologically minded young woman offered me a bag full of apples. She said that she had gone apple-picking over the weekend and wanted me to have some. I was taken aback. Neither her characteristic way of being nor the material in the session had prepared me for this. I responded, "I appreciate your bringing me this gift but I am afraid that I cannot accept it. See, our task here is to understand, enlighten ourselves to your mental functioning and, thus, come to grips with your difficulties. We cannot, therefore, move into actions, especially ones whose meanings are unknown to us. Now, I regret if my stance hurts your feelings, but I do not apologize because my intent is not to hurt you." She listened carefully and nodded in agreement. I then spontaneously added, "For instance, apples. What comes to mind about apples?" She answered "Adam's apple! . . . Adam and Eve . . . forbidden fruit." She smiled, blushed, and left shaking her head, saying, "I understand, I understand."

In this case, my refusal of the patient's gift led to the strengthening of her observing ego. However, refusal might not always be right. Other ways of handling the situation include exploration of motives and meanings along with acceptance of the gift (Kritzberg 1980) or taking the gift and postponing interpretation to later in the treatment (Talan 1989). Yet another possibility is to keep the gift as a mutual property for the time being with the decision of full acceptance or refusal to be made later.

A more intriguing realm is that of the analyst giving a gift to the patient. Freud himself offered food to the Rat man (1918), money to the Wolf man (reported in Brunswick 1928), and books and photos of himself to other patients (Blanton 1971). Child analytic literature contains many illustrations of such gift giving (A. Freud 1923, 1963, Issacs 1933, Weiss 1964) with both beneficial as well as disruptive results. The adult psychoanalytic literature, in contrast, offers few such reports. Smolar (in press) has reviewed this topic extensively and gives many examples from his practice. However, his gifts to the patients were intangible ones (e.g. extra time, self-disclosure, attending a wedding, etc).[49] In contrast, Settlage (2001) gave an actual pottery vase to a patient around the time of his geographical relocation. The intervention seemed to have unmistakable countertransference elements (see my comments on it, Akhtar 2001b, pp. 95–114) but did provide immense relief to the anguished patient.

Deliberate Use of Physical Objects in the Treatment of Adult Patients

In the psychoanalytic psychotherapy of pathological grief reactions, it is useful to have the patient bring his *linking objects* to the analyst's office.

> With the patient's permission, the therapist may keep it in the therapy room, saying that its magical properties exist only in the patient's perception of it. Introduced into the therapy process at last, it is placed between patient and therapist long enough for the patient to feel its spell. He may even be asked to touch it and to report anything that comes to his mind. I am even now astonished at what intense emotion that is now generated serves to unlock the psychological processes that, until now, have been contained in the linking object itself. Emotional storms may continue for weeks; at first diffuse, they later become differentiated, and with the therapist, the patient can identify anger, guilt, sadness, and so on. The linking object will then at last lose its power, whether the patient chooses to discard it altogether or not. (Volkan 1981, pp. 209–210)

I have myself treated a patient whose deceased mother's toothbrush and half-empty bottle of cold cream played a significant psychological role in the treatment (quoted in Volkan 1981, pp. 178–200). It should, however, be emphasized that linking objects can also be part of the clinical picture in mourning that results not from death but from other devastating forms of separation. The following case, in which physical objects played an important part in

---

49. Of course, patients might view ordinary things given by the analyst (e.g. a bill, a card on which an appointment is written) to them also as gifts. However, only the objects knowingly given by the analyst as gifts are under consideration here.

the treatment, illustrates this point (a different aspect of this case
has been included in Chapter One).

Case 8

A socially withdrawn, white, divorced accountant in her mid-
forties was persuaded by her sister to seek help for a rather severe
depression of about a year's duration. This was precipitated by her
being abruptly left by her married lover of quite some time. Since
then she had been in constant agony, pining for him, crying, and
contemplating suicide. After some initial stabilizing measures, twice
weekly psychotherapy was begun.

For a long time, our work remained focused on this relationship. Session after anguished session, the patient spoke of this man.
They used to meet for a fixed number of hours each week. They
laughed, played, talked, and made deeply satisfying love. Theirs had
been an "ideal relationship" and now she was hopelessly unable to
let go of it. Indeed, she had held on to everything associated with
him: the pillowcase on which he last rested his head, his used
napkin, the tissue papers with which he had cleaned himself
whenever they made love, his comb, a newspaper he had left in her
apartment, and so on. Her place—indeed her heart—was a shrine
and he was a god.

As these details unfolded amid heart-wrenching crying, all I could
do was affirm to her experience and empathize with her loss.
Whenever a discordant note appeared in her descriptions of this
man (e.g., his inconsistencies, lying, racial slurs), I underscored it,
hoping it would help her de-idealize him and facilitate mourning.
She, however, responded to such interventions with hurt and denial
of the significance of his "other side." Soon, I saw the premature
nature of my interventions and began keeping material regarding
his "bad" side to myself.

Over the subsequent months, she brought to my office the linking
objects that connected her with him, often with much emotional
flooding. This gradually diminished her preoccupation with him.
Still, she was unable to get rid of the things that linked her with
him. Clearly, he had been profoundly important to her. But why?
With this, a floodgate opened to themes involving a highly de-

formed self-image consequent upon profound childhood neglect and abuse. Significantly, as this information unfolded, the patient talked only to her being bad, ugly, mean, and so on. It had never occurred to her that she had been abused and neglected. Only much later in treatment did she begin to question how her parents had raised her: being sent to a summer camp at age 4, going to get a haircut by herself at age 6, total absence of physical affection (except from a black maid), and frequent beatings by her father. She now felt that her "badness" was taking the blame for how things were and letting her parents off the hook. This realization led, on the one hand, to the emergence of violent rage toward her parents, and, on the other hand, to an intensified idealization of her departed lover (now also seen by us as a reincarnation of the kind black maid of her childhood).

Significantly, she tenaciously avoided the transference allusions of either extreme object representation. She kept me in a neutral though benevolently positive position, sort of like the black maid. Only gradually did it become clear that, having practically no one else in her life, she deeply feared violence from putting me in the "bad" (mother) role and abject dependency from placing me into the "good" (lover) role. We continued working in the extratransference realm. After some angry confrontations with her parents, she began to be more tolerant, though understandably never too kind, toward them. Her relationship with her sister and brother-in-law now began to deepen and they slowly came to serve as surrogate parents for her. In this relationship, she became more tolerant of ambivalence. She gradually got rid of the useless items belonging to her lover. She also began to talk of his weaknesses and her disappointment in him. As these changes occurred, she referred to herself as "neither black nor white but striped like a zebra." Indeed, she developed a fascination for zebras and began collecting little replicas of them!

Non-Human Experiences in the Clinical Process

The usual understanding of the various relationships between the patient and analyst (transference, countertransference, therapeutic alliance, real relationship, and so on) rests upon viewing the two parties as animate and human. This is certainly true most of the time. However, there occur moments in the treatment situation where one or the other party stops being human, even animate, in the other's subjective experience. Concepts such as *mirror trans-ference* (Kohut 1971), and *cocoon transference* (Modell 1976), by their very names, imply this sort of occurrence. A more gross form of such *dehumanization*[50] is the blind fury of the patient who, in viciously attacking the analyst, loses all sight of the latter's humanity. Here the patient treats the analyst as if he were made of wood or steel, as if he were an inanimate object and had no feelings at all. In doing so, the patient enacts the role of an enraged parent who, in his or her harsh treatment of the patient, (as a child) had lost all sense of limits (Pine 1995). Fantasies accompanying such rage clearly betray this dynamic.

Case 9

A borderline young man in twice weekly psychotherapy exploded with rage when I refused to yield to his request for painkillers. In a menacing tone, he threatened to take my eyeballs off and crush them under his shoes. As I listened, there floated in my mind a picture of myself as a Raggedy-Ann doll (note, the female doll, perhaps standing for mother transference) lifted up by him as he enucleated my eyes. That the enactment was recapitulating an earlier parent–child interaction was evident by the size differential between us (in the fantasy) and the associated dehumanization by the doll imagery in the countertransference. Moreover, the patient himself seemed to be undergoing a diabolical transformation into a torture machine.[51]

---

50. In a forthcoming paper (Akhtar 2003), I have delineated four types of *dehumanization:* defect-based, regressive, instinctualized, and strategic. The first is seen in feral children, the second in psychoses, the third in serial killing, and the fourth in terrorism to ward off the dread of empathy with the victim of one's attack.

51. One way to *re-humanize* the patient is to name the affect that the patient is experiencing (Katan 1961) and, if that does not seem sufficient, to gently take the patient's name while talking to him or her (Volkan 1976). This draws a cognitive wedge between the diabolically transformed self and the sector of sanity that still exists under such circumstances.

Less dramatic and, at times, infinitely more subtle moments occur in the course of many treatments when the patient stops experiencing the analyst as a human being and relates to him only as an environmental provision. Interpretations made at such moments must convey the analyst's understanding of this dynamics.

Case 10

To a patient who was profoundly upset about an upcoming separation, I once said: "It seems to me that sometimes I am like an ocean to you, in which you swim freely like a fish; at other times, I am like a jar and you the water nicely contained in it. In either case, my leaving feels profoundly threatening to you, since it is like an ocean drying up for a fish or a jar breaking for the water in it." The patient sobbed but indicated feeling understood. A significant thing to note about this interpretation is that it referred to her transference to me as an environment rather than as a person and in doing so relied heavily on Winnicott's (1963) concept of the *holding environment.*

Another example involves a narcissistic patient struggling with the issue of *optimal distance* (Akhtar 1992a, Bouvet 1958, Escoll 1992, Mahler 1968), especially as it threatened her with fears of fusion on the one hand and of stark aloneness on the other.

Case 11

Once, when she described her chronic hesitation in relating deeply to me as perpetually standing on a diving board without jumping in the pool, I said: "Perhaps in this picture I am the pool. I think what frightens you is that the pool might be so deep that you would drown or so shallow that you would crash against its bottom and hurt yourself. If somehow you could be reassured that the pool is neither too shallow nor too deep, then you might jump in and swim around." Of course, having discerned a different anxiety might have led me to include her concern, for instance, over her own swimming skills, the presence or absence of a swimming instructor in the pool, or the elegance of her diving. However, my sense was that she was not relating to me in transference as a specific individual but more as an uncertain containing environment, hence, the choice of my phrases.

In sum, the analyst needs to keep in mind that there are times in treatment that non-human experiences dominate the transference-countertransference relatedness. In psychotic patients, such allusions might be bizarre and very literal (Searles 1960). In non-psychotic patients, they are subtle and fleeting though, by no means, of any less importance to the clinical process.

CONCLUDING REMARKS

This survey has highlighted the fact that inanimate objects serve a variety of psychosocial purposes. These include functions that are merely instrumental, silently stabilizing, psychostructurally reparative, instinctually gratifying, symbolically expressive, and sublimation related. While the net I have cast here is wide, many aspects of this intriguing topic have not been captured by it. Three such matters are (1) the psychological significance of formal characteristics of physical objects, (2) the role of culture-at-large in determining the significance of inanimate objects in human mental life, and (3) the impact of gender on these formulations.

The Form of Things

The issue of formal characteristics is multifaceted. Dimensions of size, texture, color, and appearance need to be considered. Take size, for example. Objects that are small in size evoke unconscious identifications with our child selves. They come to embody our infantile omnipotence and, for men, help deny the genital inferiority of childhood. It is as if they "confirm" that size does not matter after all. Looking at very small cars (e.g. the British Mini) and little dollhouses evokes such childlike wonder. Truly small electronic devices (e.g. cameras and tape recorders that fit in the palm of one's hand) can fuel voyeuristic fantasies and are therefore found very exciting. Largeness has its own psychological consequences. It is usually equated with the view of parents during childhood and thus evokes intimidation and respect.[52] Ostow (2001) notes that the affect of awe is felt by

> exposure to structures whose size is almost incommensurate with human dimensions, so large perhaps that they cannot be included within a normal visual field at a reasonable distance. They are usually natural formations such as mountains, bodies of water, or, on a smaller scale, buildings such as great cathedrals. The cathedrals seem to have been built in such a way as to inspire awe. (p. 201)

Like size, texture, shape, and color of inanimate objects play important roles in determining their psychological significance.[53] For instance, *transitional objects* (Winnicott 1953) are usually soft, *autistic objects* (Tustin 1980) hard. Long objects (e.g. swords, spears, poles, oars, pens) seem suitable for symbolizing the penis and round objects (e.g. melons, oranges, balls) for symbolizing breasts. Matters are far from simple though. For instance, balloons often signify breasts but their lightness and playfulness can also be listed as "contra-depressive symbols" (Winnicott 1935, p. 136). The texture of the object also matters. Softness and smoothness often carry feminine or maternal qualities and hardness and roughness masculine or paternal qualities. Similarly, the color of physical objects invites its own affective and linguistic projections (e.g. red for danger and excitement, yellow for cowardice, green for envy). Exploration of this in pop psychology and the world of interior

---

52. Significantly, the devastating terrorist attacks against the United States on September 11, 2001, involved two of its tallest buildings. Also note the worldwide distress at the Taliban's destruction of ancient Buddha statues in Bamian Valley, statues that were the tallest of their type. Among the multitude of factors that determine the choice of such targets (and, the depth of distress their destruction causes), their extraordinary height figures prominently.

53. Yet another factor is how close an inanimate object comes to be appearing alive. Robots, for instance, belong to a certain gray area and evoke much fascination from observers. Transformers, a 1970s genre of children's toys, owe their great popularity to this very reason. This effect can reach uncanny proportions. The human-like wax statues in Madame Tussaud's Museum are a testimony to our profound unconscious attraction toward the mixing-up of the animate and inanimate worlds. Spitz (1963) states that the "fascination about the idea of the inanimate creating the illusion of life; and also about the living posing as inanimate permeates a great deal more of our thinking than we are usually aware" (p. 147).

decoration notwithstanding, there is something warranting further thought here, especially the extent to which the significance of a particular color is universal versus culturally determined.

The Role of Culture

The role inanimate objects play in human mental life might vary from culture to culture. Unanswered questions abound in this realm. For instance, is the number of possessions deemed enough for a human being decided by his or her culture? What is the cut-off point for having too many or too few things? How long should a possession be kept? How soon does an acquisition become obsolete? Why does an automobile get accorded the status of an antique after 30 years in the United States and after 50 years in United Kingdom? Are physical objects man's servants or, ultimately, man theirs? What is the existential status of that which is one minute a part of us (e.g. hair, nails) and the next minute merely a thing? Are there different periods in life for which asceticism and material acquisition are advocated? To what extent do the projections evoked by inanimate aspects vary from culture to culture? How come it is that in the West, with proper marketing strategy, practically anything can be sold[54] and in the East, with proper spiritual attitude, practically anything can be worshipped? How does popular culture portray inanimate objects? How important really is the bicycle in De Sica's *Bicycle Thief,* the music box in Costa-Gavras' *The Music Box,* and the piano in Campion's *The Piano?* And so on.[55]

The Impact of Gender

Gender also seems to affect the psychological use of physical objects. Take, for instance, the fact that kleptomania is more common in

---

54. In the category of masonry and stone alone, the range extends from the pieces of the solemn Berlin Wall to the faddish absurdity of the Pet Rock.

55. Language should also be included here. The relationship between words and things is a complex and vast topic including matters such as words being treated as things; things for which one language has words and another does not; the category of metaphor (and the prosodic qualities of language in general) and other literary devices of poetry (Akhtar 2000); and so on.

women, fetishism among men. Is it simply that women steal the
father's penis and men assign a penis to mother? Or, is there more
involved here? Yet another example is the use of razor blades for
delicate self-cutting, a syndrome much more frequent in women
(Favazza 1992). Contrast this to the use of guns and knives in serial
killing, typically a male perversity (Stone 1979). Perhaps such
differences go back to the dissimilar ways in which the two sexes
encounter physical reality of their bodies and the external world
from the very early childhood onward. For instance, different
clothes and toys are chosen by parents for boys and girls, and these
choices mold their identity and social roles. The important thing to
note is that there is a dialectic here: object assignment shapes
gender and gender affects object usage. At the same time, unanswered questions exist in this realm too, especially vis-à-vis the
interactions among formal characteristics of object, culture, and
gender (i.e. the three variables under consideration here).

A Parable

I wish to conclude by citing an incident from Gandhi's life. The
story, bringing the various aspects of this paper together in a zen-like
gestalt of simplicity and wisdom, goes like this.

Toward the last years of his life, Gandhi had become world-
renowned. In India, he was nearly worshipped. Everyone called him
Bapu, an endearing term for father. Everyone wanted to see him.
Hundreds waited in front of his residence to catch merely a glimpse.
Ever inventive, Gandhi found a solution to this. He instructed
his secretary that he would do his paperwork and respond to his
correspondence while sitting in the front yard. Soon this was
arranged. A cordon was erected around the space where Gandhi
worked with his secretary. People passed by quietly gazing at him in
awe, many bowing down to touch the ground where he had walked.
His secretary would read aloud the mail that had arrived and
Gandhi would dictate a few lines to him in response.

One day the secretary opened an envelope. Two sheets of paper,
attached to each other by a pin, came out. He began to read the
letter, gasped, and became silent. Quickly, he crumpled the sheets of
paper and threw them in the wastebasket. Gandhi asked him the
reason for this and was told that the letter was highly vituperative

and contained obscenities directed at him. The secretary suggested that they move on to the next piece of mail but Gandhi insisted upon reading the letter himself. Once he had finished, he took the pin out and threw the two sheets of paper away. His secretary was amazed that he did not look upset at all. "Bapu, has the hatred in this letter not hurt you?" Gandhi smiled and said that he was not affected because he was certain that the epithets and curses in the letter had no application to him at all. He added that the man who wrote the letter knew this too and, to make up for his assault, had sent along the gift of a pin. It was as important to not let the hatred contaminate oneself as it was to enjoy the gift of this pin.

Did this episode actually happen or is it the sort of folklore that accrues regarding the lives of great people over time? Did the letter writer unconsciously intend what Gandhi attributed to him? Was Gandhi being genuinely forgiving or was it a clever ploy to salvage an embarrassing social situation? These questions are certainly worthwhile. However, to my mind, a more important question here is whether we can recognize that in the midst of the inevitable suffering of life, solace and even joy often come to us in the form, so to speak, of a pin?

Part IV

UNFAMILIAR PROCESSES

7

FROM SIMPLICITY THROUGH CONTRADICTION TO PARADOX

For individuals with deficient object constancy (Akhtar 1994, Mahler 1958, Mahler and Furer 1968, Mahler et al. 1975, Settlage 1977, 1993) and associated borderline personality organization (Kernberg 1967), starting psychoanalytic treatment is a profoundly significant event. The availability of someone empathic, reliable, and constant in the person of the analyst is often an entirely new experience for them. It stirs up a wide gamut of intense, often contradictory, emotions: disbelief and excitement, anaclitic yearnings and anxious withdrawal, hate transferred from early frustrating objects and hope that such hate will not destroy this relationship, and so on. Those with less ego impairment manifest these attitudes only after the treatment has gone on for a while and the initial resistances have been dissolved. Those with greater ego weakness display these attitudes readily. Sooner or later both types of patients settle into one or the other extreme of such polar variation of content (Akhtar 1992b, Kernberg 1975). Some give voice to a manifesto of desperate hope,

object hunger, and idealization. Others fill the therapeutic space
with rage, paranoia, and sadomasochistic enactments.

THE SEQUENCE OF EVENTS

A feature common to both types of dialogue mentioned previously
is a certain simplicity and directness of the material. What is being
said appears self-evident and seems to have no further layers.
Indeed,

> there is a special quality of directness both in style and in choice of
> the words. It is the "frankness" of the person who has nothing to hide
> and therefore in an obstinate way can press his point without risking
> the burden of evidence being turned back on him. (Killingmo 1989,
> p. 72)

The patient seems to possess an impressive degree of certainty
about his statements (e.g. his need for love, his reasons for
mistrusting others, his belief that nobody likes him, etc.) and this
has a compelling effect upon the analyst's usually skeptical attitude
of listening. The temptation to put this attitude aside makes the
analyst fear becoming gullible and "supportive." The insistence on
exercising this attitude results in the analyst's making interpretive or
unmasking interventions that seem to injure the patient, who feels
invalidated and accused.

A further development occurs as a consequence of interpretive
resolution of early resistances coupled with the influence of regression that ordinarily sets in as the analytic work proceeds. The patient
who was needy, timid, and full of hope from the analyst begins to
experience and express hateful and destructive wishes in the
transference. Likewise, the patient who was mistrustful, cynical, and
mocking begins to reveal his affectionate and guidance-seeking
tendencies involving the analyst. Such logically incompatible attitudes result from the use of splitting. They are, however, not limited
to the arena of affective ambivalence. They also underlie the
patient's beginning vacillations between compliance and negativ-
ism, creativity and mindlessness, waiting and regret, mimicry and
idiosyncrasy, and so on. Significantly, the patient does not seem to

notice that anything contradictory to his usual stance has happened. Indeed, he shows a "striking lack of concern" (Kernberg 1976, p. 20) about such oscillations and about the implicit compartmentalization of his psychic reality. It is the analyst who picks up the patient's contradictions. He then helps the patient observe these splits, thus making the cleavage (and reasons for it) a topic of the analytic exploration. Through a commitment to the "principle of multiple function" (Waelder 1936), which broadens his conceptual horizon and deepens his containing capacities, and through "bridging interventions" (Akhtar 1995, p. 150), the analyst helps the patient bring the two sides of the psychic laceration together.

As this work proceeds, a third psychic configuration becomes discernible by the analyst. Now he can see not only the co-existence of the two polarities (e.g. love and hate, close and far, past and future) but also that even in what seems to be one pole of experience subtle reverberations of the other are unmistakably present. The patient's desperate attempts to control and coerce the analyst, for instance, now appear not only sadistic but also a rudimentary variety of love. Conversely, the patient's idealization now begins to appear not only a childlike search for an all-good object and a defense against hostility but also a form of subtle mocking in itself. This is the level of paradox.

Let me reiterate. At the level of simplicity, the material appears monotonous, repetitive, and devoid of psychic layers. At the level of contradiction, incompatible clusters alternate at the same level of awareness and abstraction, as well as along a commonly shared dimension of experience (e.g. affect, time, space, morality, etc.). This state of affairs, however, might not be readily noticeable by the patient himself. At the level of paradox, multidimensional and contradictory meanings co-exist but at different levels of awareness and abstraction (Kafka 1989). It is the manner in which these three levels evolve during the treatment of borderline patients that forms the focus of this paper. The thesis offered here is essentially twofold. First, the paper proposes that the psychic reality of the borderline patient evolves in a three-step ("simplicity-contradiction-paradox") process during the analytic treatment. Second, it suggests that this psychic movement takes place at first within the analyst's reverie and only with the aid of the analyst's *holding* (Winnicott 1960a), unmasking, *bridging* (Akhtar 1995, Kernberg 1975) and depth-rendering interventions, as well as through the vicissitudes of identification as it occurs in the patient's psychic reality.

SOME CAVEATS

First and foremost, it must be emphasized that there exist many overlaps and grey areas among simplicity, contradiction, and paradox. For instance, a paradox often has a patina of *simplicity* (a favorite idiom of Zen mysticism) and "strictly speaking, any contradiction is a paradox" (Kafka 1989, p. 41). The three phenomena are not as sharply distinct as didactic necessity makes them appear here. Second, the degree of their clarity and the velocity of their sequential progression (or dynamic ebb and flow) vary greatly from patient to patient. There is no set timetable to these evolutions. Third, while a hierarchical order from simplicity through contradiction to paradox is certainly implied, these steps are not intended to reflect "phases" of analytic treatment. To be sure, progression along these lines occurs with treatment but such advance is far from linear. Interpretive resolution of conflictual areas enhances the patient's capacity to feel and think in newer ways, including experiencing paradox. Defensive regressions are accompanied by return to the level of simplicity. Progressive and regressive shifts often occur within a single session where an empathically attuned oscillation of the analyst's attention becomes a tool for discerning them and guiding the analyst's interventions. Fourth, the capacities for simplicity, contradiction, and paradox do not seem evenly distributed over the various content-based areas of the mind. Thus a patient with a remarkable sense of humor, which capitalizes on paradox, might display a striking degree of simplicity in insisting on receiving a particular gratification from the analyst. Or, one who seems astute in pointing out contradictions in others might show little capacity to observe those of his own. Seen in this manner, simplicity, contradiction, and paradox appear to reflect not only progressive steps but variously organized levels or areas of mind as well. To take this line of thinking a bit further, it is possible to view simplicity as reflecting the level of deficit (Killingmo 1989), contradiction as reflecting the level of conflict (Kernberg 1975), and paradox as that of ego mastery and sublimation (Kafka 1989). Finally, a word of caution about the following clinical material is in order. Not only is the material highly disguised (hence not suitable for being borrowed for research purposes), but it is also quite condensed. This might result in an appearance of a greater back-and-forth dialogue than was really the case during the session. In such schematic depiction of the material, the hesitations and affective undertones are unfortunately compromised. The session is also atypical in my work with this patient. Usually she is operating at the level of paradox and is hence capable of participating in relatively unmodified analytic work. At other times, she is regressed to the level of simplicity and is therefore amenable only to holding and affirmative interventions. In this particular session, however, there is a movement from simplicity through contradiction to paradox (i.e. from literalness to analyzability). While my holding, unmasking, bridging, and depth-rendering interventions seem to have facilitated this move, the "recognition that some significant therapeutic steps involve, in retrospect, a paradox should not be mistaken for advocacy of contrived irrationality" (Kafka 1964, p. 577).

CLINICAL MATERIAL

During a session in the third year of her analysis, a patient (who at other times profoundly idealized me) begins to be in touch with her nakedly violent impulses toward me. Uncharacteristically, she does not attribute the origin of her rage to something I have said or done. She can see it as coming from within herself. This encourages her. However, she feels frightened of the ferocity of her fantasies. What if she really hurt me? She hesitates, remains quiet for a while. I feel that she is stuck and is looking for me to somehow help her proceed further. I therefore respond by saying that perhaps she needs me to reassure her that I could contain and absorb her aggression which, after all, exists parallel to her deep fondness for me. Not satisfied with this, she insists that there is no way that I could truly reassure her since her fantasies are really violent and dangerous.

With some encouragement, the patient proceeds to tell me that maybe she will get up and slap me on my face or maybe one day she will come in with a knife and stab me. As she describes these and other scenarios, I am struck by the fact that she is assuming that I will let her do all this to me. This picture of total passivity on my part is in striking contrast with her idealized view of me, in which she sees me as agile and powerful. I therefore ask her what she imagines me doing in the face of such actions on her part and she is surprised to find that, in these fantasies, she has pictured me as totally passive. She responds by saying: "Okay, Okay, I know you will stop me, fight me off. This does not reassure me though since I can be quite devious and can do harmful things surreptitiously." She then proceeds to enumerate further imaginary scenarios in which I become the helpless victim of her clandestine violent assault. She raises a question: What if she really put these fantasies into action? She repeats the question. Sensing a plaintive conviction in her voice, I begin to wonder if her concerns about the future are defensive against acknowledging actual acts from the past. Is her search for reassurance a confession in disguise? Inquiry along this line leads her to acknowledge that a few months ago she had stolen my scarf from the waiting room. "Now, doesn't that hurt you?" the patient asks me in a tone that is a bit teasing and yet peculiarly hopeful. It is as if she wants to hear me say yes. I respond by saying that while it is indeed plausible that I am bothered about the scarf being stolen, I might also feel pleasure in knowing its whereabouts after all this time, tickled by the implicit flattery, and happy about her honesty. The patient is taken aback. She sobs but soon returns to her insistence that there is no way that I could reassure her that she would not be able to hurt me. What if, unbeknown to me, she put a bomb in my car? What if she clobbered me with a baseball bat from behind as I was walking on the street? She goes on and on.

Now, I become aware of a still deeper layer in the patient's communication. While undeniably pained and anxious, she is beginning to take her first steps in the realm of play. While seemingly dependent upon me for reassurance, she is asserting the inevitability of our psychic separateness. While talking about hurting me, she is actually showing concern for me. While displaying anxious helplessness, she wants to hear that she is indeed capable of making an impact on me. While seeking omnipotence from me, she is becoming tolerant of its lack and, implicitly, of the illusory nature of the psychoanalytic process. Realizing all this, I respond to the patient by saying: "I think you are right. I cannot completely reassure you that you cannot or even will not hurt me." As the patient nods emphatically, I go on to say: "However, what seems significant here is that you are showing a capacity to understand and perhaps even accept that I have no way of providing the reassurance you are seeking from me. Even more importantly, in seeking reassurance regarding your hostility, you also seem to be showing concern and love for me." The patient nods strongly in agreement. The affective atmosphere of the office somehow seems to have shifted from anxiety, pain, and potential danger, to a slightly sad but also optimistic mutuality. It seems that we have overcome something, though I privately have little doubt that this achievement can soon be lost and that this psychic threshold might need to be crossed again and again.

HOLDING, UNMASKING, BRIDGING, AND DEPTH-RENDERING INTERVENTIONS

Two sets of phenomena are evident in this clinical vignette. The first pertains to the shift in the patient's material from simplicity through contradiction to paradox. At the level of simplicity, she needed reassurance from me that she would not hurt me. Contradiction appeared on the scene when she could see her having portrayed me as passive and impotent while holding an idealized and omnipotent view of me as well. Similarly, a temporal contradiction became apparent when her worry about the future turned out, at least in part, to be based upon concerns regarding the past. Finally, her emphatic agreement with my later comments (e.g. that her search for reassurance while insisting that it could not be provided implied a step toward relinquishment of symbiotic omnipotence, or that her talk of hostility also contained a core of concern for me) displayed a move to the psychic level of paradox.

The second phenomenon highlighted by this vignette pertains to the role of analyst's reverie in deciphering the shifts in the patient's material and in guiding the analyst's interventions. After all, the discernment of contradiction and of arrival at paradox took place at first in my feeling and thinking state. Their communication to the patient in subtle ("I wonder what you picture me doing as you are slapping me or stabbing me with a knife") or direct ("In this search for reassurance regarding your hostility you also seem to be showing concern and love for me") ways followed.

Four meta-interventions are involved here: *holding, unmasking, bridging,* and *depth-rendering.*

(i) Foremost is the function of *holding* (Winnicott 1960). This refers to the analyst's containment of the patient's scattered associations, diverse affects, and regressive movements, in an empathic and unquestioning manner. The provision of a safe and non-retaliatory ambience where even violent fantasies can be peacefully elucidated might itself have provided considerable reassurance to the patient and permitted ego advance.

(ii) Then there is *unmasking* the contradiction. By ordinary methods of defense analysis or by merely seeking a clarification (e.g. my asking the patient what he imagined me doing while he was stabbing me), the analyst might make the patient cognizant of a certain psychic discrepancy that has already become intuitively evident to the analyst. The patient's gaining this awareness might, in turn, prompt his or her observing ego to strive toward mending the cleavage, at first on an intellectual and then on an affective level (and sometimes vice versa).

(iii) Closely associated with this is the use of *bridging* (Akhtar 1995, Kernberg 1975) interventions, which emanate from the analyst's capacity to retain the patient's split and contradictory self- and object-representations in mind (since the patient has a tendency to "forget" affectively one or another extreme of his experience). Their aim is to undo the psychic compartmentalization caused by splitting. Such interventions involve the analyst's subtle display that he, at least, has not "forgotten" the opposite transference is accompanied by a gentle verbal reminder of the patient's love for the analyst (e.g. my "reminding" the patient, who was talking about stabbing me, that he also liked me very much), and elucidation of the latter is accompanied by a mild, almost passing, remark regarding the patient's hostility.

(iv) Finally, there is the use of what I would call *depth-rendering* interventions. Unlike bridging interventions, which aim to connect contradictory clusters along a single dimension (e.g. affect, morality), depth rendering interventions impart the knowledge to the patient that multiple meanings coexist in his or her communication, though at differing levels of awareness and abstraction. Rather than arranging contradictory material in a parallel fashion, depth-rendering interventions impart such material a figure-ground relationship. To use a phrase of Kristeva's (1987), such interventions aim at "layering of significance" (p. 6). Bridging interventions address material that has been consciously felt and conveyed by the patient. They are therefore closer to the concept of clarifications. Depth-rendering interventions, in contrast, add something new to the patient's awareness, something preconscious, and are therefore closer to the concept of interpretation proper. Such a depth-rendering intervention involved my saying to the patient that while asking me for reassurance he was also displaying acceptance of the fact that I could not provide it and in talking about his hostility he was showing concern for me as well.

A brief vignette from the analysis of a different patient further illustrates the use of such a depth-rendering intervention. This material too shows the simplicity-contradiction-paradox movement, though in a more subtle manner.

Ms. K. begins the last session of her nearly ten year–long analysis by saying that on her way to my office, she felt as if she were coming to a funeral. She describes her experience of there being an air of finality, solemnity, and loss to the afternoon. As I remain silent, Ms. K. goes on to recount her experiences at a couple of funerals she has attended. She sobs. I too feel sad, but do not say anything. Gradually, her associations shift to her getting a doctorate soon and then to graduation dinners, commencement ceremonies, etc. She begins to be animated. Soon, however, she catches herself and observes that this talk of happy endings (graduations) is defensive against her sadness (funerals). Significantly, she adds that while this might be the case, the two sides most likely represent the two sides of her feelings regarding parting from me for good: "happy and sad, sad and happy." I now say, "Yes, it does seem like that" and, after a momentary pause, add "but you know, all well-timed funerals are graduations of a sort and all graduations contain funeral-like elements." Ms. K. nods in agreement. The sense of our being together in each other's apartness is evident as the end of the session approaches.

Here the patient begins at the level of *simplicity* (sadness at funerals, joy at commencements). Then, spontaneously (and/or with the continued provision of my holding), she observes the coexistence of the two disparate clusters. This is the level of *contradiction.* Noticing the defensive link between them, she becomes able to mend the split ("happy and sad, sad and happy"). Subsequently, she arrives at the level of *paradox* at which happiness and sadness inevitably contain elements of each other. Facilitating this move is my depth-rendering intervention ("You know all well-timed funerals are graduations of a sort and all graduations contain funeral-like elements"). Such depth-rendering interventions usually follow holding, unmasking, and bridging measures. Together these four functions of the analyst's transform the patient's splintered, vacillating, and simplistic psychic existence into one that is diverse, affectively rich, and multi-layered. In effect, they have a growth-promoting effect upon the patient's psychic organization.[56]

A close parallel to these processes (and their effects) can be witnessed in a mother's facilitation of her infant's advance from the earliest state of psychic unintegration to that of becoming a coherent psychic unit in its own right (Winnicott 1960a). While such role of the mother vis-à-vis infants and toddlers is well recognized, maternal ego participation seems no less significant for the stabilization and deepening of her older child's psychic reality. The following non-clinical vignette illustrates this and provides a developmental substrate to the analytic interventions outlined previously. Two children are talking to each other in their mother's presence.

---

56. Only at the level of paradox does the patient become analyzable in the traditional sense of the word, i.e. capable of a collaborative inquiry into the concealed meanings and multi-layered connections within the association material and the transference experience. It is for this reason that in the session described here my interventions are not actually interpretive but largely clarifying and affirmative. They render plausibility rather than decipher concealed meanings. Thus questions such as why was the patient (mentioned in the first vignette) feeling angry, what did stealing the scarf mean, what did hitting or stabbing me symbolize, and how was all this related to the patient's childhood etc. remain unaddressed in this session. These are left for later inquiry.

The 6-year-old boy announces that he will be a doctor when he grows up. His prim and "mature" 10-year-old sister promptly objects, saying to the mother, "But he said yesterday that he wants to be a pilot." The little boy gets tense. The mother smiles and responds, "Well, you know there are doctors in the Air Force too!"

Amply evident in this discourse is a progression from simplicity (the wish to be a doctor) through a transitional stage of contradiction (doctor–pilot) to paradox (doctor in the Air Force). Also evident is that the sister and mother form an operant pair whose interventions facilitate this move. Together the duo can be seen as a collated counterpart to the analyst's unmasking (sister), bridging, and depth-rendering (mother) activities. Both kinds of "therapeutic interventions" were needed for the dialogue to have progressed from the level of simplicity to that of paradox.

The mention of two kinds of therapeutic interventions brings me to the last point of my paper. It seems that regarding the understanding and treatment of individuals with severe character pathology, psychoanalytic thought has adopted two divergent paths. The first path, embodying a synthesis of certain Kleinian notions with contemporary ego psychology, is exemplified by Kernberg (1975, 1976, 1984) and those who have extended his work (Volkan 1976, Yeomans et al. 1992). The second is represented by the psychoanalysts of the British Middle Group—Balint (1958), Winnicott (1965), Guntrip (1969), and their exponents, Casement (1991), Wright (1991), Bollas (1992)—and, in this country, by Modell (1976), Kohut (1977), Adler (1985), and Schulz and Lewin (1992). These two conceptual approaches can be seen as representing, respectively, the "classic" and the "romantic" visions of psychoanalysis (Strenger 1989). The "classic" vision prompts a skeptical listening attitude, considers the analyst's personality only a vehicle of his technique, views motivation in terms of wishes and psychopathology in terms of conflict, regards deep regression during treatment undesirable, sees acting out as an unproductive spilling over into life of material that is better restricted to the verbal transactions of treatment, minimizes the analyst's role as a new object, yields interventions that address resistance and facilitate psychic uncovering, and considers increased rationality and realism to be the goal of treatment. The "romantic" vision, in contrast, mobilizes a listening attitude of credulousness, regards the personal warmth of the therapist as crucial, views motivation in terms of ego needs and psychopathology in terms of deficit, sees deep regression during treatment as offering the possibility of a psychic rebirth, views acting out as a manifestation of the patient's hope for reparation, emphasizes the analyst's role as a new object, yields intervention that renders the patient's experience plausible by empathic affirmation and reconstruction, and considers enhanced authenticity and vitality to be the goal of treatment.

It is my conviction that the practicing analyst, in his view of these divergent approaches, needs to traverse a *simplicity-contradiction-paradox* sequence of the type described previously. At the simple, though not necessarily incorrect, level, he might view the two approaches to be applicable to different kinds of patients. The first approach might seem better suited for neurotic and the second approach for borderline, narcissistic, and schizoid patients. At the level of contradiction, both approaches might seem suitable for one and the same patient but at different times during the treatment (Killingmo 1989). The first approach, with its emphasis upon the search for hidden meaning, would seem to work better when the patient is better organized and operating at the level of conflict. The second approach, with its accent on empathy and holding, would be the preferred mode of engaging the patient at the level of deficit and during states of extraordinary turmoil and regression. Finally, at the level of paradox, both approaches would be simultaneously operative in the analyst's mind. Every patient's every association and every behavior will be subject to a form of listening, understanding, and intervening. The choice of which perspective to address the material from and what facet to bring to the patient's attention would then depend on the analyst's intuitive evaluation of the patient's capacity to hear, assimilate, and utilize the information.

CONCLUDING REMARKS

This paper touches upon three separate but overlapping realms. These are (a) the progression of discourse during the analytic treatment of borderline patients, (b) the role of maternal care in the psychic integration of a growing child, and (c) the practicing analyst's attitude toward divergent psychoanalytic approaches to severe character pathology. The thesis of this contribution is two-fold. First, it proposes that the psychic reality of the borderline patient evolves in a three-step process during the analytic treatment. These steps include: (1) experiencing and presenting disparate psychic states without the awareness of inherent contradictions; (2) observing, acknowledging, and mending the splits responsible for these contradictions; and (3) developing a capacity for feeling and accepting paradox, that is, coexistence of multiple meanings at different levels of abstraction. Second, it suggests that this three-step movement vis-à-vis the associative material takes place first within the analyst's reverie and then in the patient's psychic reality. The analyst's holding, unmasking, bridging, and depth-rendering interventions, and the vicissitudes of identification, make the patient's advance possible. The chapter offers two clinical vignettes highlighting these hypotheses and their technical implications. A vignette from the non-clinical realm of a mother's interaction with her children is also included in the hope of demonstrating a developmental prototype of the analyst's interventions outlined previously. It is suggested that the practicing analyst also needs to traverse a "simplicity-contradiction-paradox" sequence in his view of the divergent theoretical approaches to the analytic understanding and treatment of severe character pathology. Chapter Eight explicates this in finer details. Indeed, in all these realms (clinical, developmental, and conceptual), a movement from simplicity to awareness of contradictions and from there to acceptance of paradox is desirable. The ideal to be strived for is that which accommodates complexity, multiple determinants, different viewpoints, and varying levels of abstraction. It is only through such striving that one can achieve a fluid, though informed, psychoanalytic theory and technique vis-à-vis patients with severe character pathology.

8

FROM SCHISMS
THROUGH SYNTHESIS
TO OSCILLATION

From the early Freud–Ferenczi debates on analytic technique, through the Klein–Balint schism in England and the Kernberg–Kohut controversy in the United States, to the contemporary tension between the classical and the intersubjective views of the analytic process, there has existed a schism in the way our field has practiced and conceptualized its own enterprise. Seen and described variously, this schism subsumes the following dichotomies: oedipal–preoedipal, psychopathological–developmental, one person–two person, verbal–non-verbal, conflict–deficit, and so on. To be sure, each such conceptual pair has its own vantage point, ups and downs in psychoanalytic history, heuristic accompaniments, and technical nuances. At the same time, these dichotomies do tend to share an important common element. One polarity of these concepts (e.g. oedipal, psychopathological, one person, verbal, and conflict) tends to tilt the analyst's listening in a skeptical direction and his interventions toward a search for hidden meanings in the patient's communications. The other polarity (e.g. preoedipal, developmental, two person, non-verbal, and deficit) tends to tilt the

analyst's listening toward credulousness and his interventions in an
affirmative direction. The implications of this schism for the theory
and craft of psychoanalytic technique are therefore quite significant.
In light of this, it is surprising that little effort has been made to
elucidate and heal this split.[57] The tendency, instead, has been to
ignore the bifurcartion, or to rigidly adhere to one particular side of
the split or, more recently, to profess a non-aligned eclecticism
where multiple models are used in the service of clinical necessity.
Such solutions have pragmatic and aesthetic advantages but miss out
on the technical coherence that synthesizing the two sides promises
to yield.

In a technically relevant and experience-near emphasis, I will
begin this essay[58] by two clinical examples that highlight the issues
involved. I will note the technical choices presented by such material
and briefly elucidate related matters of technique. Since the two
vignettes highlight only the conceptual dilemma and do not contain
information on how I resolved it, I will offer a third vignette to show
what I did say and do in a similarly puzzling situation. Finally, I will
comment upon the developmental basis of my conceptualizations
and then conclude with a short parable containing the essence of
my message.

TWO CLINICAL VIGNETTES

Case 1

A schizoid woman in the first year of her brittle and tenuous
analysis begins a session by a prolonged silence. After waiting it out
some, since I am used to her halting manner, I bring her attention
to the difficulty she seems to be experiencing in beginning to talk.
Encountering further silence, I venture, "Perhaps there is some
concern, some feeling about me that is making it difficult for you to
reveal what you are thinking and feeling." The patient remains quiet

---

57. There are a few notable exceptions in this regard (Greenspan 1977,
Killingmo 1989, Strenger 1989, Wallerstein 1983), and I will refer to these
contributions later in this essay.

58. This essay was originally written in honor of Arnold Cooper, M.D.

for another few minutes. Then, in a pained voice, she says, "Why can't you understand me without my speaking? You are an analyst. You should be able to understand what I am feeling, what I am wanting and needing from you at this time." She pauses. I remain quiet. She adds, "It hurts my feelings when you want me to speak so that you can understand me. See, when I was little I had to teach my mother—at least, I tried to—how to be my mother. Then I had to teach my father how to be my father. And, now I have to speak here so that you can understand me. That's like my teaching you how to be an analyst. It hurts my feelings. It really does, this whole thing."

While she is not vengeful, her plaintive and hurt voice makes me feel I have burdened her. By encouraging verbalization, I have imposed my agenda. Soon, however, I see the idealizing aspect of her desire. I should omnisciently discern her inner world and she, having arrived at the Vatican of depth psychology, should be healed with little further effort on her part. I begin to feel skeptical. What is all this a defense against? Does the desire to keep me fixed in an idealized healer role help her ward off hate toward me for my seeming unhelpful (allegedly, like her parents)? Is this God-like view of me a shield to deflect her erotic and non-erotic feelings about my body, which is after all only about two feet from her? With these thoughts, an intervention begins to formulate in my mind. I will, in some fashion, bring her attention to the defensive aims in her statement.

However, I decide to give myself just another moment or two to think this out further. Now it occurs to me that while my line of thinking is plausible, it involves a rather swift bypass of the patient's overt material. Maybe there is something to what she is saying. Maybe her feeling hurt by my first intervention was not simply a response to a frustrated transference wish but an understandable reaction to the deprivation of a healthy ego need. After all, aren't there certain human relationships (e.g. between infant and mother, between two naked lovers under a sheet, between a religious mendicant and his or her spiritual guide, between two friends driving for a long while on a highway, etc.) where words are not essential for communication? Clearly, this patient did not have enough such ego-strengthening experiences during childhood and is not having enough such experiences in her adult life. To be sure, we should work at her resolving the intrapsychic hurdles in her path to be more satisfied in this regard, but what about this very moment when she seems to be in need of such an experience? Is there a point in depriving her? Should my follow-up intervention not indicate that I respect her need to be understood in her silence and that I did indeed burden her by encouraging her to talk? Should I interpret the idealizing, defensive, and potentially paranoid aspect of her comments? Or, should I empathize with her hurt, and discern and acknowledge the healthy, developmentally valid aspect of her ego need? I am at a conceptual fork.

Case 2

A thin-skinned and shy, fearful but immensely needy young woman is in a five-times-a-week analysis. From time to time she feels a bit more confident of her acceptability to me. Usually this is a result of a piece of superego analysis, whereby the defensive nature of her inhibitions become more observable to her and whereby she learns of the childhood roots and current uses of terrifying inner injunctions. Mostly, she is afraid of overburdening me and immensely thankful for my attention. At other times, she expresses a need to see me more often, have longer sessions, meet me on demand, and so on. Five times a week for 50 minutes certainly does not seem enough. I encourage her to tell me more about all this. She reveals that as a child she felt horribly rejected by her mother, who sternly discouraged any physical contact between them. She sobs. We go on in this staccato fashion.

Then, one day she reveals, fearfully and with some help from me, that she has found out where I live and has driven by to take a look at my house. I experience mixed feelings upon hearing this. Mostly, I feel fascination at this manner of transference deepening. The link between this behavior and her childhood wishes to touch her mother is clear to me. When I bring this to her attention, she notices the connection too. However, the material does not deepen. Inquiries regarding what fantasies she has about my house, what or who does she really want to see, what does the house stand for, how the looking at my house might be a way of avoiding wishes to see me more fully (she is on the couch), yield meager results.

Gradually, the pattern of visiting my house becomes a regular one. Three, four times a week, including at times on weekends, she drives by the street on which I live, slowing down as she passes my house, looking at it intently. Once in a while, from inside my house I can see her driving by in her car. I feel a bit intruded upon and mildly annoyed. I listen to the reports of these visits often but gain little further access to her inner world. I present this situation to a study group where some members express alarm and question my not feeling frightened and angry. They suggest more active efforts at bringing this matter into the verbal discourse, getting at the underlying wishes of intruding upon the primal scene, cannibalism, whatever. One member recommends a prohibition of this behavior, thinking that only that will force the material back into the chamber of thought.

I find myself congenial to these ideas but not feeling truly alarmed; I am in no rush. A different approach presents itself to me. I am reminded that the patient wanted to see me more than five times a week and for longer sessions held at her demand. Was that a coercive control of me behind which lurked the fear (wish) of having killed me during the intervals? Or, was it a developmental need? In other words, was the patient's wish to have more contact a hostile defense against deeper layers of even greater hostility or was her going to my house an innovative way of having more sessions, without which she felt cognitively and emotionally disorganized? Two interventions were thus possible. One leaned toward interpreting the defensive and/or provocative nature of her actions. The other involved acknowledging the adaptive aspects of her behavior, which sought satisfaction of an ego need that I had failed to meet. Here it was again, the same conceptual fork!

SCHISMS AND SYNTHESIS

These vignettes demonstrate that clinical material offered us can be heard from two opposing perspectives. While described from various vantage points, as noted previously, these perspectives ultimately arise out of what Strenger (1989) has termed the *classic* and *romantic* visions of human nature, its maladies, and their amelioration. The classic vision, found most clearly in Kant's thought, holds striving toward autonomy and the reign of reason to be the essence of being human. The romantic vision, developed by

Rousseau and Goethe, values authenticity and spontaneity over logic and reason. Each vision exerts a powerful impact upon psychoanalytic theory.

> The *classic view* sees man as governed by the pleasure principle and the development towards maturity is that towards the predominance of the reality principle. Neurosis is the result of the covert influence of the pleasure principle. The analyst's attitude towards the patient is a combination of respect and suspicion and the analyst takes the side of the reality principle. The ethic is stoic: maturity and mental health depend on the extent to which a person can acknowledge reality as it is and be rational and wise. The *romantic view* sees man as striving towards becoming a cohesive self. Development aims at a self which consists of a continuous flow from ambitions to ideals, from a sense of vitality towards goals which are experienced as intrinsically valuable. Mental suffering is the result of the failure of the environment to fulfill the self-object function and the patient's symptoms are the desperate attempt to fill the vacuum in his depleted self. The analyst's attitude towards the patient is one of trust in his humanity and the analyst takes the side of joy and vitality. The ethic is romantic: maturity and mental health consist in the ability to sustain enthusiasm and a sense of meaning. (Strenger 1989, p. 601)

This bifurcation has profound effects on the psychoanalytic conceptualizations of psychopathology and its amelioration. The classic approach views psychopathology, even its severe forms, in terms of internal conflict (Abend et al. 1983, Arlow and Brenner 1964, Kernberg 1975) and the romantic approach (Kohut 1977, Winnicott 1965) in terms of deficit. The first approach values rationality and realism in the conduct of life and the second approach, authenticity and vitality. Therefore the two approaches have potentially different goals for treatment and different parameters for regarding a treatment successful.

Strenger (1989) notes the impact of these two visions upon the technique of psychoanalysis in the following two areas: (1) *listening attitude:* the classic attitude prompts skepticism and a listening geared to decipher "the ways in which the patient's wishes and fantasies colour his perception of reality, past and present" (p. 603); the romantic attitude mobilizes credulousness and a listening attitude geared to discern "the healthy striving for wholeness and psychic survival" (p. 603) in his communications;[59] (2) *nature of interventions*: the classic attitude yields interventions that address resistance, facilitate uncovering, and pertain to the intrapsychic "here and now," while the romantic attitude yields interventions aimed at enhancing validity and plausibility of the patient's experience by empathic affirmation and reconstruction.

Other aspects of technique, not spelled out by Strenger, also reveal differences in these two approaches: (1) *the view of transference*: the first approach views transference as a re-creation (however distorted by wish, defense, immature ego apparatus, etc.) of early object relations (Freud 1912, 1915, Klein 1948); the second approach considers the possibility that transference might also contain a search for new objects (Loewald 1960, Tahka 1993, Winnicott 1965); (2) *the view of resistance*: the classic approach values verbalization via free association and therefore views patients' silences as resistance to the process; the romantic approach emphasizes that the patient is always communicating something important to the analyst and his or her silence is but one way of doing so (Khan 1983, Winnicott 1965); (3) *the recognition of the therapist's role as a new object* is lesser in the first than in the second approach (Loewald 1960, Settlage 1994); in the classic approach, the therapist's role is technical and interpretive while in the romantic approach it is mutative via empathic relatedness and development facilitation; (4) in a related vein, the classic approach regards *the therapist's personality* significant only insofar as it is a constituent of the technique (Kernberg 1984), while the romantic approach regards the warmth, tact, and authenticity of the therapist to be of central importance (Guntrip 1969); (5) the classic approach deems *deep regression during the treatment* undesirable since it threatens therapeutic alliance and

---

59. The recent Arlow–Schwaber debate (Arlow 1995, Schwaber 1998) exemplifies this very polarity in the analyst's listening attitude. With a different slant, Spencer and Balter (1990) also underscore the tension between the "introspective" and the "behavioral" methods of observation in psychoanalysis. In the former, the analyst puts himself in the position of the analysand and derives clinical understanding from the latter's perspective. In the latter, the analyst adopts the "view of a spectator, without regard to the subject's own thoughts or feelings" (p. 402). The two methods, often yielding different sets of information, are complementary, each modifying the other in the service of deepening the grasp of the analysand's mental functioning.

contaminates reason (Kernberg 1975, 1984), while the romantic approach (Adler 1985, Balint 1968, Guntrip 1969, Searles 1986, Winnicott 1960a) regards it as essential for a new beginning to become possible; (6) while both views acknowledge *acting out* to be inevitable, the classic view deems it an undesirable spilling over into the life of material that should be brought to conscious awareness in treatment (Abend et al. 1983, Freud 1914b, Kernberg 1975, 1984, Volkan 1987), and the romantic approach views it as a desperate "manifestation of hope" (Winnicott 1963, p. 208) that the environment (now embodied by the therapist) will reverse the damage it has done; and (7) the two approaches carry different *countertransference* risks; the main risk of the classic approach is that the analyst might become judgmental and a haughtily superior arbiter of "reality," and the main risk of the romantic approach is that the analyst might become overindulgent and unduly identified with the child self-representations of the patient.

These distinctions highlight that an exclusive adherence to either of the two approaches necessarily entails technical tradeoffs. A dedicatedly "romantic" approach can preclude uncovering, interpretive work, and a strictly "classic" approach can overlook the importance of empathic, stabilizing measures. Fortunately, admixture of the two approaches is discernable in the work of some integrative theorists. For instance, Modell (1976), while betraying an overall romantic bent, recognizes the importance of oedipal transferences, a proposition of the classic type. Volkan (1987), though classic in his approach, emphasizes the redemptive power of a deep regression, a notion of the romantic type.

Most practicing clinicians also intuitively attempt to strike their own variety of a balance between these two positions. Indeed, the two approaches can be reconciled with the possibility of rapprochement on three levels of increasing complexity. The simplest stance is to view them as being suited for different kinds of patients. The technical approach derived from the classic vision appears more applicable to analyzable neurotics and, within the severe character pathology realm, to "thick-skinned" (Rosenfeld 1971) narcissistic and borderline patients. The approach derived from the romantic vision seems more suited for fragile borderline, retiring schizoid, and "thin-skinned" (Rosenfeld 1971) narcissistic patients. At a more complex level, it seems that both approaches are suitable for one and the same patient, only at different times during the treatment. The classic approach, with its emphasis on the search for hidden meaning, works better when the patient is more organized and allied with the therapist. The romantic approach, with its accent on affirmation and empathy, would be the preferred mode of engaging the patient during states of extraordinary turmoil, self-absorption, and regression. At an even more sophisticated level, it can be said that every patient's every association and every behavior can, and should, be understood from both approaches. The choice of which perspective to address the material from and what facet to bring to the patient's attention then depends on the therapist's intuitive evaluation of the patient's capacity to hear and assimilate the information. Issues of optimal distance (Akhtar 1992a, Bouvet 1958, Escoll 1992, Mahler et al. 1975) and tact (Poland 1975) are clearly of paramount importance here. One thing, however, is certain and that is that the

> choice between the classic and the romantic attitude is not to be made once and for all. It must depend at every moment on an assessment of where the patient is in this respect . . . this tension is not to be resolved, as it reflects the tension between the human ability and need for full experience and the capacity for self-reflection which is essential to maturity and wisdom. (Strenger 1989, pp. 607, 609)

In a different but overlapping context, Wallerstein (1983) has voiced reservations about an exclusive focusing upon the oedipal or preoedipal determinants of psychopathology. Wallerstein emphasizes that

> In the flow and flux of analytic clinical material we are always in the world of "both/and." We deal constantly, and in turn, both with the oedipal where there is a coherent self, and the preoedipal, where there may not yet be; with defensive regressions and with developmental arrests; with defensive transferences and defensive resistances and with recreations of earlier traumatic and traumatized states. (p. 31)

Another reminder of this sort, this time about the controversy over the deciphering and interpreting of transferences related to conflicts and deficits, comes from Killingmo (1989) who states:

As the structural level will fluctuate within one and the same patient
from one point of time to another or from one area of the personality
to another, the analyst has to be in a state of constant receptivity to
oscillate between the two strategic positions. (p. 77)

When the patient's transferences reflect the conflict-based sector
of his personality, the technical approach should be one of skeptical
listening, search for concealed meanings, and interpretive interventions. On the other hand, when the patient's transferences
reflect deficit-based sectors of his personality, the technical approach should be characterized by credulous listening, validation
of the patient's psychic reality, and affirmative interventions. At
such moments,

> issues of subtle meaning, affect and wish, are of secondary impor-
> tance to issues of internal intactness or disruption related to a lack of
> a differentiated ego structure secondary to a lack of constant,
> delineated, internal representations . . . the analyst does not wish
> to focus his attention on the patient's drive derivatives when the
> patient's main concern is fragmentation. (Greenspan 1977, p. 387)

The doctrinaire tendency of either/or thinking must be put aside
in favor of a technique that oscillates in rhythm with the patient's
level of psychic organization.

Such crisscross between addressing differently organized clusters
of patient's material is also inherent in Settlage's (1992, 1994)
pointing out that the therapeutic process and the developmental
process are complimentary and proceed hand in hand. Transference interpretation increasingly reveals the analyst as a new
object that the patient can use for developmental purposes. Settlage
notes that

> With each undoing of some aspect of pathology, there is opportunity
> for development in that same area. With each increment of develop-
> ment, the personality structure is strengthened. The strengthened
> structure increases the patient's tolerance for the therapeutic expo-
> sure of repressed, anxiety-creating urges, fantasies and feelings,
> further therapeutic work is followed in turn by more development,
> and so on. (1992, p. 355)

Following Loewald (1960), Settlage suggests that the analyst should fluctuate between maintaining a neutral position toward the patient's transferences and establishing a "developmental relationship" (1994, p. 42) with the healthier sectors of the patient's personality. Through the former stance, he will acquire the ability to make interpretations. Through the latter, he will encourage patients' developmental initiatives and acknowledge developmental achievements.

Yet another observation of the same type, though stated in somewhat different terms, comes from Bach (1994), who states that

> A considerable period of holding or attunement, which is *not* the same as passivity, mirroring, corrective emotional experience, or role playing, may be necessary in order to provide the patient with the [needed] psychic space. . . . If the patient is consistently confronted with the analyst's reality before the psychic space has developed, then two common miscarriages of analysis may ensue. In the first the patient becomes acquiescent and agrees, but does not develop a genuine sense of self and a prolonged pseudo-analysis results. In the second the patient disagrees and eventually either acts out or conforms, but becomes internally isolated, suspicious, and schizoid. (p. 158)

Bach emphasizes that attunement of another person to one's inner emotional state results in a feeling of cohesion, trust, and psychic solidity. This foundation is essential to handling later disillusionments, including those inherent in healthy development. The same scheme applies to the conduct of analysis. In other words, provision of attunement and facilitation of trust in the validity of the patient's own experience is a prerequisite for its interpretive deconstruction.

Therefore, it seems that whether it be the polarity between classic and romantic (Strenger 1989), oedipal and preoedipal (Wallerstein 1983), conflict and deficit (Killingmo 1989), insight and empathy (Kernberg 1975, Kohut 1977), attunement and interpretation (Bach 1994), or psychopathological and developmental (Loewald 1960, Settlage 1992, 1994), the ideal to be strived for is the acceptance of complexity, of paradox, of multiple determination, and by implication, of a fluid though informed and thoughtful technique.

In an eloquent elucidation of the changing views of the therapeutic action of psychoanalysis, Cooper (1988b) makes an essentially similar plea.[60] Comparing Strachey's (1934) and Loewald's
(1960) seminal contributions on technique, Cooper (1988b) notes
that Strachey's model of therapeutic action

> seems straightforward, based on classical instinct theory and resis-
> tance analysis, and interlarded with a bit of Kleinian object relations
> theory. The role of the analyst is as a neutral, benign interpreter of
> reality, internalized as a temporary new object, helping to make the
> unconscious conscious, and modifying the superego. Classical ana-
> lytic neutrality is preserved. (p. 19)

In contrast, the model analyst for Loewald offers himself to the
patient as a contemporary object. He works by being

> an emotionally related object, with an important gradient of organi-
> zational maturity between him and his patient, mindful of the
> patient's core of potential being, which he senses as a parent does,
> oriented toward the future, offering the patient opportunities to
> create new integrations on the armature of maturity that the analyst
> provides. His task is empathic communication, uncovering, and
> guidance towards new synthesis. (Cooper 1988b, p. 26)

Cooper concludes that these two sets of ideas regarding how
psychoanalysis works remain "parallel rather than integrated . . .
(and that) . . . it is a major task of psychoanalysis today to unify
these two forms of description" (p. 26).[61]

---

60. By this time, the reader would have become aware of the profusion of
quotations from various authors. This is a deliberate literary device. In letting the
voices of distinguished theoreticians (e.g. Bach, Cooper, Greenspan, Herzog,
Killingmo, Settlage, Wallerstein, Wright) speak literally for themselves, without
paraphrase or interpretation, I have sought to create a heuristic chorus in support
of my main technical and theoretical assertions.

61. Pressures other than intellectual might add to the necessity for synthesizing
diverse views of analytic theory and technique. In a contribution on the future of
psychoanalysis, Cooper (1990) suggests that the increasing presence of IPA
societies as full-fledged members of the North American analytic community will
eventually make it necessary for American analysts to get acquainted with the
continental and Latin American views of analytic theory and technique.

BACK TO THE CLINICAL SITUATION

Case 3

In the throes of a regressive transference, a patient entered my office enraged and waiving a finger. Approaching the couch, she said, "I have a lot on my mind today and I want to do all the talking. I don't want you to speak even a single word!" A little taken aback, I mumbled "Okay." The patient shouted, "I said, 'not one word' and you have already fucked up this session!" Now sitting on my chair behind her, I was more rattled. "Did I do wrong by speaking at all?" I asked myself. As the patient lay on the couch, angry and stiff, I started to think. Perhaps she is so inconsolable today, so intent upon forcing me into the role of a depriving person, that she found a way to see even the gratification of her desire as its frustration. I was, however, not entirely satisfied with this explanation and therefore decided to wait, and think further. It then occurred to me that maybe she was rightly angered by my saying okay. In my agreeing to let her have omnipotent control over me, I had asserted my will and thus paradoxically deprived her of the omnipotence she seemed to need. I was about to make an interpretation along these lines, when it occurred to me that by sharing this understanding, I would be repeating my mistake: making my autonomous psychic functioning too obvious. As a result, I decided to only say, "I am sorry," and left the remaining thought unspoken. The patient relaxed and the tension in the room began to lessen. After 10 minutes of further silence, the patient said, "Well, this session has been messed up. I had so many things to say." After a further pause, she said, "Among the various things on my mind" . . . and thus the session gradually "started." By the time we ended, things were going pretty smoothly.

Now, I am aware that a novice too could have said, "I am sorry," but I believe the underlying discernment of ego needs would be missing there. In apologizing, I was acknowledging that I had failed her by not understanding that she needed to have no boundaries, as it were, between us at all; she was the kind of patient (at least in that moment) who "need(s) to be allowed to establish a provisional omnipotence over the analyst" (Casement 1991, p. 277). Moreover, by thus meeting the patient where she experientially was, my comment facilitated her moving up to a level where she could collaborate with me in an exploration of her psychic reality, *including* her rage at me and her injured sense that I was, in general, withholding love and affection from her. Affirmation thus prepared the ground for interpretation.

More on technique

One other aspect of technique deserves attention. In all three vignettes included here, there is a turning point in my subjective attitude.[62] In the first case, this occurs when I begin to leave the interpretation that the patient's demand is based upon an infantile wish in favor of viewing it as emanating from a legitimate ego need (see Akhtar 1999b for an elucidation of the need–wish distinction). In the second case, a similar shift is evident in my moving from the view that the patient's driving by my house expresses a warded off unconscious fantasy to the view that it is a manifestation of a need for greater contact with the analyst without which the self-experience would become incoherent and disorganized. In the third case, the patient's rage at my verbally agreeing to remain silent throughout the session was at first viewed by me as her paranoid inconsolability and only later as a reaction to my failing to meet her anaclitic ego needs. The turning point is evident in all three instances.

There are two ways to understand this internal shift. Not surprisingly, these take a classic and romantic view of my own subjectivity. In the former, the shift appears to result from an anxious giving up on the analysis of negative transference by resorting to patient-pleasing narratives. In the latter, the shift seems an accommodation to the level of the patient's structural organization. The momentary delay in arriving at the second formulation is caused by my analytic ego being transiently overwhelmed by affect and hence vulnerable to making what were to me relatively standard interpretations.[63] In

---

62. This turning point is obvious, owing to the severity of the cases cited. In ordinarily analyzable neurotic patients, the holding and affirmative functions of the analyst remain "silently" in place and permit the interpretive work to go on in the foreground.

63. Such transitional object-like use of familiar concepts has been commented upon by Michels (1983) in his elucidation of the scientific and clinical functions of

this connection, it is important to note that, in all three instances, I was not comfortable with the first line of understanding *and* surprised myself by the second formulation. Moreover, the second line of thinking did *not* exclude the first. It only prepared the ground for the interpretation as is clearly shown in the third vignette.

Such willingness and ability of the analyst to "oscillate between two strategic positions" (Killingmo 1989, p. 77), that is, those of affirmation and interpretation, have developmental correlates that can provide a rationale for mending the schism that has plagued psychoanalytic technique and its theories from its inception.

A DEVELOPMENTAL POSTSCRIPT

The technical polarities of listening with credulousness and responding with affirmative interventions versus listening with skepticism and responding with interpretive interventions seem to have as their respective developmental prototypes the maternal and paternal styles of relating to young children. Herzog's (1984) elucidation of the "homeostatic" and "disruptive" attunements of parents to their growing child is especially illuminating in this context. Through video-monitored child-observational studies, Herzog has demonstrated that mothers usually join in with a toddler in his or her ongoing play (e.g. building a tower with wooden blocks), thus giving the child a "continuity of being" (Winnicott 1965, p. 54), validity, and harmony with the environment ("homeostatic attunement"). Fathers, on the contrary, characteristically disrupt the playing toddler's equilibrium by cajoling him or her into *joining them* in a new activity ("disruptive attunement"). Homeostatic attunement has affirming qualities necessary for the sustenance and

---

psychoanalytic theory for psychoanalysts. In this light, the conceptual shift described previously can be seen as reflecting my own freedom from handed-down ideas in favor of experientially derived insights in the clinical here and now. While this indeed might have been the case, my sense is that more was involved here. The two patterns of understanding and responding reflected different analytic traditions and, as I propose to demonstrate in the latter parts of this essay, had different developmental prototypes.

consolidation of self-experience. Disruptive attunement has enhancing qualities necessary for broadening and deepening of self-experience. The influence of the two types of attunements is additive and contributes to the fluid solidity of a healthy self-experience.[64] Herzog further observed that fathers distract the child from the game he or she is playing only when the mother is with the child. In her absence, and especially with younger children, fathers too start playing the child's own game (i.e. resort to homeostatic attunement). This suggests that homeostatic attunement is an experiential prerequisite for disruptive attunement.

Extrapolating these developmental observations to the clinical situation suggests the following. The analyst's credulous listening and his "holding" (Winnicott 1960a) and "affirmative" (Killingmo 1989) interventions are akin to the maternal "homeostatic attunement" insofar as they too aim to validate, strengthen, and stabilize the self-experience. The analyst's skepticism regarding the patient's conscious material and his unmasking interpretive interventions seem akin to the paternal "disruptive attunement" insofar as these too cause cognitive expansion by introducing new material into the patient's awareness. Herzog's conclusion that homeostatic attunement is a prerequisite for the disruptive attunement also finds a parallel in the clinical situation wherein the analyst's holding and affirmative (i.e. homeostatic) functions must be securely in place in order for his interpretive (i.e. disruptive) efforts to be fruitful. The patient's inner sense of the analytic relationship must be stable (or should be stabilized) for him or her to utilize the destabilizing impact of interpretation which, by definition, brings something new to the patient's attention. The patient must possess or be helped to possess a "safety feeling" (Sandler 1960, p. 4) before the risk of encountering the repudiated aspects of his self-experience. Couched in the developmental metaphor, the analyst's exercise of maternal functions seems to be a prerequisite for his or her exercise of paternal functions.

---

64. Indeed, the two attunements might even be necessary for the two sides of identity—subjective self-sameness and self-objectification (Bach 1994, Erikson 1956, Lichtenstein 1963) —to optimally develop.

Designating such maternal and paternal interventions as "two poles of therapeutic technique" (1991, p. 280), Wright traces their respective origins to Freud and Winnicott.

> Freud, it seems to me, stands for the father with his forbidding and prohibitions; Winnicott stands for the mother and her caring, nurturing, and loving. Freud is the mediator of the reality principle to which the child must adapt; Winnicott is the protector of a kinder, more lenient space, which keeps reality, to some extent, at bay. (p. 280)

In Wright's view, analysis involves a renewal of the process of psychic formation. It provides the space within which new forms or symbols of the self may be created. However, for fully separated and representative symbols, as well as less separated and iconic symbols in the human discourse to emerge, be understood, and coalesce, the analytic technique requires both maternal and paternal elements. The maternal element (holding, facilitating, enabling, and surviving) "posits faith in the background process. Things will happen if you wait" (p. 283). The paternal element (searching, confronting, deciphering, and interpreting) underlies the analyst's skepticism, his struggles with the patient's resistances, his confrontations with the turbulent world of intrapsychic conflict. Wright goes on to suggest that the two modes of intervention might be appropriate at different times and foster different modes of symbolizing. However, maternal holding of the psychically banished elements has to precede a meaningful looking at them with the aim of further self-understanding.[65] "Containing holding" is a prior condition for "transformative looking" (p. 300). Moreover, the maternal and paternal elements of technique "provide a point and counterpoint in analysis between two styles and two visions and neither wins the day completely" (p. 280). It should also be remembered that such "maternal" and "paternal" attributes are not gender-based in a literal sense. There are male analysts who seem more "maternal"

---

65. To be sure, this is far from the technical stance adopted by self psychologists. For them, the empathic approach is not merely aimed at stabilizing the patient and consolidating his or her psychic experience *before* an interpretive mode can be introduced. For them the empathic approach is mutative in its own right.

and female analysts who seem more "paternal" in technique. At the same time, it is true that most analysts, regardless of their actual gender, possess both these attributes and strive to incorporate them in their technical approaches.[66]

Wright's bringing together of the Freud–Winnicott technical schism seems to have seamless underpinnings in Herzog's (1984) developmental observations. Together, their views also resonate with Greenspan's (1977), Wallerstein's (1983), Killingmo's (1989), Settlage's (1992), and Bach's (1994) differently couched statements mentioned earlier. In the end, it all boils down to placing consolidation before deconstruction, empathy before insight, affirmation before interpretation, and "mother" before "father," while recognizing that *both* experiences are as necessary in psychoanalytic treatment as they are in the course of development.[67] In the treatment of patients with reasonably well-established object constancy, these oscillations are mild; to extend the developmental metaphor, the "mother" is already in the room and "father" can proceed with his disruptive attunement. In sicker cases, "mother" has to be brought in before the introduction of paternal disruptive attunement;[68] I have elsewhere described such analytic work with individuals with

---

66. Cultural factors might also play a role here. For example, the "maternal" element of technique seems overrepresented by the analysts of Hungarian heritage (e.g. Ferenczi and Balint) and the "paternal" element by the analysts of Germanic descent (e.g. Freud and Kernberg).

67. Teaching is yet another arena in which oscillation between homeostatic and disruptive attainment has profoundly salutary effects. A good teacher tells the students what they already know and thus generates a feeling of self-worth and confidence in them (homeostatic attainment). Then, in a swift movement, the teacher presents new information to the student, challenging and expanding the student's intellectual horizons (disruptive attainment). More importantly, a good teacher is one who knows the velocity and intensity of oscillations between homeostatic and disruptive attunements suitable for his students.

68. The use of the terms *mother* and *father* here is largely metaphorical. While the attunement between parents and their children and between the analyst and analysand have similarities, the two relationships exist at different levels of complexity, involve different types of ego-relatedness, take place in different realms, and are in place for ultimately different purposes. The discernment of a remote echo of maternal and paternal styles of relating in certain analytic interventions is not to be construed as genetic reductionism, role playing, and transference manipulation.

defective object constancy in detail (Akhtar 1994, 1996, 1998). In either case, the treatment requires both types of interventions, though in neurotic patients less visibly so. A psychoanalytic technique that opts for only one side of this duality misses the clinical boat even if it rests safely on the shores of a pristine theory.

CONCLUDING REMARKS

In this chapter, I have attempted to highlight the existence of a central schism in the theory and practice of psychoanalytic technique. There exists a conceptual bifurcation at the core of psychoanalysis. It has been viewed from differing vantage points and portrayed as subsuming various dichotomies (oedipal–preoedipal, conflict–deficit, one person–two person, classic–romantic, etc.). While each such conceptual pair has its own heuristic accompaniments, these dichotomies share a profoundly important element. They have divergent effects upon the analyst's mode of listening and the nature of his or her interventions. These and other related technical implications are the topic of this chapter. With the help of three clinical vignettes and by coalescing the isolated voices of many distinguished theoreticians, this chapter attempts to elucidate and heal this split. It proposes three levels of increasingly sophisticated resolution of the technical divergence resulting from this schism. I recommend an informed oscillation between the two polarities of psychoanalytic technique, an oscillation that must remain in consonance with the patient's shifting ego organization. Now, in a final reiteration of my thesis, I conclude with a parable. There is a young boy and he has a beloved uncle. Each Easter, the uncle comes to visit his nephew and before entering the house goes to the backyard, where he hides some eggs so that they can go on a scavenger hunt. The boy loves searching for the hidden eggs with his uncle and looks forward to Easter each year. One year, the uncle arrives as usual, hides the eggs in the backyard, and enters the house. To his dismay, he finds the nephew bedridden, both his legs crushed in a car accident. What should the uncle do now? Pick the nephew up, put him in a wheelchair, take him to the backyard, and initiate the scavenger hunt as usual? Or, should the uncle sit down with the boy, ask him about the accident, and tell him about his own experiences of sickness and injury? If the uncle does the former, they might find the eggs but something deeper in the boy's experience will be missed. In contrast, if the uncle gives up his own enthusiasm for the scavenger hunt and sits down with the nephew, empathizes and chats, it is quite likely that when he gets up after a while, to go to the bathroom, he will hear the boy ask in a feeble voice, "Uncle, what about the eggs this year?"

Part V

UNTAPPED
POTENTIALS

9

MENTORSHIP

While inborn talents, early identifications, and childhood conflicts and their resolutions all contribute to an individual's choice of vocation, it is only after the consolidation of ego-ideal at the end of adolescence (Blos 1967, 1985, Erikson 1959b) that the work-related path of one's life actually becomes clear. However, this clarity is not etched in stone. It requires refinement and, if the intrapsychic flash has to evolve into a sustained glow, praxis in reality. What the young adult with a dream needs is a mentor, that is, someone who can show him the ropes and help him actualize his dream. Colloquial wisdom recognizes this, but there are few in-depth explorations of what exactly a mentor is or what he does; the *Title Key Word and Author Index to Psychoanalytic Journals—1920–1990* (Mosher 1991) does not have a single article under the headings of "mentor," "mentoring," or "mentorship." This chapter is aimed to fill this lacuna in the psychoanalytic literature.[69]

---

69. This essay was originally written in honor of Professor N.N. Wig of India, who was my first mentor in psychiatry.

WHAT IS A MENTOR?

The dictionary definition of the word *mentor* includes phrases such as "tutor, coach . . . trusted counselor or guide" (*Webster's*, 1987, p. 472). This spirit is reflected in the ordinary usage of the word to denote someone older, more experienced, and wiser than one's self who has been especially instrumental in one's personal and professional growth. A mentor is a development-facilitating object that helps consolidate the cognitive and social facets of one's work-related identity, especially during adolescence and young adulthood. The relationship between a mentor and his or her protégé is a special one and suffused with healthy narcissism of the dyad. There is a shared sense of purpose between them, with the mentor facilitating the protégé's work, achievement, and success in a largely non-exploitative manner. In the book, *The Seasons of a Man's Life*, Levinson (1978) states:

> Mentors are essential others who strengthen the resolve to work at difficult tasks . . . In a "good enough" mentoring relationship, the young man feels admiration, respect, appreciation, gratitude, and love for the mentor . . . The elder has the qualities of character, expertise, and understanding that the younger admires and wants to make part of himself. The young man is excited and spurred on by the shared sense of his promise. (p. 100)

By carving out the similarities and differences between a mentor on the one hand and a teacher, a father,[70] a lover, and an analyst on

---

70. In evoking "father" and not "mother" here, I am not suggesting that older and experienced women cannot be mentors to either younger men or women. My use of the word *father* is only partly literal. In a greater part, it is based upon the fact that, in the course of development, mother is a given object while father is a discovered object. Relationship with the former revolves around soothing, relatedness, affirmation, and psychic consolidation. In contrast, relationship with the latter revolves around instruction, search, development of autonomy, and efforts at pragmatic mastery of the world at large. Thus, even a female mentor largely performs functions that are paternal in nature. In this connection, it is noteworthy that in Homer's *The Oddessy*, Athena, the goddess of wisdom, took the male form of "mentor" in order to become a guide and role model for Odysseus's son, Telemachus.

the other hand, I seek to elucidate the mentor's psychosocial role. I also comment briefly upon the gender-based and the culturally determined variables in this realm and conclude with underscoring the implications of such an individual to a young adult's life.

MENTOR VERSUS TEACHER

A teacher, by definition, is one who teaches. He imparts a piece of knowledge to someone who does not possess it. Such knowledge might involve facts or theories. It might pertain to principles and guidelines or to skills and craftsmanship. Old texts might be prescribed and historical antecedents evoked. Or, the focus might be contemporary. Regardless of these scenarios, the task of the teacher is relatively clear-cut. If it is done with skill, resilient empathy with pupils,[71] and personal joy, all the better.

A mentor, in contrast, is more than a teacher. In fact, at times, a mentor might not even be involved in directly teaching the apprentice; the latter might have become acquainted with the former's work from a distance (e.g. by reading his published works). "Admiration of Freud's intellectual and scientific integrity, his relentless pursuit of truths even when confronted by stigma and resistance, has fostered the careers of many younger psychoanalysts who never met him" (Galatzer-Levy and Cohler 1993, p. 243). Even when a mentor is explicitly didactic, he comes across as having undertaken a task larger than transfer of knowledge. He excites the student, recognizes unevoked potentials, nurtures talent, and sponsors his student toward the outer intellectual and organizational limits of the latter's vision. A mentor works with his student outside the

---

71. In the arena of teaching, oscillation between two forms of engagement, namely "homeostatic" and "disruptive" attunements (Herzog 1984), has highly salutary effects. A good teacher tells the students what they already know, thus generating a feeling of self-worth and confidence in them (homeostatic attunement). Then, in a swift movement, the teacher presents new information to the student, challenging and expanding the student's intellectual horizons (disruptive attunement). More important, a good teacher is one who knows the velocity and intensity of oscillation between homeostatic and disruptive attunements suitable for his or her students.

formal teaching arena (e.g. classroom) and on topics beyond those formally prescribed. Unlike a teacher who prides himself in paying equal attention to all his pupils, the mentor is biased in favor of a specific, chosen student; Albom's (1998) memoir of the last days of his mentor, Morrie, captures such distinctions in poignant details.

MENTOR VERSUS FATHER

The role of a father (Blos 1985, Ross 1979, 1982) overlaps with that of a mentor in remarkable ways. The father helps a growing child separate from his mother and emerge from the affectively charged "symbiotic orbit" (Mahler et al. 1975) into a world of sharper cognition, heightened exploration, and attempt at mastery of external reality (Akhtar 1995, pp. 77–78). Similarly, a mentor puts an end to rote forms of learning, challenges indolence, and spurs active exercise of intellect. By virtue of possessing desirable skills and being ahead in life's game, so to speak, the father offers himself as a role model;[72] the growing child can project his lost infantile omnipotence onto him. Such "forward projection" (Chassaguet-Smirgel 1984) of narcissism offers hope, future orientation, and a rationale for aspiration and effort in life. The mentor, like the father, also becomes a role model. He knows. He can do what one cannot do. He is strong and seems unruffled by the hurdles of adversity and hardship. In other words, both father and mentor become objects of idealization and therefore emulation and identification.

Their roles overlap in three other ways. First, the father lends his name to his offspring and thus gives credibility and filiation to the latter's existence. The mentor too leaves his imprimatur upon his apprentice, whose work comes to belong in a particular lineage,[73] so

---

72. While a son is the greater beneficiary of such modeling, a daughter also needs to identify with the father in his executive skills vis-à-vis the extrafamilial world (Bernstein 1983).

73. This is evident in the academic tradition of putting the department chairman's name on papers published by members of the faculty. While this does have potentially exploitative aspects, its deeper psychodynamic significance in terms of oedipal affiliation must not be overlooked.

to speak. Second, both the father and the mentor have to be outgrown sooner or later by the offspring. Such overtaking might be a result of higher achievements of the offspring/apprentice or simply a reflection of the aging process by which the father/mentor in his advancing years begins to recede in the background. In other words, the outdoing might be absolute or relative. Ideally, such outdoing is not bloody and hostile;[74] indeed, the disengagement from early parental internalizations should be compatible with continued affectionate ties with them and a continuation of the family legacy, even if in a more personalized idiom (Poland 1977). Finally, at the time of major milestones of adult life (e.g. marriage), a father's "blessing" (Blos 1985, p. 12) is invariably sought. This serves multiple purposes ranging from relief of guilt (over the unconscious equation of success with patricide) to establishment of a deeper fraternity with the older man. Similarly, the benediction of a mentor seems needed at the time that a major shift in a professional career is about to take place.

All this goes to demonstrate the profound similarities that exist between the role of a mentor and a father. However, there are also important differences. The father is an integral and drive-invested part of the child's (and, later the young adult's) internal representational world. He has played a prominent role in the early separation–individuation process as well as in the vicissitudes of the Oedipus complex, and therefore, the superego formation (Freud 1913, 1924, 1930). In contrast, the mentor is an object discovered during the young adulthood when the psychic structure is already firmly in place. He is less invested with primitive conflicts and possesses greater "transformational" (Bollas 1979) potential toward a young adult who is disengaging himself from idealized parental imagos. Also, not being involved in the real-life variables of money, place of residence, familial responsibilities, and so on, the mentor, unlike the father, is less likely to be tainted with daily aggression. Idealization of a mentor can be maintained longer. This permits for internalizations to accrue and form structures. Moreover, unlike the

---

74. This may be hard to avoid if the mentor (or the father) is either highly renowned or overwhelmingly controlling (see the 1996 movie *Shine* and also its discussion by Akhtar and Powell 1999), or both. Some of Freud's early disciples had to break off with him for the same reason.

father, the value of whose bedrock presence gets submerged during early adulthood, the mentor occupies a prominent place in the psychic life of the young adult. A mentor might even serve as an agent of helping create distance from the father until the young adult's self is further consolidated. A mentor's presence thus beneficially delays the discovery of hitherto denied yet profound identifications with the father that emerge during middle age with full intensity (Akhtar and Samuel 1996, Kernberg 1980a).

MENTOR VERSUS LOVER

Unsettling as it may seem, but the fact is that a mentor also shares many role-related characteristics with a lover.

> This similarity arises because the poignancy that surfaces when a student finds a mentor feels like a new love. The two partners share an unblemished idea of what will become. It is an exhilarating time of possibilities. The freshness makes the relationship glow as there is no history of nasty arguments or clashing of values. Like the genesis of a romantic relationship, the mentor–protégé relationship enters a honeymoon period of joint discovery. Small arguments are laughed at and overlooked. Each day the individuals are filled with a growing love for each other. It is an infatuation. Unlike a romantic relationship where amorous feelings dominate, however, the student is in awe of the professor and the professor is filled with hope and charmed by the student. The student senses the possibility of achieving his own aspirations with this stronghold by his side. And, any hidden and repressed insecurities of the professor are soothed by having the reverence of this youngster. (Karen Groff, personal communication, August 2002)

The mentor and the lover both offer a specific and intense bond to the one seeking them out. Both facilitate the development of mutuality with a sense of mature "we-ness" (Bergman 1980) with their respective others. Both show a glow of excitement about the relationship and have dreams for its future. And, when the relationship comes to a tragic end, the battles between a mentor and a student who have fallen out of each other's favor appear similar to marital partners undergoing a divorce.

There are important differences in the two roles as well. Romance and sexuality, the cornerstones of the relationship between lovers, exist only at a lambent and deeply unconscious level, if at all, between the mentor and his protégé. Moreover, the penetrative and receptive aims of the two parties are relatively clear in the mentor–student relationship, while they tend to become more diffusely distributed between lovers, especially during their sexual encounters. Finally, while both relationships strive toward a mutually conceived creative product, such product is an intellectual one (e.g. a co-authored book) in the mentor–student relationship and a physical one (i.e. a baby) in the romantic relationship. One leads to a sociocognitive linkage that can be disowned, the other to a biological bond that is unbreakable.

MENTOR VERSUS ANALYST

Like a psychoanalyst, the mentor is in part a developmental, new external object and, in part, a transferentially re-created, old internal object. In the former capacity, the mentor performs all the developmental tasks typical of an analyst (Pine 1999); maintaining optimism, giving language to the protégé's unexpressed aspirations, viewing the potential for growth as lifelong, surviving aggressive attacks of the pupil, and celebrating new achievements on the latter's part (Settlage 1992, 1994). In the latter capacity, he "accepts" transference projections peacefully and remains empathically attuned to not only the student's conscious and verbalized purposes and intents but also to those aims and designs that do not exist on a conscious level in the latter's mind. Unlike the analyst, however, the mentor does not interpret defenses nor does he reconstruct the childhood origins of his student's fears and aspirations (Haesler 1993). Yet he gains knowledge of his mentee's background and helps him transcend it by using wit, gentle cajoling, role-modeling, and lighthearted confrontation. The focus of the analyst is upon the underbelly of the ego that deals with unconscious fantasies and conflicting drives. The focus of the mentor is upon the outer rind of the ego that is engaged with the external reality and thrives on the pleasure of work and mastery. Unlike the analyst who rarely offers advice, the mentor is explicitly supportive and encouraging in both professional and personal matters and suggests specific strategies for managing professional life (Perkoff 1992, Reynolds 1994).

SOME UNADDRESSED REALMS

The foregoing comparisons of a mentor to a teacher, father, lover, and analyst reveal that a mentor shares characteristics with each of them yet differs from each of them in significant ways. He is equidistant from all of these other roles.[75] His function consists of creating a specific bond, showing excitement, imparting knowledge, offering himself as a role model, expanding the psychic horizon of his follower, accepting the projection of internal objects upon his person, and acting as a developmental object in the professional life of a young adult. This is, of course, true only if the narcisstic motives and rescue fantasies play a lesser role than genuine altruism in the makeup of the mentor. Such a role comes closest to the Indian concept of a *guru,* though without the latter's unsurpassable superiority and religious connotations (see Isherwood 1980 for an eloquent description of a disciple's relationship with his *guru*). Compensation to a *guru* often takes the form of monetary payment or assistance with the day to day chores of life. This is not the case with the apprentice's relationships with a mentor.

Many aspects of the mentorship position, however, still remain unclear. For instance, is the experience of a "good-enough" relationship with one's father a prerequisite for one to be able to find and use a mentor? Would an extraordinary father-hunger, say in a child abandoned by his or her father, intensify the need for a mentor? Would it, at the same time, make it difficult to use the mentor as such, burdening him with greater than ordinary paternal transference? Are there gender differences that govern the need for a mentor? Little data is available to answer this last question, but it

---

75. When the mentor departs from this position and becomes more of a father or even a lover, the relationship becomes pathological and is destined for severe psychosocial difficulties.

is my impression that young men need a mentor more often and more strongly than do young women. The reasons for this observation, assuming that it is valid, might come from both societal and intrapsyhcic realms. In most societies, men are still the ones required to succeed vocationally and to have more visible professional achievements. Hence they might require more help and guidance. Psychically, the greater degree of separation in men from early objects, especially the primary maternal introject, makes for lesser regressive oneness experiences, argued recently (Chirban 2000) to be beneficial for psychic growth; this might increase their need for submissive narcissistic bonds with older men. The unconscious homosexual gratification afforded by such relationships also brings them to par with women, who owing to their bodily similarity with the primary love object, retain an uncanny, liquid closeness with other women including the subliminal homosexual gratification such deeper links might provide. Women might also seek more guidance from their peers than men, whose inherent and socially reinforced competitive strivings might inhibit them in this regard. The threatened breakthrough of erotic impulses in a male mentor/ female apprentice dyad might also discourage the formation of such relationships. Here issues of culture and gender seem to intersect. It appears that such relationships might be more common in Western cultures, where sexual gratification is readily available elsewhere and thus erotic tensions might not accrue to uncomfortable degrees in a mentor–student relationship.

Regardless of the variable of gender, certain cultures seem to be more conducive than others to one's acquisition of a mentor. In social groups that permit a greater tolerance of infantile and feminine receptive attributes in a pupil and encourage greater authoritative charisma in a teacher, a mentor–apprentice relationship tends to emerge more sharply. Even within the same culture, there might be endeavors (e.g. classical music, psychoanalysis, organized politics) in which one's development is more mentor-dependent than in others (e.g. film direction). Such questions merit further attention if the complex psychosocial role of the mentor is to be adequately understood. The present contribution should therefore be regarded as only a first step in that direction.

CONCLUDING REMARKS

A couple of years ago, I had to travel to a Latin American country for a professional meeting. I decided to ask my then 18-year-old daughter if she would like to come along and see a new country. She agreed but, sensibly, put a condition that she would come if a friend could come along; that way, she would have company since I would be busy most of the day anyway. However, the friend, a budding artist, had no monetary resources available to undertake this trip. Since I liked this friend, I offered to cover his expenses. He was immensely thankful and asked me how he could ever pay me back for such a big favor. I first said that he did not have to pay me at all, but when he insisted, I told him that there was a quick and easy way and a slow but more meaningful way of repaying this debt. Which one did he want to know? He said both. The first way, I said, is that you make me a painting and I will regard it to be worth the amount of money I am spending on you. That way we will be even. And, the other way, he asked? Well, I said, "How old are you?" "Nineteen," the boy replied. I responded, "Look, I am 51, so let me suggest that when you become 51, find a 19-year-old boy and take him where he cannot go. Tell me, which way of paying me back do you wish to use?"

10

FORGIVENESS

Psychoanalysis has had little to say about forgiveness. The topic is neither listed in the index of the standard edition of Freud's works nor in the *Title Key Word and Author Index to Psychoanalytic Journals—1920–1990* (Mosher 1991).[76] This omission is puzzling since issues closely linked to forgiveness (e.g. trauma, mourning, guilt, need for punishment) have been of utmost concern to psychoanalysis. Reasons for this neglect are unclear, though many possibilities exist. First, the tradition among psychoanalysts to treat Freud's work as a touchstone before positing their own views creates the risk of topics not addressed by the master being ignored. *Forgiveness* is one such phenomenon. The word itself appears a mere five times in the entire corpus of his work (Guttman et al. 1980)[77] and then too in a colloquial rather than a scientific manner. Second, forgiveness is a hybrid psychological concept with unmistakable interpersonal and social referents. Thus it borders on areas where psychoanalytic theory traditionally has been at its weakest and prone to heuristic

---

76. A computerized update extending up to 1998 fares no better in this regard.

77. In contrast, *punishment* finds 253 mentions. This speaks volumes not only to Freud's own *punishing* (Gay 1988, p. 140) conscience but to a certain puritanical bent of the classical psychoanalytic theory itself.

omissions.[78] Third, originating in clinical concerns, psychoanalysis
has devoted greater attention to morbid psychic phenomena (e.g.
anxiety, hate) at the cost of positive and life-enhancing emotions
(e.g. courage, altruism). This bias, admittedly rectified to a certain
extent by the recent writings on wisdom (Kohut 1971), tact (Poland
1975), hope (Casement 1991), and love (Kernberg 1995a), is also
reflected in the literature's inattention to forgiveness. Finally, the
benevolence implicit in forgiveness gives religious overtones (a lá
"to err is human, to forgive divine") to the concept. This link,
strengthened in the mind if one regards "sin" as the fraternal twin
of forgiveness, might also have given psychoanalysts considering the
topic a pause.

Nonetheless, the phenomenon of forgiveness remains dynamically, technically, and socially important enough to warrant serious
attention from the discipline. This chapter is aimed to fill this
lacuna. I will begin by highlighting the psychodynamics of giving
and seeking forgiveness. I will then attempt to elucidate the
evolutionary and developmental correlates of these phenomena.
Following this, I will discuss the various psychopathological syndromes involving forgiveness. Finally, I will address the technical
significance of these conceptualizations and conclude with some
remarks about areas needing further investigation.

DEFINITION AND DYNAMICS

Webster (1998) defines *forgiveness* as the "act of forgiving" (p. 458)
and the root word, *forgive*, in the following way: "1a: to give up
resentment of or claim to requital for (i.e. an insult) b. to grant
relief from payment of (i.e. a debt), 2: to cease to feel resentment
against (an offender)" (p. 458). The definition indicates that active
intent ("to give up . . ." "to grant . . ." etc.) is involved in forgiving. It also suggests that forgiveness comprises two mental operations, namely the resolution of an unpleasant angry emotion within
oneself *and* a changed attitude toward an offending party that is

---

78. The term *identity* has had a checkered history in psychoanalytic theorizing
for the same reason (Akhtar 1999a).

then allowed freedom from one's claims over it. While this is not made explicit, the change in affect seems to precede the change in object relationship. Another matter of note is that little mention is made of the association between forgiving and forgetting. The widespread colloquial counsel for one to "forgive and forget" not withstanding, the fact is that forgetting of a traumatic event, especially too early in the course of mourning and forgiveness, betrays defensive distortion of internal and external reality. To be sure, once forgiveness is granted, the injurious event no longer preoccupies the conscious mind. However, with a diminished affective charge, the memory of it remains available at a preconscious level; this serves as a potential signal and informs the ego when a similarly traumatic situation is about to arise again.[79] Yet another issue is the distinction between the dynamics of bestowing forgiveness and the dynamics of seeking forgiveness. The first is related to mourning a trauma and the second to the emergence of remorse over one's own hostility.

Bestowing Forgiveness

In dealing with forgiving, one is immediately faced with the psychology of someone who has something (in actual or psychic reality, or both) to forgive, that is, some trauma, disenfranchisement, or injustice. One is also faced with a perpetrator who is to be forgiven. Thus in order to understand forgiving, one has to take into account the "victim," the "perpetrator," and the trauma that has been inflicted upon the former. This applies equally to whether the scenario of forgiving unfolds in a clinical or a sociopolitical situation (Akhtar 1999b, Volkan 1997).

---

79. An alternate view is voiced by Hunter (1978), who states that "forgetting is an almost invariable accompaniment of forgiving, and forgiving leads to it, the process not being complete unless forgetting results. This is literally forgetting and not repressing, and is analogous to the letting go and forgetting that takes place through mourning." (p. 167). Interestingly, it is a Dutch novelist, Cees Nooteboom, who brings the two views (i.e. what is forgiven should be forgotten and what is forgiven should be remembered) together in a deliciously paradoxical manner. Nooteboom (1980) says that the injury that has been forgiven should be forgotten but the fact that is has been forgotten should be remembered!

The Rabin–Arafat handshake at the 1995 peace accord between Israelis and Palestinians at the White House is emblematic of mutual forgiveness between fierce opponents, both of whom held themselves to be the victim and the other the perpetrator. Their reconciliation involved diminution of resentment toward each other, letting go of grudges, making compromises, renouncing omnipotent claims, and settling for less than ideal handouts from life. In Kleinian terms, this is a move from the paranoid to the depressive position (Klein 1948). In paranoid position, "goodness" is claimed for oneself and "badness" is totally externalized. The world is viewed in black-and-white terms. The self is regarded as a victim and the other as an oppressor. Mistrust, fear, rage, greed, and ruthlessness predominate. In a depressive position, it is acknowledged that the self is not "all good" and the other not "all bad." Capacity for empathy appears on the horizon. There also emerge feelings of gratitude for what one has indeed received, guilt and sadness for having hurt others, and reparative longings to redress the damage done. Reality testing improves and the capacity for reciprocal relationships develops.

In clinical as well as social situations of adult life, three factors seem important in making it possible to advance from traumatized victimhood to forgiveness. These are *revenge, reparation,* and *reconsideration.* Although "politically incorrect," some revenge is actually good for the victim.[80] It puts the victim's hitherto passive ego in an active position. This imparts a sense of mastery and enhances self-esteem. Revenge (in reality or fantasy), allowing the victim to taste the pleasure of sadism, also changes the libido-aggression balance in the self-object relationship. The victim no longer remains innocent and the perpetrator no longer the sole cruel party. Now both seem to have been hurt and to have caused hurt. This shift lays the groundwork for empathy with the enemy and reduces hatred. Forgiveness is the next step.

The second factor that facilitates forgiving is reparation. Acknowledgment by the perpetrator that he has indeed harmed the victim is

---

80. Note Nietzsche's remark that "A small revenge is humaner than no revenge at all" (1905, p. 71), and Heine's (quoted in Freud, 1930, p. 110) witticism that "One must, it is true, forgive one's enemies—but not before they have been hanged."

important for the latter's recovery from the trauma (Herman 1992, Madanes 1990). It undoes the deleterious effects of "gaslighting" (i.e. denying that anything destructive has been done to someone). To harm someone and then to question his or her perception of it is a double jeopardy, tantamount to "soul murder" (Shengold 1989). Note in this connection the pain caused to Jews by those who deny the Holocaust and, in a clinical parallel, the anguish induced in a sexually abused child whose "non-abusive" parent refuses to believe the occurrence of such event. Recognizing the Holocaust and acknowledging the sexual abuse, in contrast, improve reality testing and facilitate mourning. Such a move is given further impetus if the perpetrator shows signs of remorse, apologizes, and offers emotional recompense, material reparation, or both.[81] This testifies to the verity of the victim's grievance and functions as a graft over his or her psychic wound. Receiving apology (and reparation) thus adds to the perceptual clarity of the victim's ego. ("I was right in perceiving what was going on to be wrong.") Alongside such cognitive vindication, being apologized to puts the victim in an active position with choice to forgive or not forgive. The passive underdog of yesterday becomes the active bestower of pardon. This improves self-esteem which, in turn, permits further mourning.[82] Yet another manner in which an apology exerts a healing effect is by shifting the psychic locale of the representations of trauma from the actual to the transitional area of the mind. Without labeling it as such, Tavuchis (1991) hints at such a shift when he says that

> An apology, no matter how sincere or effective, does not and can not undo what has been done. And yet, in a mysterious way

---

81. Material reparation (e.g. giving gifts following a dispute) alone, however, is far less effective in eliciting forgiveness than a sincere apology with no offer for tangible compensation (Sanders 1995).

82. Empirical research has demonstrated that apologies, when they are constructed appropriately, reduce the victim's motivation to blame, punish, or retaliate against the transgressor (Darby and Schlenker 1982, 1989, Ohbuchi et al. 1989); improve the victim's perception of, and empathy with, the transgressor's character (McMillen and Helmreich 1969, O'Malley and Greenberg 1993, Scher and Darley 1997); and increase the victim's willingness to forgive the transgressor (McCullough et al. 1997, Sanders 1995).

and according to its own logic, this is precisely what it manages to do. (p. 5)

The "mystery" here is that after an apology is made, the trauma begins to get recorded in both the real and the unreal registers of the mind; that is, it acquires a transitional quality. In this realm it can be more easily played with, looked at from various perspectives, and, finally let go.

The libido-aggression shift as a result of taking some revenge, and the rectified perceptual and narcissistic economy as a consequence of receiving reparation, together result in the capacity for better reality testing. This makes a reconsideration of the memories of one's traumas possible. Kafka's (1992) view that we repeat not what we have repressed but what we remember in a particular rigid way is pertinent in this context. Its implication for the clinical as well as the social situation is that to let go of grudges we do not need to recall what has been forgotten, but an amplification, elaboration, and revision of what indeed is remembered and re-enacted over and over again. In tandem, these three factors (revenge, reparation, and reconsideration) improve reality testing, facilitate mourning of earlier injustices, enhance ownership of one's own destructiveness (Steiner 1993), permit the capacity for concern for the opponent, and allow "mature forgiveness" (Gartner 1992) to emerge and consolidate.

Seeking Forgiveness

The wish to be forgiven implies that the subject has become cognizant of having done something hurtful (an act of omission or commission) in actual or psychic reality (or both) toward another individual. It also implies that the latter is significant enough for the perpetrator to want to restore the pre-existing relationship with him or her. Seeking forgiveness therefore emanates from not only a capacity for remorse but from a libidinal component in one's feelings for one's victim. Freud (1913) underscored this by saying that "When one forgives a slight that one has received from someone of whom one is fond" the underlying mechanism is "to substract, as it were, the feeling with the lesser intensity [hostile] from that with the greater [affectionate] and to establish the remainder in consciousness" (p. 62). Moses (1999) emphasizes that in seeking forgiveness, the perpetrator must genuinely own the responsibility of the wrong done by him, and express this not only privately but in an explicit and public form; the apology should be highly specific, accompanied by remorse, and a truly felt commitment to avoid doing the harmful act again. Seeking forgiveness thus involves the working-through of narcissistic resistances to recognizing one's being at fault, tolerance of humility (a "one-down" position being inherent in apologizing), and ego resources to offer reparation. This last point is clearly spelled out in various Judeo-Christian and Islamic scriptures; Mishne Torah (*Hilchot Teshuvah: 2*, p. 42), for instance, declares that

> Someone who injures a colleague, curses a colleague, steals from him, or the like, will never be forgiven until he gives his colleague what he owes him and appeases him. (Maimonides, c. 1200)

Like forgiving, seeking forgiveness is not easy and requires much intrapsychic work. Moreover, once forgiveness is received, the next step is to accept it. To assimilate the new knowledge about the self and the other requires letting go of the masochistic pleasure of guilt, renouncing a debased self-view, and acknowledging the kindness of the hitherto vilified victim of one's own destructiveness.

ORIGINS

Evolutionary Foundations

In nature, conflicts arise as self-interested individuals compete over limited supplies of food, space, mating partners, social status, refuge from enemies, and other scarce resources. Such conflicts are sharper within the same species since the needs of individual members are similar. However, when the advantages of joint action outweigh the costs of social life, groups and families evolve. Occurrence of conflict between individual members, in such settings, hampers cooperation and threatens to damage social bonds.

To resolve such conflicts, behavioral strategies for conflict resolution have been evolved by a variety of species ranging from prosimians to great apes. These strategies enable them to repair the damage caused by conflict, restore peaceful contact, and preserve social relationships (deWaal and Aureli 1996, Silk 1998). Chimpanzees kiss their opponents after conflicts (deWaal and van Roosmalen 1979), baboons grunt quietly to their victims minutes after the attack (Cherney et al. 1995) and golden monkeys embrace or groom their former adversaries (Ren et al. 1991). Such "signals of benign intent" (Silk 1998, p. 346) serve a socially homeostatic function. While there is risk here of confusing behavioral events with their postulated function, observational studies, both in experimental settings and in natural habitat, suggest that the "peaceful post-conflict signals" (Silk 1998, p. 347) do have a calming effect upon former opponents by reducing uncertainty about whether aggression will continue or whether it is over. Cords (1992) has conducted elegant experimental studies that demonstrate that post-conflict affiliative behaviors from the perpetrator monkeys' side influence the victimized monkeys to feed together with the former. Among baboons, vocalizations serve a similar conciliatory function (Silk et al. 1996). The facilitating effects of such behaviors upon resumption of cooperation after a dispute are more marked (Silk 1998) than those upon long-term social relationships, though there is some support (deWaal et al. 1989) for the latter too. What remains clear is that perpetrators' attempts to make amends are responded to by their victims by resumption of contact and "forgiveness" in non-human primates.

Individual Psychic Development

In light of the ebb and flow of aggression within the mother–infant dyad, it is imperative that forgiveness exist on the part of both if the loving and nurturing aspect of their relationship has to be safeguarded. The mother has to forgive her baby's aggressive assaults upon her and the child has to forgive the mother for her empathic shortcomings and actual limitations. This might seem self-evident, yet the fact is that few psychoanalytic investigators invoke the concept of forgiveness in discussing the metabolism of aggression within the mother–infant dyad.

Klein (1937) is an outstanding exception in this regard. She noted that the infant develops pleasant fantasies involving the mother in consequence to satisfaction and hostile fantasies in response to frustration. The latter are tantamount to death wishes. Moreover, in his omnipotence, the baby feels that what he does in fantasy has really taken place; that is to say, he feels that he has actually destroyed the object. Initially such destructive fantasies alternate with pleasant fantasies, each being aroused in affectively charged circumstances of corresponding unpleasureable and pleasureable states. Gradually, however, the child can hold both views of his mother together in his mind. Conflict between love and hate now develops. Guilt enters as a new element into the feeling of love. Klein noted that

> Even in the small child, one can observe a concern for the loved one which is not, as one might think, merely a sign of dependence upon a friendly and helpful person. Side by side with the destructive impulses in the unconscious mind both of the child and of the adult, there exists a profound urge to make sacrifices, in order to help and to put right loved people who in phantasy have been harmed or destroyed. (1937, p. 311)

Klein stated that generosity toward others arises from identification with kindness of one's parents but also from a desire to undo the injuries one has done to them in fantasy when they were being frustrating. She termed this dually determined attitude as *making reparation*[83] (Klein 1937, p. 313). Implicit in her views is the idea that the one who has attacked in a hostile fashion (i.e. the child) now comes to recognize his hostility, recover his love for his objects, and experience a wish to repair the damage done to him. He forgives him (for their having frustrated him) while simultaneously seeking his forgiveness (for his aggression toward him). Klein traced the source of the child's aggression to both preoedipal, especially oral, and oedipal frustrations. She also elucidated the mother's "drive to reparation" (p. 318), tracing it to her identifications with generative parents as well as her own feelings of guilt over aggression toward

---

83. Klein (1937) demonstrated the dynamics of "reparation" in not only the mother–child relationship, but in the father's relationship to his children, childhood and adolescent peer relationships, adult friendships, and choice of a mate as well.

them and her child. She emphasized that the desire to make reparation diminishes the despair arising out of guilt and enhances hope and love in life. In this context, the value of forgiveness becomes paramount:

> If we have become able, deep in our unconscious minds, to clear our feelings to some extent towards our parents of grievances, and have forgiven them for the frustrations we had to bear, then we can be at peace with ourselves and are able to love others in the true sense of the word. (Klein 1937, p. 343)

Besides Klein, Winnicott and Mahler have contributed, albeit indirectly, to understanding the ontogenetic origins of forgiveness. Winnicott's (1971) notion of the "survival of object" speaks to this matter. The *ordinarily devoted mother* (Winnicott 1960) allows herself to be used (and, in the infant's mind, even used up) by her essentially ruthless and cannibalistic infant. His "destructiveness" comes from both the nature of his robust hunger and from his rage at her inevitable failures. She nonetheless survives such rage and destruction, remaining available to be discovered again and again. Going through such use-destruction and refinding cycles of the object, the child begins to sense the forgiving attitude of the mother and thus learns to accept forgiveness. Also, in identification with her, he begins to develop the ego capacity for containing and metabolizing aggression, a necessary preliminary step in forgiving her and, by extension, others. Winnicott's (1963) views on the development of the capacity for concern further elaborate these issues. According to him, there are actually two sets of experiences that contribute to the development of concern, healthy amounts of guilt, and a desire for reparation. One is the "survival" of the object-mother in the face of the child's oral sadism. The second is the continued interest in the child's spontaneity on the part of the environment-mother.

Just as Winnicott's ideas illuminate *forgiveness-related phenomena* without actually using the term itself, Mahler's (1975) description of the maternal resilience during the child's rapprochement subphase touches upon this issue. The child's maddeningly contradictory demands for closeness and distance, protection and freedom, and intimacy and autonomy are met by the mother with a nonretaliatory stance. Her containment of the aggression mobilized within her allows the child to gradually see her as neither engulfing nor abandoning and himself as neither a passive lap baby nor an omnipotent conqueror of the world. A deeper, more realistic view of mother is now internalized. With this, external dependency upon her diminishes. The contradictory self-images are also mended; growing object constancy is accompanied by self-constancy. It is this capacity for object constancy that allows for accommodating (and forgiving) the aggression stirred up by frustrations at the hands of the object.

In essence, Klein, Winnicott, and Mahler all seem to suggest that the metabolism of aggression in the crucible of the mother–infant dyad lies at the root of forgiveness versus vengeance. If the aggression is well metabolized and love predominates in their relationship, forgiveness would be experienced and identified with. If not, seeds of revenge-seeking tendencies are sowed.

However, such emphasis upon the "oral" foundations of the capacity for forgiveness should not be taken to mean that developments during later developmental phases do not contribute to the ontogenesis of forgiveness. Indeed, they do. In the anal phase, the child is faced with the monumental discovery that something belonging to oneself, namely feces, is "not good" and has to be renounced. Passage through this developmental turmoil consolidates the capacity to "let go" in general. Later, in the oedipal phase, the child has to sooner or later forgive the parents for their sexual betrayal of him or her[84] and they, in turn, have to forgive him or her for the desires to intrude. The compensations received by each party (protection, love, guidance by the child; narcissistic and generative pleasure of helping an offspring by the parents) are crucial in letting go of the pain caused to the child and parent by exclusion and rivalry respectively.

---

84. At first, of course, the child "does not forgive his mother for having granted the favor of sexual intercourse not to himself but to his father" (Freud 1910, p. 171). Such "forgiveness" arises only with passage of time and with the aforementioned compensations to the child.

Relationship between the Evolutionary
and the Individual Origins

There exist striking parallels between the "peaceful post-conflict signals" (Silk 1998) of non-human primates (e.g. grunting, grooming) and the conciliatory behaviors of children after they have had a fight with their peers. These behaviors, including verbal apologies, gift-giving, and affectionate physical contacts (e.g. hugs, gentle touches), enhance the probability that former opponents will re-establish contact following aggression and might also contribute to preserving the long-term relationship between the opponents.

While the similarity between the conciliatory gestures of non-human primates and those of children is indeed significant, the heuristic path from this observation onward is fraught with difficulties. The risk of circular reasoning, reductionism, and tautological leaps is great. Unanswered questions abound. Is it reasonable, for instance, to equate the two behaviors owing to their superficial similarities? Could what the monkeys and apes show be labeled *proto-forgiveness*, an archaic prototype of human forgiveness? Since the complexity of peaceful post-conflict signals increases as the monkeys approach anthropoid proximity, say in the form of great apes, is it possible that human forgiveness is merely the next step in this evolutionary ladder? Or, could the move from paranoid to depressive position, which is supposed to underlie human infantile reparation, also exist in non-human primates? Since in attributing such processes to preverbal human infants we are largely in the realm of speculation, could similar processes be hypothesized to exist in animals? While such matters await exploration, one thing seems certain: the purpose of all forgiveness, *mentalized* (Fonagy and Target 1997) or not, is to assure cooperation. This was something the primitive man, with his relative weakness vis-à-vis the larger forces of nature, badly needed. In order to establish groups and, later, families, he needed to overlook ("forgive") minor conflicts with other members of his species. And, in an ontogenetic repetition of phylogeny, the human infant, dependent as he is upon others' care of him, needs to be forgiving; holding grudges against mother would not get a child very far!

All in all, therefore, it seems that the attitude of forgiveness has survival value and might have acquired a "hardwired" status from this evolutionary imperative. The ritualization, complexity, and psychic elaboration of forgiveness, however, is greater in human beings than in non-human primates, though both show evidence of such capacity. The evocation of this capacity seems to have its own prerequisites (e.g. maternal love in case of human beings). Without them, the intrinsic capacity might atrophy or develop along pathological lines.

PSYCHOPATHOLOGICAL SYNDROMES INVOLVING FORGIVENESS

Psychopathological syndromes involving forgiveness include (1) inability to forgive, (2) premature forgiveness, (3) excessive forgiveness, (4) pseudo-forgiveness, (5) relentless forgiveness-seeking, (6) inability to accept forgiveness, (7) inability to seek forgiveness, and (8) imbalance between capacities for self-forgiveness and forgiveness toward others.

Inability to Forgive

Some people just cannot forgive. They continue to harbor resentment toward their offenders for months, years, and often for their entire lifetime. They hold onto a grudge (Socarides 1966) and are given to chronic hatred (Akhtar 1999a, Blum 1997, Kernberg 1992), though they might not be overtly vindictive. Diagnostically, this group includes individuals with severe personality disorders, especially paranoid personality, severe antisocial personality, and those with the syndrome of malignant narcissism (Kernberg 1989). When given to overt revenge-seeking, such individuals disregard all limits in their destructive pursuit of their offender. Melville's (1851) Captain Ahab is an example-par-excellence of such unrelenting "narcissistic rage" (Kohut 1972), including its self-destructive consequences. Toward the end of his vengeful saga, Ahab puts his hatred into words:

> Towards thee I roll, thou all destroying but unconquering whale; to the last I grapple with the; from hell's heart I stab at thee; for hate's sake, I spit my last breath at thee. Sink all coffins and all hearses to

one common pool! and since neither can be mine, let me then tow
to pieces while still chasing thee, though tied to thee, thou damned
whale! (Melville 1851, p. 575)

Premature Forgiveness

A second syndrome is characterized by individuals who seem too
readily prepared to forgive and forget injuries afflicted upon them.
Obsessional neurotics, with their characteristic reaction formation
against aggression, tend to fall in this category. They quickly
"forgive" others since not doing so would force them to acknowledge that they feel hurt and angry. Such conflict-based premature
forgiveness is a compromise formation (between aggressive impulses and superego prohibitions against them) and can be clinically analyzed as such. A more severe form of premature forgiveness
is defect-based. Individuals with such a malady feel no entitlement,
lack a "healthy capacity for indignation" (Ambassador Nathaniel
Howell, personal communication, April 1996), and cannot hate
(Galdston 1987). They do not adequately register that they have
been wronged. Their object-hunger is intense and their dependence upon others great. Hence, they are all too willing to let go of
hurts and injustices. Diagnostically, this group includes weak, unen-
titled, schizoid, and "as-if" (Deutsch 1942) personalities with a
childhood background of multiple and unreliable caretakers.

Excessive Forgiveness

Excessive forgiveness is seen in masochistic individuals. They repeatedly forgive traumas inflicted upon them by their tormentors and
never seem to learn from experience. They live in a state of near
addiction to those who are sadistic or can easily be manipulated in
becoming sadistic (Berliner 1958, Kernberg 1992), repeatedly sub-
mitting to them for further humiliation and torture. States of
"co-dependency" in the partners of addicts also depict the masochistic dimension of excessive forgiveness. The addict continues to be
self-destructive while hoping that the drug will somehow magically
solve intrapsychic problems, and the codependent individual re-

mains relentlessly optimistic that a terrible relationship will, through
their ever-forgiving attitude, become all right. The following poem
of mine (titled "The Second Poem") portrays this very dimension of
masochistic pathology.

> Undoing
> > the psychic truth,
> (Or, speaking from a second room
> > within the self?)
> Something destructively large-hearted
> > took him by his hand,
> > > led him to the balcony of forgiveness
> Again and again.
>
> > > > > (Akhtar 1998b, p. 51)

Pseudo-Forgiveness

Yet another psychopathological group is constituted by individuals
who practice *pseudo-forgiveness*[85] On the surface, they forgive but
inwardly they maintain ill will and do not mourn (Sohn 1999). Some
of them are genuinely split into parts. One part of their mind accepts
reality and is able to let go of previous hurts and injuries while the
other, a mad part, holds on to omnipotent dreams of reversing history
altogether (Bion 1957). In a further split within itself, this mad part,
on the one hand, maintains that the glorious "pre-trauma" days can
actually be brought back,[86] and, on the other hand, ruthlessly
carries on vengeful attacks on the (alleged) offender.

Alongside such individuals are those with pronounced antisocial
trends and where pseudo-forgiveness emanates from calculated lying
and hiding of true psychic reality for strategic advantages. Joseph
Stalin's wry remark that "revenge is a dish that is best eaten cold" and
Joseph Kennedy Sr.'s advice to his son John that he should "not get
mad but get even" are examples of such perversions of forgiveness.

---

85. A parallel phenomenon is that of *caricatured modesty* (Jones 1913, p. 244)
seen in conjunction with a narcissistic personality.

86. See also the related descriptions of "someday . . ." and "if only" fantasies
(Akhtar 1996) in this regard.

Relentless Forgiveness-Seeking

Some individuals are relentlessly apologetic about ordinary errors of daily life. They betray a heavy burden of unconscious guilt. Apologizing for their actions does not relieve them of the prohibited and morally repugnant hostile and sexual intentions that lurk in their unconscious. However, the act of repeatedly seeking pardon itself can come to have hostile aims and a hidden sexual discharge value. One of Abraham's (1925) patients gave a very instructive example of this from his childhood.

> His behaviour at that time, even when he seemed to be full of guilt-feelings and repentance, was a mixture of hostile and tormenting drives. These feelings were secretly closely linked with masturbation, whilst externally they appeared to be connected with other small misdeeds in the nursery. Any trivial wrong-doing was invariably followed by the same reaction. The boy would cling to his mother and say in endless repetition: "Forgive me, mother, forgive me, mother!" This behaviour did in fact express his contrition, but it also expressed far more strongly two other tendencies. In the first place, he continued in this way to torment his mother, whilst asking her forgiveness. Furthermore, it was apparent then, as also in later years, that instead of trying to reform himself, he always preferred to repeat his faults and to obtain forgiveness for them. This was also a disturbing factor during his psycho-analytical treatment. We found, moreover, that the rapid rattling-off of the formula of atonement had been devised in imitation of the rhythm of his masturbation. Thus the forbidden sexual wish contrived to break through in this concealed form. (pp. 323–324)

Inability to Accept Forgiveness

Closely akin to those who repeatedly apologize are individuals who remain tormented, often for months and years, despite having been forgiven by others. They seem unable to accept pardon and continue to suffer from remorse and its depressive and persecutory consequences. A striking example of this is to be found in Chekov's (1927) story, *The Death of a Government Clerk*. Vicissitudes of anally regressive hostility, and the defense of reaction-formation against it, are illustrated there via the tale of a Russian postal clerk who spends his life savings to obtain a highly expensive seat in the Bolshevik opera only to sneeze and squirt his nasal secretions on the bald head of the man sitting in front of him. The protagonist apologizes and is forgiven. However, he can not settle and remains remorseful. He apologizes again and again. Each time, he is forgiven, although with ever-increasing annoyance by the bald man. The clerk writes to him and visits him in the latter's workplace to seek forgiveness just one more time. Finally, the bald man gets enraged and throws him out of his office. That evening the clerk comes home, sits on his living room sofa, and dies!

Unconscious guilt clearly plays a big role in the dynamics of these individuals. In talking about those involved in such endless self-condemnation, Cooper (1995, quoted in Akhtar 1999, p. 222) pointedly speaks of their "ferocious superegos and masochistic inclinations."

Inability to Seek Forgiveness

Individuals who lack empathy with others often do not seek forgiveness. They seem oblivious to the harm and injuries they have caused to others. Such oblivion is often the result of severe superego defects and the associated incapacity for remorse. At other times, it originates from a tenacious denial of blemishes in oneself. Such denial is aimed at managing paranoid anxieties (e.g. the fear of being severely shamed by others upon apologizing to them) and keeping a shaky self-esteem intact. Antisocial and narcissistic personalities are thus especially prone to such behavior (Akhtar 1992b, Kernberg 1984).

Imbalances in Forgiving Others Versus Forgiving Oneself

Psychopathology is also evident when there is a gross discrepancy in one's capacity to bestow forgiveness upon others and oneself. Narcissistic, paranoid, and antisocial individuals readily absolve themselves of responsibility of having caused any harm. They either deny it totally or see their hostile actions as justifiable responses to others' unfairness toward them. They readily forgive themselves but do not forgive others with the same ease. Masochistic individuals are prone to do just the opposite. Repeatedly, they turn a blind eye to their (real or imagined) tormentors, remaining devoted to them. They forgive others but continue to punish themselves relentlessly.

THE ROLE OF APOLOGY AND FORGIVENESS IN THE CLINICAL SITUATION

Concerns around forgiveness surface in the course of psychoanalytic treatment in many ways. With severely traumatized individuals, *forgiving* (or not forgiving) those who have hurt them (and the transferential reactivations of such objects) sooner or later occupies the center stage of clinical dialogue. With individuals who suffer from remorse over real or imagined injuries caused to others, *being forgiven* by actual external figures (and, in transference, the analyst) becomes a concern.[87]

Individuals who have suffered from severe trauma in childhood (e.g. sexual abuse, physical violence and cruelty, massive and sustained neglect) bring with them an internal world rife with split self- and object-representations with a predominance of hate over love and of malice over concern for their objects. Internally they cling to a retrospectively idealized "all-good" mother representation of early infancy (Mahler et al. 1975) while simultaneously holding a contradictory and aggressively charged image of her (and other early objects). The former substrate gives rise to idealizing transferences of varying forms and tenacities. The latter results in guiltless, destructive attacks against the analyst. The patient claims (often, correctly) to have been hurt, abused, and deprived of what was an inalienable right in childhood, that is, having love, an intact family, benevolent guidance, and so on. Taking a victim stance, the patient feels justified in attacking the offending parties and the analyst who

---

87. Such phenomenological division, reminiscent of Kohut's (1977) "Tragic Man-Guilty Man" dichotomy, is admittedly simplistic. In the flow and flux of analytic clinical material, we are always in the world of "both/and." Thus trauma-based revenge fantasies gradually leading to forgiving the "enemy," almost always co-exist with guilt over one's own ruthlessness and the consequent need to be forgiven. Yet, separating the two configurations does afford a didactic ease in elucidating the dynamics of respective events in the transference-countertransference axis.

inevitably comes to represent them. He or she displays an unconscious striving for totally undoing the effects of the childhood trauma or even erasing its occurrence in the first place. Suffering from pathological hope and harboring a malignant "someday" fantasy (Akhtar 1991, 1996), the patient strives to obtain absolute satisfaction from the analyst without any concern for the latter. He demands that the analyst provide exquisite empathy, love, sex, treatment with reduced fees, access to his or her home, sessions on demand, and encounters at all kinds of hours. As the patient finds the analyst to be lacking in this regard, he berates him or her as useless, unloving, and even cruel. The patient attacks not only the analyst's concern and devotion, but also those parts of his own personality that seem aligned with the analyst and can see the inconsolable nature of his own hunger. It is as if the patient has an *intrapsychic terrorist organization* (Akhtar 1999d) that seeks to assassinate his observing ego because it is collaborating with the analyst and is willing to renounce the lost, dimly remembered, and retrospectively idealized "all-good" days of early infancy in favor of realistic satisfactions in the current life. This internal destructive agency also renders the patient enormously stoic. Recourse to infantile omnipotence makes any amount of waiting bearable (Potamianou 1992). For such individuals, the present has only secondary importance. They can tolerate any current suffering in the hope that future rewards will make it all worthwhile.

What, under such circumstances, can move the patient toward forgiveness? As discussed earlier, the factors of revenge, reparation, and reconsideration working in tandem can facilitate mourning of trauma, permit acknowledgment of one's own destructiveness, release the capacity for concern for the opponent, and allow forgiveness to emerge. Revenge is taken by the patient in the form of relentless sadistic assaults on the analyst. Continued hostility toward those viewed as offenders (e.g. patient's parents in actual adult life), even if the latter are trying to make amends, is another form of grudge-holding and revenge. Reparation is available to the patient in the form of the analyst's lasting empathy and devotion that "survives" (Winnicott 1971) despite the patient's attacks upon it. Reconsideration results from recontextualization and revision of childhood memories (Kafka 1992); negative images of early caretakers now come to be supplanted with the recall of hitherto repressed positive interactions with them.

However, for such advance to occur, resistances to acknowledging love for the analyst's tolerance as well as to recognizing one's own contributions to the current (and even, at times, childhood) suffering must be interpreted. Defenses against the awareness of sadomasochistic pleasure in ongoing hatred (Kernberg 1995a), as well as the defensive functions of the unforgiving attitude itself (Jones 1928, Fairbairn 1940, Searles 1956) need to be interpreted. The fact that giving up hatred and forgiving others also opens up newer, less familiar (e.g. oedipal) psychic realms for exploration also makes the patient anxious and regressively cling to a simplistic victimhood[88] which, in turn, fuels continuing warfare with the analyst along the lines mentioned previously. While work along the lines mentioned previously usually occurs in a gradual, piecemeal fashion, occasionally a firm confrontation with an alternate way of being becomes necessary.

Case 1

Ms. E., an unmarried Catholic librarian in her mid-thirties, had felt immensely rejected by her mother as a child. Her sense was that she was all but forgotten following the birth of a brother when she was nearly three years old. Over the course of a long analysis, the patient incessantly talked of her despair at this rejection. She wanted (a desire she was able to reveal only after painstaking defense analysis) me to mother her, thus making up for all she needed and did not receive during her childhood. She wanted on-demand sessions, love, physical holding, special status, adoption, travel together, everything. Her despair at not receiving all this was thick and she slowly turned me into a highly desired but ungiving and rejecting figure. She began to hate me.

Condensed with such split maternal transference was a powerful sexual component emanating from her childhood relationship to a

---

88. Forgiving early offenders (and the analyst who embodies them in the transference) also mobilizes fears that the treatment might come to an end. See Grunert (1979) and Akhtar (1992a) for negative therapeutic reactions emanating from this dynamic.

deeply admired father who fluctuated between flirtatiously rescuing her and abruptly dropping her from attention. Not surprisingly, this led to an addictive bond with the father where idealization was tenaciously maintained and all aggression was shifted to the mother. In this mental set, the patient wanted to have sex with me, be my beloved, marry me. Lacking any countertransference resonance and replete with a desperate, coercive quality, the situation was actually one of a *malignant erotic transference* (Akhtar 1994).

Analytic work with her would fall apart again and again. Desperate longings for the pre-traumatic, "all-good" mother and the idealized father (and their substitute the "all-giving" analyst) would vehemently surface. At the same time, vicious attacks upon the rejecting mother/oblivious father (and their re-creation in the form of the "bad" analyst) would begin. In such hours, the patient often compared herself to Captain Ahab and me to Moby Dick, his nemesis. She felt her attacks were totally justified. After all, wasn't I depriving her of what she felt she needed. "What would you do if someone was threatening to cut off your oxygen supply?", she would retort. Attempts to help her see that marrying me was hardly akin to needing oxygen would be felt as further humiliation from me and fuel her hostility. Psychological-mindedness would be lost and previously gained insights would be put aside. Reconstruction of events that might have triggered the regression would be sometimes helpful in dislodging the impasse, sometimes not.

In one such session during the tenth year of her analysis, with the patient going on berating me, I firmly said to her, "Look, since you are so fond of metaphorically likening us to Captain Ahab and Moby Dick, permit me also to introduce a metaphor. Tell me, what do you think made it possible for Yitzahk Rabin and Yasser Arafat to shake hands with each other?" The patient responded in a fashion that was typical for her in states of regression. "What does that have to do with anything? Besides, I am not interested in politics anyway." I then said, "No, I think what I said is of serious significance to us. Your metaphor has to do with revenge and mutual destruction. Mine has to do with letting go of grudges, however justified, and forgiveness."

Of course, this intervention in of itself did not give rise to an immediate shift from hatred to forgiveness. It did, however, lay the groundwork for such an advance and became a landmark in her analysis to which we would return again and again in subsequent months and years. Before deeper mourning of childhood trauma (and the built-in analytic deprivations that had become condensed with them) became possible, there was a protracted transitional phase. In that phase, she developed a collaborative, mournful mutuality with me, "forgiving" me for not marrying her on the one hand and retaining a hostile and unforgiving, even if less vitriolic, stance toward me on the other hand. The latter, often worked as an *intrapsychic terrorist organization* (Akhtar 1999d), which sought to destroy not only the external peacemakers (i.e. me) but also her own internal functions aligned with the former. It was only after a protracted transitional period of this sort that the patient became able to see her own destructiveness (and recall her childhood hostile manipulativeness toward her mother). Remorse and forgiveness followed.

Throughout such work, the analyst has to remain respectful of the patient's need for apology from those who have hurt him.[89] He must demonstrate to the patient the awareness that being apologized to for a wrong does improve reality testing and that such perceptual clarity is useful for the patient, since often the original abuse was denied by the perpetrator or other family members. It also puts the recipient of apology in an active position, undoing the humiliation of passivity and lack of control.

At the same time, the analyst has to remember that not all trauma might be forgivable. The hurt, pain, and rage felt, for instance, by a Holocaust survivor in encountering a Nazi camp guard is hardly subject to ordinary psychic metabolism. There might be other individual circumstances of torture, abuse, and humiliation that are less public but nonetheless equally unforgivable. Upon encountering such scenarios in the clinical situation, the analyst must not uphold a manic ideal of kindness. Indeed, he might even help the patient feel not too guilty about his lack of forgiveness.

---

89. The sexual abuse literature pays special attention to this issue, with some family therapists (e.g. Madanes 1990) requiring the perpetrator to actually, even ritualistically, apologize to the victim in front of other family members.

Premature forgiveness should also draw the analyst's attention. Here the analytic task[90] is to bring the patient's attention to it so that the roots of his too readily forgiving others (including the analyst) may be explored. If the tendency is based upon splitting and denial, then the sequestered aggression needs to be brought into the treatment; this is what Kernberg (1992) means by attempting to change a *schizoid* or *psychopathic transference* into a *paranoid transference*. If, however, the tendency is owing to a genuine lack of entitlement, then the roots of that should be explored. Similarly, pseudo-forgiveness, based upon maintaining two mental registers and secretly holding on to grudges, needs to be exposed by confrontation and defense analysis. The same holds true if the analyst notices gross discrepancies in the patient's capacity to forgive himself versus others or vice versa. Underlying narcissistic-masochistic proclivities are what seem to deserve attention in such instances. Issues of unconscious guilt over real or imagined childhood "crimes" (including separating from a needy parent, surviving a deceased parent or sibling, and the more usual oedipal transgressions) need to be kept in mind while listening to those who are chronically apologetic and cannot forgive themselves despite others' having forgiven them.

Besides such patient-related scenarios, the analyst has to deal with forgiveness from his own side in two ways. One involves the controversial matter of apologizing to the patient and seeking forgiveness. The other, perhaps even more contested and heuristically elusive, is the analyst's providing the patient an opportunity to apologize and seek forgiveness from him. An example of the former stance is evident in Case 3 in Chapter Eight.

In discussing the place of apology in psychoanalysis, Goldberg (1987) delineates two possible stances. One stance, exemplified in the clinical material previously mentioned, emanates from the

---

90. Some might question such agenda-based approach to clinical work. After all, the aim in psychoanalytic listening involves "not directing one's notice to anything in particular" (Freud 1912b, p. 111) and dealing with all material alike. At the same time, there is also a legacy of "strategy" (Levy 1987) in psychoanalysis that dictates measured, deliberate tracks of interventions in certain circumstances. It is my impression that most clinicians strike an intuitive balance between a free-floating and strategic approach to clinical listening and interventions.

234   NEW CLINICAL REALMS

analytic perspective which suggests that via empathic immersion,
the analyst may attain an ability to see the patient's world as he or
she does *and* the major burden of achieving and sustaining such
intersubjective agreement rests upon the analyst. In this view the
failure of intersubjectivity would largely be the analyst's responsibility and thus necessitate an apology from the analyst. The second
stance, mentioned by Goldberg, holds the analyst to be more
informed about "reality" and thus viewing transference, however
plausible its content might be, as a distortion of that reality. In this
perspective, the differences in perception between the patient and
the analyst never call for an apology from the analyst. Deftly and
convincingly, Goldberg argues the untenability of either extreme
position, concluding that while the wish to apologize may be
countertransference based, it does have a place at certain times in
certain treatments. Of course, the patient's experience of the
analyst's apology needs to be then explored and handled in a
relatively traditional way.

Next, as mentioned, is the question of the analyst's providing the
patient an opportunity to apologize for his erstwhile destructive
attacks upon the analyst.[91] Kernberg (1976) approaches this point
when he describes the appearance of intense remorse in the later
phases of analysis of narcissistic patients. They become aware of how
badly they have treated others in their life, including the analyst,
and wish to seek their forgiveness. However, it was Winnicott (1947)
who most directly addressed this matter. He declared that a patient
who has been hostile for a long time during treatment must, when
he or she becomes better integrated, be told how he has burdened
the analyst throughout their work.[92] Winnicott says that this is

> obviously a matter fraught with danger, and it needs the most careful
> timing. But I believe an analysis is incomplete if even towards the end

---

91. In work with children, such attacks might involve the analyst's office and
even his body.

92. Blum (1997) has recently raised questions about Winnicott's recommenda-
tion. His critique, especially of the handling of the particular case on which
Winnicott's views are based, is well reasoned. Nonetheless, I believe that while the
particular clinical example used by Winnicott might not have been the best for the
purpose, the idea he was proposing does have merit.

it has not been possible for the analyst to tell the patient what he, the analyst, did unbeknown for the patient whilst he was ill, in the early stages. Until this interpretation is made the patient is kept to some extent in the position of infant—one who cannot understand what he owes to his mother. (p. 202)

Ideally, the patient should arrive at such understanding by himself and as a result of diminishing hate and growing empathy for others. However patients who are too narcissistically vulnerable to sincerely "apologize" to the analyst and seek forgiveness might actually benefit by their analyst's providing them an occasion to do so by acknowledging his having felt burdened by them as the treatment was going on. Such intervention should not emanate from hostile countertransference. It should come from a depressive working-through of the reality that the analyst has indeed felt put upon, at times even abused, by the patient during the course of their work.

CONCLUDING REMARKS

Despite covering considerable ground, I remain aware that many important areas pertaining to forgiveness have remained unaddressed in this paper. The first such area pertains to *gender*. Little is known about the qualitative or quantitative similarities and/or differences in the two sexes in this regard. Women's deeper capacity for commitment in love relations and for making context-based decisions in the moral sphere (Gilligan 1982) suggest that they might possess a greater capacity for forgiveness than men. However, further clinical and empirical data is needed to confirm or refute this impression.

The second such area pertains to the *sociopolitical realm*. The importance of a perpetrator apologizing and making reparation to its victim is emphatically clear in the recent German apologies and reparations to the victims of Holocaust, the North American expression of remorse for the tyranny of slavery, the offer by the United States of recompense to the Japanese Americans interred in camps during World War II, and the work of Bishop Desmond Tutu's Truth and Reconciliation commission in South Africa. At a less dramatic level is the prayer written by Archbishop Renbert Weakland of Milwaukee, which builds on Pope John Paul II's request that Catholics observe this year's Ash Wednesday by reflecting upon the pain inflicted on Jews by Christians over the last millennium. To quote one of the eight stanzas of this prayer:

> I ask for forgiveness for all the statements that implied that the Jewish people were no longer loved by God, that God had abandoned them, that they were guilty of deicide, that they were, as a people, being punished by God. Amen. (Weakland, quoted in Gallagher 2000, p. 17)

Interdisciplinary studies, where sociopolitical processes inform psychoanalysis and psychoanalysis informs the latter (see Volkan 1997 in this connection), are thus badly needed to enrich the understanding of phenomena related to mourning, apologizing, and seeking and receiving forgiveness.

The third area pertaining to forgiveness that needs closer examination is that of *cross-cultural variations* in the patterns of remorse and reparation. Many questions arise in this context. Are all cultures equally forgiving? Are there transgressions and faults that are selectively more or less forgivable in a given culture? Do some cultures provide socially recognized forgiveness rituals while others do not? Is forgiving faster in the former cultures? Little data exists to answer such questions. It does, however, seem that cultural factors shape the use and formal characteristics of apologies. Barnland and Yoshioko (1990), for instance, have demonstrated that while Japanese and American subjects agree on the kinds of situations that require apologies, they differ to some extent in the kind of apologies that they regard to be appropriate in such situations.

Finally, the application of psychodynamic insights regarding forgiveness to the *justice system* at large and forensic psychiatry in particular merits further inquiry. Comparing the justice system in the United States to that in Japan and Korea, Harding (1999) finds the former to be characteristically retributive and the latter to have a greater restorative bent. Not unaware of the limitations of the restorative justice, Harding nonetheless feels that it is important that opportunities be provided to the offender to understand the significance of the victim's experience and to make appropriate gestures of remorse and atonement. Chase (2000) reports upon the "victim-offender conferencing" program (developed in the United States during the mid-1970s) in which the court brings offenders and their victims together with a neutral facilitator. During the meeting the offender is offered an opportunity to apologize to his victim. Overall, however, the legal system remains somewhat ambivalent about the offender's expression of remorse. More work is needed in this realm.[93]

While these areas await further exploration, one thing appears certain from the material covered in this essay. Forgiveness is an integral element of mourning and therefore necessary for psychic growth. Forgiving others for their hurtful actions and forgiving oneself for one's causing pain to others, are integral to moving on in life and to opening oneself for new experiences. Inability or unwillingness to forgive keeps one tied to past and impedes development. Nowhere is this fixating element of an unforgiving attitude—here, regarding oneself—better described than in the following parable from the life of Buddha.

A man approached Buddha while he was sitting, eyes closed, under a Banyan tree, meditating. Amid sobs and tears, the man reported that his son was very ill and the local healers had given up on the child. The boy was about the die. The man pleaded for divine intervention from Buddha. He cried, wailed, touched Buddha's feet. Buddha, however, sat motionless and neither opened his eyes nor said anything in response. The man left, only to appear the next day filled with rage. His son had died and he held Buddha's inactivity responsible for it. He shouted obscenities, cursed Buddha, and still finding no visible response, spat at him in disgust and left.

Time passed and a day came, a few years later, when the man returned to visit Buddha again. Now he was very remorseful. He said that, over time, he had gradually realized that by remaining silent, Buddha was conveying to him two important messages, that there is little he could do in a situation if those who knew about physical ailments had given up, and that there are no words to offer solace

---

93. The fact that Fordham University School of Law in New York City recently held a conference on "The Role of Forgiveness in the Law" is encouraging in this regard.

to a man whose son is about to die. The man was guilt-ridden for his having spat on Buddha. Crying and holding Buddha's feet, he begged for forgiveness. It was then that Buddha opened his eyes and spoke. He said: "You spat on a river and the water flowed away. The man I was then is gone with time. I am different. You did not spit on me and hence I have no authority to forgive you. But it makes me sad that while you have learnt many things, you are still standing on the same spot on the riverbank. You are being consumed by a moment that has long departed. It is not I, but you, and only you, who can release yourself from this bondage. Do you think you can do it?"

REFERENCES

Abend, S., Porder, M.S., and Willick, M.S. (1983). *Borderline Patients: Psychoanalytic Perspectives.* New York: International Universities Press.

Abraham, K. (1925). Psychoanalytical notes on Coue's system of self mastery. In *Clinical Papers and Essays on Psycho-Analysis,* pp. 306–327. London: Hogarth Press, 1955.

———. (1927). *Selected Papers* (Chapters 4 and 11). London: Hogarth Press.

———. (1953). *Selected Papers on Psychoanalysis,* pp. 226–234. New York: Basic Books.

Abrams, S. (1978). The teaching and learning of psychoanalytic developmental psychology. *Journal of the American Psychoanalytic Association* 26:387–406.

Adler, G. (1985). *Borderline Psychopathology and Its Treatment.* New York: Jason Aronson.

Akhtar, S. (1983). Preface. In *New Psychiatric Syndromes: DSM III and Beyond,* pp. vii–ix. New York: Jason Aronson.

———. (1984). The syndrome of identity diffusion. *American Journal of Psychiatry* 141:1381–1385.

———. (1989). Narcissistic personality disorder: descriptive feature and differential diagnosis. *Psychiatric Clinics of North America* 12:505–529.

———. (1991). Three fantasies related to unresolved separation-individuation: a less recognized aspect of severe character pathology. In *Beyond the Symbiotic Orbit: Advances in Separation-Individuation Theory — Essays in Honor of Selma Kramer, M.D,* eds. S. Akhtar, and H. Parens, pp. 261–284. Hillsdale, NJ: The Analytic Press.

———. (1991a). Panel report: sadomasochism in perversions. *Journal of the American Psychoanalytic Association* 39:741–755.

———. (1992a). Tethers, orbits, and invisible fences: clinical, developmental, sociocultural, and technical aspects of optimal distance. In *When the Body Speaks: Psychological Meanings in Kinetic Clues*, eds. S. Kramer, and S. Akhtar, pp. 21–57. Northvale, NJ: Jason Aronson.

———. (1992b). *Broken Structures: Severe Personality Disorders and Their Treatment*. Northvale, NJ: Jason Aronson.

———. (1993). *Conditions*. Chicago: Adams Press.

———. (1994). Object constancy and adult psychopathology. *International Journal of Psycho-Analysis* 75:441–455.

———. (1995). *Quest for Answers: Understanding and Treating Severe Personality Disorders*. Northvale, NJ: Jason Aronson.

———. (1996). "Someday . . ." and "if only" fantasies: pathological optimism and inordinate nostalgia as related forms of idealization. *Journal of the American Psychoanalytic Association* 44:723–753.

———. (1998a). From simplicity through contradiction to paradox: the evolving psychic reality of the borderline patient in treatment. *International Journal of Psycho-Analysis* 79:241–252.

———. (1998b). *Turn to Light*. Chicago: Adams Press.

———. (1999b). The distinction between needs and wishes: implications for psychoanalytic theory and technique. *Journal of the American Psychoanalytic Association* 47:113–151.

———. (1999). *Inner Torment: Living Between Conflict and Fragmentation*. Northvale, NJ: Jason Aronson.

———. (1999a). *Immigration and Identity: Turmoil, Treatment, and Transformation*. Northvale, NJ: Jason Aronson.

———. (1999c). The immigrant, the exile, and the experience of nostalgia. *Journal of Applied Psychoanalytic Studies*, 1:123–130.

———. (1999d). The psychodynamic dimension of terrorism. *Psychiatric Annals* 29:350–355.

———. (2000). Mental pain and the cultural ointment of poetry. *International Journal of Psychoanalysis* 81:229–243.

———. (2001a). Things are us: a friendly rejoinder to Marianne Spitzform's paper "The ecological self: metaphor and developmental experience." *Journal of Applied Psychoanalytic Studies* 3:205–210.

———. (2001b). From mental pain through manic defense to mourning: discussion of Settlage's chapter "Defenses evoked by early childhood loss: their impact on life-span development." In *Three Faces of Mourning: Melancholia, Manic Defense, and Moving On*, ed. S. Akhtar, pp. 95–113. Northvale, NJ: Jason Aronson.

———. (2002). Dehumanization: causes, manifestations, and remedies. In *Silence or Violence: Psychoanalytic Contributions to the Understanding of Terrorism and Related Phenomena*, eds. S. Varvin, and V. Volkan. London: International Psychoanalytic Association (in press).

Akhtar, S., and Brenner, I. (1979). Differential diagnosis of fugue-like states. *Journal of Clinical Psychiatry* 40:381–385.

Akhtar, S., and Byrne, J.P. (1983). The concept of splitting and its clinical relevance. *American Journal of Psychiatry* 140:1016–1018.

Akhtar, S., and Powell, A. (1999). Four fathers: the depiction of father-child relationship in some recent movies. *Mind and Human Interaction* 9:82–93.

Akhtar, S., and Samuel, S. (1996). The concept of identity: developmental origins, phenomenology, clinical relevance, and measurement. *Harvard Review of Psychiatry* 3:254–267.

Akhtar, S., and Smolar, A. (1998). Visiting the father's grave. *Psychoanalytic Quarterly* 67:474–483.

Akhtar, S., and Thomson, J.A. (1980). Schizophrenia and sexuality: a review and a report of 12 unusual cases—part 1. *Journal of Clinical Psychiatry* 41:123–143.

———. (1982). Overview: narcissistic personality disorder. *American Journal of Psychiatry* 139:12–20.

Akhtar, S., and Volkan, V.D. (2003a). *The Mental Zoo: Animals in the Human Mind and Its Pathology*. Madison, CT: International Universities Press.

———. (2003b). *The Cultural Zoo: Animals in the Human Mind and Its Sublimations*. Madison, CT: International Universities Press.

Albom, M. (1998). *Tuesdays with Morrie*. New York: Bantam Books.

Altman, L.L. (1977). Some vicissitudes of love. *Journal of the American Psychoanalytic Association* 23:35–52.

Amirthanayagam, I. (1995). What happened to all my life. In *Living in America: Poetry and Fiction by South-Asian American Writers*, ed. R. Rustomji-Kerns, pp. 37–38. Boulder, CO: Westview.

Amsterdam, B.K., and Levitt, M. (1980). Consciousness of self and painful self-consciousness. *Psychoanalytic Study of the Child* 35:67–85.

Angel, A. (1934). Einige bemerkungen uber den optimismus. *International Journal of Psycho-Analysis* 20:191–199.

Arieti, S. (1974). *American Handbook of Psychiatry*, pp. 114–140. New York: Basic Books.

———. (1974). *Interpretation of Schizophrenia*, second addition. New York: Basic Books.

Arlow, J. and Brenner, C. (1964). *Psychoanalytic Concepts and the Structural Theory*. New York: International Universities Press.

Arlow, J.A. (1985). The concept of psychic reality and related problems. *Journal of the American Psychoanalytic Association* 33:521–535.

———. (1986). The poet as prophet: a psychoanalytic perspective. *Psychoanalytic Quarterly* 55:53–68.

———. (1995). Stilted listening: psychoanalysis as discourse. *Psychoanalytic Quarterly* 64:215–233.

Bach, S. (1977). On the narcissistic state of consciousness. *International Journal of Psycho-Analysis* 58:209–233.

———. (1994). *The Language of Perversion and the Language of Love.* Northvale, NJ: Jason Aronson.

Balint, M. (1959). *Thrills and Regression.* London: Hogarth Press.

———. (1968). *The Basic Fault: Therapeutic Aspects of Regression.* London: Tavistock.

Barnland, D.C., and Yoshioko, M. (1990). *Apologies: Japanese and American styles. International Journal of Intercultural Relations* 14:193–206.

Bell, R., and Peltz, D. (1974). *Extramarital sex among women. Medical Aspects of Human Sexuality* 8.

Beltz, S. (1969). *Five year effects of altered marital contracts. In G. Neubeck (ed.), Extramarital Relations.* Englewood Cliffs, NJ: Prentice Hall.

Benezech, M., DeWitte, J., Etchepare, J.J., and Bourgeois, M. (1989). A case of lycanthropy with deadly violence. *Annales Medico—Psychologiques* 147:464–470.

Bennett-Levy, J., and Marteau, T. (1984). Fear of animals: what is prepared? *British Journal of Psychology* 75:37–42.

Berdy, M.D. (1984). Women who are drawn to unavailable men. *Medical Aspects of Human Sexuality* 18:138–146.

Bergler, E. (1952). *The Writer and Psychoanalysis.* Madison, CT: International Universities Press.

———. (1969). *Selected Papers of Edmund Bergler.* New York: Grune & Stratton.

Bergler, M. (1947). Further contributions to the psychoanalysis of writers. *Psychoanalytic Review* 34:455–465.

———. (1950). Does "writer's block" exist? *American Imago* 7:1–19.

Bergman, A. (1980). Ours, yours, mine. In *Rapprochemement: The Critical Subphase of Separation-Individuation,* eds. R.F. Lax, S. Bach, and J.A. Burland, pp. 199–216. New York: Jason Aronson.

Bergmann, M. (1997). Creative work, work inhibitions, and their relation to internal objects. In *Work and Its Inhibitions: Psychoanalytic Essays,* eds. C.W. Socarides, and S. Kramer, pp. 191–208. Madison, CT: International Universities Press.

Bergmann, M.S. (1971). Psychoanalytic observations on the capacity to love. In *Separation-Individuation*, eds. J.B. McDevitt, and C.F. Settlage. New York: International Universities Press.

———. (1982). Thoughts on super-ego pathology of survivors and their children. In *Generations of the Holocaust*, eds. M.S. Bergmann, and M.E. Jucovy, pp. 287–311. New York: Basic Books.

Berliner, B. (1958). The role of object relations in moral masochism. *Psychoanalytic Quarterly* 27:38–56.

Bernard, M., Claney, B., et al. (1978). *Human Sexuality for Health Professionals*, p. 211. Philadelphia, PA: W.B. Saunders Co.

Bernstein, D. (1983). The female superego: a different perspective. *International Journal of Psycho-Analysis* 64:187.

Bernstein, I. (1983). Masochistic pathology and feminine development. *Journal of the American Psychoanalytic Association* 31:467–486..

Berrios, G.E. (1985). Tactile hallucinations: conceptual and historical aspects. *Journal of Neurology and Neurosurgical Psychiatry* 45:395–403.

Bick, E. (1968). The experience of the skin in early object relations. *International Journal of Psycho-Analysis* 49:484–486.

Bion, W. (1957). Differentiation of the psychotic from the non-psychotic personalities. *International Journal of Psycho-Analysis* 38:266–275.

———. (1963). *Elements of Psycho-analysis*. London: Heinemann.

———. (1967). *Second Thoughts*. London: Heinemann.

———. (1970). *Attention and Interpretation*. London: Karnac.

Blanck, G., and Blanck R.. (1974). *Ego Psychology: Theory and Practice*. New York: Columbia University Press.

Blanton, S. (1971). *Diary of My Analysis with Sigmund Freud*. New York: Hawthorne Press.

Bleuler, E. (1930). *Textbook of Psychiatry*. Transl. A.A. Brill. New York: McMillan

Block, J. (1978). *The Other Man/The Other Woman*. New York: Grosset & Dunlap.

Blos, P. (1967). The second individuation process of adolescence. *Psychoanalytic Study of the Child* 22:162–186.

———. (1985). *Son and Father: Before and Beyond the Oedipus Complex*. New York: Free Press.

Blum, H. (1976). Masochism, the ego ideal, and the psychology of women. *Journal of the American Psychoanalytic Association* 24:157–191.

———. (1981). Object inconstancy and paranoid conspiracy. *Journal of the American Psychoanalytic Association* 29:789–813.

———. (1997). Clinical and developmental dimensions of hate. *Journal of the American Psychoanalytic Association* 45:359–375.

Bollas, C. (1979). The transformational object. *International Journal of Psycho-Analysis* 60:97–107.

———. (1992). *Being a Character: Psychoanalysis and Self Experience.* New York: Hill and Wang.

Borges, J.L. (1973). Things. In *Jorge Luis Borges: Selected Poems,* ed. A. Coleman, p. 277. New York: Viking Press.

Bourdon, K., Boyd, J., Dae, D., Burns, B., Thompson, J., and Locke, B. (1988). Gender differences in phobias: results of the ECA Community Survey. *Journal of Anxiety Disorders* 2:227–241.

Bourgeouis, M.L. Duhamel, P., and Verdoux, H. (1992). Delusional parasitosis: folie a deux and attempted murder of a family doctor. *British Journal of Psychiatry* 161:709–711.

Bouvet, M. (1958). Technical variations and the concept of a distance. *International Journal of Psychoanalysis* 39:211–221.

Britton, R. (1989). The missing link: parental sexuality in the oedipus complex. In *The Oedipus Complex Today,* ed. J. Steiner, pp. 83–101. London: Karnac.

———. (1994). Publication anxiety: conflict between communication and affiliation. *International Journal of Psycho-Analysis* 75:1213–1224.

Brodsky, J. (1973). Elegy: for Robert Powell. In *A Part of Speech,* pp. 135–137. New York: Farrar, Strauss, and Giroux.

Brunswick, R.M. (1928). A supplement to Freud's "History of infantile neurosis." In *The Psychoanalytic Reader,* ed. R. Fliess. New York: International Universities Press, 1948.

Cairns, D.L. (1999). Representations of remorse and reparation in classical Greece. In *Remorse and Reparation,* ed. M. Cox, pp. 171–178. London: Jessica Kingsley Publishers.

Calvino, I. (1972). *Invisible Cities.* Transl. W. Weaver. New York: Harcourt, 1974.

Cameron, N. (1963). *Personality Development and Psychopathology.* Boston: Houghton Mifflin.

Campbell, R.J. (1989). *Psychiatric Dictionary,* Sixth Edition, p. 415. NY: Oxford University Press.

Casement, P.J. (1991). *Learning from the Patient.* New York: Guilford Press.

Chase, D. (2000). Restorative justice: use of apologies in criminal law. *Virginia Lawyers Weekly* February 21, 2000.

Chasseguet-Smirgel, J. (1984). *Creativity and Perversion.* New York: W.W. Norton.

Chekov, A. (1927). Death of a government clerk. *Anton Chekov: Early Short Stories* 1883–1883, ed. S. Foote, transl. C. Garnet. New York: The Modern Library.

Cheney, D.L., Seyfarth R.M., and Silk, M.B. (1995). The role of grunts in reconciling opponents and facilitating interactions among adult female baboons. *Animal Behaviour* 50:249–257.

Chirban, S.A. (2000). Oneness Experience: looking through multiple lenses. *Journal of Applied Psychoanalytic Studies* 2:247–264.

Christensen, H.T. (1958). *Marriage Analysis* (2nd Edition). New York: The Ronald Press.

Colarusso, C.A. (1997). Separation–individuation processes in middle adulthood: the fourth individuation. In *The Seasons of Life: Separation-Individuation Perspectives*, eds. S. Akhtar, and S. Kramer, pp. 73–94. Northvale, NJ: Jason Aronson.

Colarusso, C.A., and Nemiroff, R.A. (1979). *Adult Development: A New Dimension in Psychodynamic Theory and Practice*. New York: Plenum.

Coll, P.G., O'Sullivan, G., and Browne, P.J. (1985). Lycanthropy lives on. *British Journal of Psychiatry* 147:201–202.

Cook, M., and Mineka, S. (1987). Second order conditioning and over-shadowing in the observational conditioning of fear in monkeys. *Behavior Research and Therapy* 25:349–364.

Cooper, A. (1981). *Narcissism, in American Handbook of Psychiatry*, vol VII. Edited by S. Arieti, et al. New York: Basic Books.

———. (1984). Narcissism in normal development. In *Character Pathology: Theory and Treatment*, ed. M.R. Zales, pp. 39–56. New York: Brunner/Mazel.

———. (1988b). Our changing views of the therapeutic action of psychoanalysis: comparing Strachey and Loewald. *Psychoanalytic Quarterly* 57:15–27.

———. (1988a). The narcissistic-masochistic character. In *Masochism: Current Psychoanalytic Perspectives*, eds. R.A. Glick, and D.I. Meyers, pp. 117–138. Hillsdale, NJ: The Analytic Press.

———. (1989). Narcissism and masochism: the narcissistic-masochistic character. *Psychiatric Clinics of North America* 12:541–552.

———. (1990). The future of psychoanalysis: challenges and opportunities. *Psychoanalytic Quarterly* 59:177–196.

Cooper, A.M., and Ronningstam, R. (1992). Narcissistic personality. In *American Psychiatric Press Review of Psychiatry*, Volume II, eds. A. Tasman, and M. Riba, pp. 80–97. Washington DC: American Psychiatric Press.

Cords, M. (1992). Post-conflict reunions and reconciliation in long-tailed Macaques. *Animal Behaviour* 44:57–61.

Cuber, J.F., and Harroff, P.B. (1965). *The Significant Americans*. New York: Appleton-Century-Crofts.

Darby, B.W., and Schlenker, B.R. (1982). Children's reactions to apologies. *Journal of Personality and Social Psychology* 43:742–753.

———. (1989). Children's reactions to transgressions: effects on the actor's apology, reputation, and remorse. *British Journal of Social Psychology* 28:353–364.

Davey, G. (1992). Characteristics of individuals with fear of spiders. *Anxiety Research* 4:299–314.

Davey, G., Forster, L., Mayhew, G., et al. (1993). Familial resemblancs in disgust sensitivity and animal phobias. *Behavior Research and Therapy* 31:41–50.

DeLeon, J., Antelo, R.E., and Simpson, G. (1992). Delusion of parasitosis or chronic tactile hallucinosis: hypothesis about their brain physiopathology. *Comprehensive Psychiatry* 33:25–33.

Delprato, D. (1980). Hereditary determinants of fears and phobias: a critical review. *Behavior Therapy* 11:79–103.

Denford, S. (1981). Going away. *International Journal of Psychoanalysis* 59:325–332.

Dening, T.R., and West, A. (1989). Multiple serial lycanthropy: a case report. *Psychopathology* 22:344–347.

Deustch, H. (1942). Some forms of emotional disturbance and their relationship to schizophrenia. *Psychoanal Quarterly* 11:301–321.

———. (1951). *Psychoanalysis of Neuroses.* London: Hogarth Press.

deWaal, F.B. (1989). *Peacemaking among Primates.* Cambridge, MA: Harvard University Press.

deWaal, F.B., and Aureli, F. (1996). Consolation, reconciliation, and a possible cognitive difference between macaques and chimpanzees. In *Reaching into Thought*, eds. A.E. Russon, K.A. Bard, and S.T. Parker, pp. 80–110. Cambridge: Cambridge University Press.

deWaal, F.B., and van Roosmalen, A. (1979). Reconciliation and consolation among chimpanzees. *Behavioral Ecology and Sociobiology* 5:55–66.

Diagnostic and Statistical Manual of Mental Disorders—IV. (1994), pp. 85–91, 532. Washington, DC. American Psychiatric Association.

Domangue, B. (1985). Hypnotic regression and refrajing in the treatment of insect phobias. *American Journal of Psychotherapy* 39:206–214.

Dorpat, T.L. (1976). Structural conflict and object relations conflict. *Journal of the American Psychoanalytic Association* 24:885–874.

Durham, M.S. (1990). The therapist and the concept of revenge: the law of talion. *The Journal of Pastoral Care* 44:131–137.

———. (2000). *The Therapist's Encounters with Revenge and Forgiveness.* London: Jessica Kingsley Publishers.

Eidelberg, L. (1968). *Encyclopedia of Psychoanalysis.* New York: The Free Press.

Eisler, R. (1978). Man into Wolf. Santa Barbara, CA: Ross-Erikson.

Ekbom, K.A. (1938). Der presenile dermatozoenwahns. *Acta Psychiatrica et Neurologica Scandinavica* 13:227–259.

Eller, J.J. (1929). Neurogenic and psychogenic disorders of the skin. *New York Medical Journal* 129:481–485.

Ellis, A. (1969). Healthy and disturbed reasons for having extramarital relations. In *Extramarital Relations*, ed. G. Neubeck. Englewood Cliffs, NJ: Prentice-Hall.

Ellis, B. (1991). *American Psycho*. New York: Random House.

Emde, R. (1984). The affective self. In *Frontiers of Infant Psychiatry*, eds. J.D. Call, E. Galenson, and R.L. Tyson, pp. 38–54. New York: Basic Books.

English, O. (1945). *Emotional Disturbances during the Phallic Period: Emotional Problems of Living*, pp. 119–127. New York: Norton and Company.

Erikson, E.H. (1950). Growth and crises of the healthy personality. In *Identity and the Life Cycle*, pp. 50–100. New York: International Universities Press.

———. (1956). The problem of ego identity. In *Identity and the Life Cycle*, pp. 104–164. New York: International Universities Press, 1959.

———. (1959a). *Identity and the Life Cycle*. New York: International Universities Press.

———. (1959b). *Childhood and Society*. Boston: Little Brown.

Escoll, P. (1992). Vicissitudes of optimal distance through the life cycle. In *When the Body Speaks: Psychological Meanings in Kinetic Clues*, eds. S. Kramer, and S. Akhtar, pp. 59–87. Northvale, NJ: Jason Aronson.

Eysenck, H.J. (1965). *The Causes and Cures of Neurosis*. London: Routledge & Kegan Paul.

———. (1976). The conditioning model of neurosis. *Behavior Research and Therapy* 14:251–267.

Faber, M.D. (1988). The pleasures of rhyme: a psychoanalytic note. *International Review of Psycho-Analysis* 15:375–380.

Fahy, T.A. (1989). Lycanthropy: a review. *Journal of the Royal Society of Medicine* 82:39–39.

Fairbairn, W.R.D. (1940). Schizoid factors in the personality. In *An Object Relations Theory of Personality*, pp. 3–27. New York: Basic Books, 1952.

———. (1952). *An Object Relations Theory of the Personality*. New York: Basic Books.

Favazza, A.R. (1992). Repetitive self-mutilation. *Psychiatric Annals* 22:60–63.

Feldman, S. (1964). The attraction of "the other woman." *Journal of the Hillside Hospital* 13:3–17.

Fenichel, O. (1934). Defense against anxiety, particularly by libidinization. In *The Collected Papers of Otto Fenichel, First Series*, eds. H. Fenichel, and D. Rapaport, pp. 303–317. New York: W.W. Norton, 1953.

248 REFERENCES

———. (1945). *The Psychoanalytic Theory of Neurosis*, pp. 163–204. New York: W.W. Norton and Company.

Ferenczi, S. (1911). On obscene words. In *First Contributions to Psychoanalysis*, pp. 132–153. London: Hogarth Press.

———. (1916). *First Contributions to Psychoanalysis*, p. 204–213. New York: Brunner/Mazel.

———. (1926). *Theory and Technique in Psychoanalysis*, pp. 360–361. London: Hogarth Press.

———. (1928). The elasticity of psycho-analytic technique. *International Journal of Psycho-Analysis* 14:197.

Fielding, J. (1983). *The Other Woman*. New York: Signet Books.

Fischer, N. (1991). The psychoanalytic experience and psychic change. Paper presented at The 27th IPA Congress, Buenos Aires, Argentina, August 18–22.

Flugel, J.C. (1930). *The Psychology of Clothes*. London: Hogarth Press.

Flynn, F.G., Cummings, J.L., and Scheibel, J. (1989). Monosymptomatic delusions of parasitosis associated with ischemic cerebrovascular disease. *Journal of Geriatric Psychiatry and Neurology* 2:134–139.

Fonagy, P. and Target, M. (1997). Attachment and reflective function: their role in self-organization. *Development and Psychopathology* 9:679–700.

Freeman, D. (2003). Cross cultural perspectives on the bond between man and animals. In *The Cultural Zoo: Animals in the Human Mind and Its Sublimations*. Madison, CT: International Universities Press.

Freinhar, J.P. (1984). Delusions of parasitosis. *Psychosomatics* 25:47–53.

French, M. (1980). *The Bleeding Heart*. New York: Ballentine Books.

Freud, A. (1936). *The Ego and the Mechanisms of Defense*. New York: International Universities Press.

———. (1952). The role of bodily illness in the mental life of children. *Psychoanalytic Study of the Child* 7:69–81.

———. (1963). The concept of developmental lines. *Psychoanalytic Study of the Child* 18:245–265.

———. (1965). Normality and pathology in childhood. In *The Writings of Anna Freud*, vol 6. New York: International Universities Press.

———. (1928). *The Psychoanalytical Treatment of Children*. New York: International Universities Press, 1959.

Freud, S. (1895a). Project for a scientific psychology. *Standard Edition* 1:283–398.

———. (1895b). Obsessions and phobias: their psychic mechanisms and their aetiology. *Standard Edition* 3:74–84.

———. (1900). Interpretation of dreams. *Standard Edition* 5:620.

———. (1905). Three essays on the theory of sexuality. *Standard Edition* 7:135–243.

———. (1907). Delusions and dreams in Jensen's "Gradiva." *Standard Edition* 9:7–96.

———. (1908a). Creative writers and day dreaming. *Standard Edition* 9:143–154.

———. (1908b). On the sexual theories of children. *Standard Edition* 9:209–226.

———. (1909a). Analysis of a phobia in a 5-year-old boy. *Standard Edition* 10:5–149.

———. (1909b). Notes upon a case of obsessional neurosis. *Standard Edition* 10:155–257.

———. (1910). A special type of object choice made by men. *Standard Edition* 11:163–175.

———. (1912a). The dynamics of transference. *Standard Edition* 12:97–108.

———. (1912b). Recommendations to physicians practicing psychoanalysis. *Standard Edition* 12:111–120.

———. (1913). Totem and Taboo. *Standard Edition* 13:1–161.

———. (1914a). On narcissism: an introduction. Standard Edition 14:67–103.

———. (1914b). Remembering, repeating, and working through. *Standard Edition* 12:145–156.

———. (1915). Observations on transference love. *Standard Edition* 12:157–171.

———. (1917). Mourning and melancholia. *Standard Edition* 14:237–260.

———. (1918). From the history of an infantile neurosis. *Standard Edition* 17:7–122.

———. (1920a). The psychogenesis of a case of homosexuality in a woman. *Standard Edition* 18.

———. (1920b). Beyond the pleasure principle. *Standard Edition* 18:7–64.

———. (1923). The ego and the id. *Standard Edition* 19:12–68.

———. (1924a). The economic problem of masochism. *Standard Edition* 19:157–170.

———. (1924b). The dissolution of the Oedipus complex. *Standard Edition* 19:173–182.

———. (1926). Inhibitions, symptoms, and anxiety. *Standard Edition* 20:77–175.

———. (1927). Fetishism. *Standard Edition* 21.

———. (1928). Dostoevsky and parricide. *Standard Edition* 21:177–194.

———. (1930). Civilization and its discontents. *Standard Edition* 21:57–145.

———. (1931). Libidinal types. *Standard Edition* 21:215–220.

———. (1933). Femininity. *Standard Edition* 22.

Friedman, D. (1966). Treatment of a case of dog phobia in a deaf mute by behavior therapy. *Behavior Reseach Therapy* 4:141–150.

Frosch, J. (1964). A note on reality constancy. In *Psychoanalysis: A General Psychology—Essays in Honor of Heinz Hartmann*, eds. R.M. Loewenstein, L.M. Newman, M. Schurr, and A.J. Solnit, pp. 349–376. New York: International Universities Press.

Gabbard, G.O. (1989). Two subtypes of narcissistic personality disorder. *Bulletin of the Menninger Clinic* 53:527–532.

Galatzer-Levy, R., and Cohler, B. (1993). *The Essential Other*. New York: Basic Books.

Galdston, R. (1987). The longest pleasure: a psychoanalytic study of hatred. *International Journal of Psycho-Analysis* 68:371–378.

Gallagher, M. (2000). Prayer asks forgiveness for anti-Semitism. *The Philadelphia Inquirer,* March 5, 2000, p. J-7.

Gartner, J. (1992). The capacity to forgive: an object relations perspective. In *Object Relations Theory and Religion: Clinical Applications*, eds. M. Finn, and J. Gartner. Westport, CT: Praeger Publishers.

Gay, P. (1988). *Freud: A Life for Our Time*. New York: Norton.

Geahchan, D. (1968). Deuil et nostalgia. *Rev. franc. Psychanal.* 32:39–65.

Ghalib, A.U.K. (1841). *Diwan-e-Ghalib*. New Delhi: Maktaba Jamia, 1969.

Gieler, U., Knoll, M. (1990). Delusional parasitosis as "folie a trois." *Dermatologica* 181:122–125.

Gilligan, C. (1982). *In a Different Voice*. Cambridge: Harvard University Press.

Glenn, J. (1984). A note on loss, pain, and masochism in children. *Journal of the American Psychoanalytic Association* 32:63–75.

———. (1991). Transformations in normal and pathology latency. In *Beyond the Symbiotic Orbit: Advances in Separation-Individuation Theory— Essays in Honor of Selma Kramer, M.D.*, eds. S. Akhtar, and H. Parens, pp. 171–188. Hillsdale, NJ: The Analytic Press.

Glover, E. (1954). The indications for psychoanalysis. *Journal of Mental Science* 100:393–401.

Goldberg, A. (1987). The place of apology in psychoanalysis and psychotherapy. *International Review of Psychoanalysis* 14:409–422.

Goldfarb, W. (1963). Self-awareness in schizophrenic children. *Archives of General Psychiatry* 8:47–60.

Goldman, A. (1984). *Personal communication*.

Gonsalez, S., Lastra, M., and Ramos, V. (1993). Parasitic delusions: literature review and report of new cases. *Actas Luso-Espanolas de Neurologia, Psiquiatria y Ciencias Afines* 21:52–62.

Gorelick, K. (1989). Rapprochement between the arts and psychotherapies: metaphor the mediator. *The Arts in Psychotherapy* 16:149–155.

Gray, S. (1992). *Monster in a Box.* New York: Vintage Books.

Green, A. (1986). Moral narcissism. In *On Private Madness*, pp. 115–141. New York: International Universities Press.

Greenacre, P. (1951). Respiratory incorporation and the phallic phase. *Psychoanalytic Study of the Child* 6:180–205.

——. (1955). *Swift and Carroll.* New York: International Universities Press.

——. (1957). The childhood of the artist: libidinal phase development and giftedness. In *Emotional Growth*, vol 2, pp. 465–486. New York: International Universities Press, 1971.

——. (1958a). The family romance of the artist. In *Emotional Growth*, vol 2, pp. 505–532. New York: International Universities Press, 1971.

——. (1958b). The relation of the impostor to the artist. In *Emotional Growth*, vol 2, pp. 533–554. New York: International Universities Press, 1971.

——. (1959). Play in relation to creative imagination. In *Emotional Growth*, vol 2, pp. 555–574. New York: International Universities Press, 1971.

Greenspan, S.I. (1977). The oedipal-preoedipal dilemma: a reformulation in the light of object relations theory. *International Review of Psycho-Analysis* 4:381–391.

Grinberg, L. (1964). Two kinds of guilt: their relations with normal and pathological aspects of mourning. *International Journal of Psycho-Analysis* 45:367–371.

Grolnick, S.A., Barkin, L., and Muensterberger, W. (1978). *Between Reality and Fantasy: Transitional Objects and Phenomena.* New York: Jason Aronson.

Grosskurth, P. (1986). *Melanie Klein: Her World and Her Work.* New York: Alfred Knopf.

Grunert, U. (1979). The negative therapeutic reaction as a reactivation of a disturbed process of separation in the transference. *Bulletin of the European Psychoanlaytic Federation* 65:5–19.

Guntrip, H. (1969). *Schizoid Phenomena, Object Relations, and the Self.* New York: International Universities Press.

Guttman, S. A., Jones R.L., and Parrish, S.M., eds. (1980). *The Concordance to the Standard Edition of the Complete Psychological Works of Sigmund Freud.* Boston: G.K. Hall.

Haesler, L. (1993). Adequate distance in the relationship between supervisor and supervisee. *International Journal of Psycho-Analysis* 74:547–555.

Hagman, E. (1932). A study of fears of children of pre-school age. *Journal of Experimental Education* 1:110–130.

Hamilton, J. (1969). Object loss, dreaming, and creativity: the poetry of John Keats. *Psychoanalytic Study of the Child* 24:488–531. New York: International Universities Press.

———. (1976). Early trauma, dreaming and creativity: works of Eugene O'Neill. *International Review of Psycho-Analysis* 3:341.

———. (1979). Transitional phenomena and the early writings of Eugene O'Neill. *International Review of Psycho-Analysis* 3:341.

Harding, J. (1999). Remorse and rehabilitation. In *Remorse and Reparation,* ed. M. Cox, pp. 107–115. London: Jessica Kingsley Publishers.

Hartmann, H. (1939). *Ego Psychology and the Problem of Adaptation.* New York: International Universities Press.

———. (1958). *Ego Psychology and the Problem of Adaptation.* New York: International Universities Press.

Heaney, S. (1995). *A Redress for Poetry.* New York: Farrar, Strauss, and Giroux.

Hendricks, I. (1943). Work and the pleasure principle. *Psychoanalytic Quarterly* 12:311–329.

Herman, J. (1992). *Trauma and Recovery.* New York: Basic Books.

Herzog, J. (1984). Fathers and young children: fathering daughters and fathering sons. In *Foundations of Infant Psychiatry, vol 2,* eds. J.D. Call, E. Galenson, and R. Tyson, pp. 335–343. New York: Basic Books.

Hinde, R. (1989). Relations between levels of complexity in the behavioral sciences. *The Journal of Nervous and Mental Disease* 177:655–667.

Hinsie, L.E., and Campbell, R.J. (1970). *Psychiatric Dictionary,* Fourth Edition. New York: Oxford University Press.

Hoffer, W. (1950). Development of the body ego. *Psychoanalytic Study of the Child* 5:18–23.

Hoffman, R.G. (1991). Companion animals: a therepautic measure for elderly patients. *Journal of Gerontological Social Work* 18:195–205.

Hollander, E., Wong, C. (1995). Body dysmorphic disorder, pathological gambling, and sexual compulsions. *The Journal of Clinical Psychiatry* 56:7–12.

Hollander, L.S. (1976). The other woman: personality characteristics and parent–child relationships of single women repeatedly involved with married men. *Dissertation Abstracts International* 12:6383-B (University Microfilms NO. 76–13880).

Hopkinson, G. (1973). The psychiatric syndrome of infestation. *Psychiatria Clinica* 6:330–345.

Horowitz, M.J. (1989). Clinical phenomenology of narcissistic pathology. *Psychiatric Clinics of North America* 12:531–539.

Horstein, O.P., Hofmann, P., and Joraschky, P. (1989). Delusions of parasitic skin infestation in elderly dermatologic patients. *Zeitschrift für Hautkrankheiten.* 64:981–989.

Hugdahl, K., and Karker, A. (1981). Biological vs. experimental factors in phobic conditioning. *Behavior Research and Therapy* 19:109–115.

Hunt, J. (1969). *The Affair.* Bergenfield, NJ: The New American Library.

Hunt, W. (1995). The diffident narcissist: a character-type illustrated in the Beast in the Jungle by Henry James. *International Journal of Psycho-Analysis* 76:1257–1267.

Hunter, R. (1978). Forgiveness, retaliation, and paranoid reactions. *Journal of the Canadian Psychiatric Association* 23:267–273.

Illis, L. (1964). On porphyria and the aetiology of werewolves. *Proc. Research of Sociological Medicine* 57:23–26.

Inman, L.D. (1997). "A room of one's own" revisited. In *Work and Its Inhibitions: Psychoanalytic Essays,* eds. C.W. Socarides, and S. Kramer, pp. 115–131. Madison, CT: International Universities Press.

Isherwood, C. (1980). *My Guru and His Disciple.* New York: Farrar, Strauss, and Giroux.

Issacs, S. (1933). *Social Development of Young Children.* London: Routledge.

Jackson, P.M. (1978). Another case of lycanthropy. *American Journal of Psychiatry* 135:134–135.

Jelliffe, S.E., and Brink, A.B. (1917). The role of animals in the unconscious, with some remarks on theriomorphic symbolism as seen in ovid. *Psychoanalytic Review* 4:253–271.

Jenkins, J.L. (1986). Pysiological effects of petting a companion animal. *Psychological Reports* 58:21–22.

Jibiki, I., Yamaguchi, N. (1992). A case with delusion of parasitosis as a reactive psychosis following scabies infection. *European Journal of Psychiatry* 6:181–183.

Joffee, W.G., and Sandler, J. (1965). Pain, depression, and individuation. In *From Safety to Superego,* ed. J. Sandler, pp. 154–179. New York: The Guilford Press.

Jones, E. (1913). The God Complex. In *Essays in Applied Psychoanalysis,* ed. E. Jones. New York: International Universities Press, 1964, pp. 244–265.

———. (1928). Fear, guilt, and hate. In *Papers on Psychoanalysis.* Baltimore, MD: Williams & Wilkins, 1950.

———. (1937). *On the Nightmare.* London: Hogarth Press.

———. (1948). The theory of symbolism. In *Papers on Psychoanalysis,* 5th edition. London: Bailmiere, Tindall & Cox.

Joseph, B. (1981). Towards the experiencing of psychic pain. In *Psychic Equilibrium and Psychic Change. Selected Papers of Betty Joseph,* eds. M. Feldman, and E.B. Spillius, pp. 88–97. London: Routledge, 1989.

————. (1982). Addiction to near-death. *International Journal of Psycho-Analysis* 63:449–456.

Joseph, E.D. (ed.). (1967). Indications for psychoanalysis. In *Kris' Study Group of the New York Psychoanalytic Institute, Monograph 2.* New York: International Universities Press.

Jung, C.G. (1954). *The Development of Personality.* London: Routledge & Kegan Paul.

Kafka, J. (1964). Technical applications of a concept of multiple reality. *Int. J. Psychoanal.* 45:575–578.

————. (1989). *Multiple Realities in Clinical Practice.* New Haven: Yale University Press.

Kafka, J.S. (1992). *Multiple Realities.* New York: International Universities Press.

Kagan, J. (1984). *The Nature of the Child.* New York: Basic Books.

Kahn, C. (1997). Emigration without leaving home. In *Immigration Experiences: Personal Narrative and Psychological Analysis,* eds. P.H. Elovitz, and C. Kahn, pp. 255–273. Cranbury, NJ: Associated University Press.

Kakar, S. (1997). *Shamans, Mystics, and Doctors: A Psychological Inquiry into India and Its Healing Traditions.* London: Oxford University Press.

Kanazawa, A., and Hata, T. (1992). Coexistence of the Ekbom syndrome and lilliputian hallucination. *Psychopathology* 25:209–211.

Kaplan, H., and Sadock, B. (1989). *Comprehensive Textbook of Psychiatry V,* pp. 844–845. Baltimore, MD: Williams and Wilkins.

Keck, P.E., Pope, H.G., Hudson, J.I., McElroy, S.L., Kulick, R., et al. (1988). Lycanthropy: alive and well in the twentieth century. *Psychological Medicine* 18:113–120.

Kernberg, O.F. (1967). Borderline personality organization. *Journal of the American Psychoanalytic Association* 15:641–685.

————. (1970). Factors in the treatment of narcissistic personality disorder. *Journal of the American Psychoanalytic Association* 18:51–85.

————. (1970a). A psychoanalytic classification of character pathology. *Journal of the American Psychoanalytic Association* 18:800–822.

————. (1974). Mature Love: prerequisites and characteristics. *Journal of the American Psychoanalytic Association* 22:743–768.

————. (1975). *Borderline Conditions and Pathological Narcissism.* New York: Jason Aronson.

————. (1976). *Object Relations Theory and Clinical Psychoanalysis.* New York: International Universities Press.

————. (1980a). *Internal World and External Reality.* New York: Jason Aronson.

————. (1980b). Love, the couple, and the group: a psychoanalytic frame. *Psychoanalytic Quarterly* 49:78–108.

————. (1984). *Severe Personality Disorders: Psychotherapeutic Strategies*. New Haven, CT: Yale University Press.

————. (1985). Hysterical and histrionic personality disorders. In *Psychiatry, vol. I*, eds. R. Michels, and J.O. Cavenar, pp. 1–12. Philadelphia: Lippincott.

————. (1989). The narcissistic personality disorder and the differential diagnosis of anti-social behavior. *The Psychiatric Clinics of North American* 12:553–570.

————. (1991). Sadomasochism, sexual excitement, and perversion. *Journal of the American Psychoanalytic Association* 39:333–362.

————. (1992). *Aggression in Personality Disorders and Perversions*. New Haven, CT: Yale University Press.

————. (1995a). *Love Relations: Normality and Pathology*. New Haven, CT: Yale University Press.

————. (1995b). Hatred as a core affect of aggression. In *The Birth of Hatred: Developmental, Clinical, and Technical Aspects of Intense Aggression*, eds. S. Akhtar, S. Kramer, and H. Parens, pp. 53–82. Northvale, NJ: Jason Aronson.

Khan, M.M.R. (1969). On symbiotic omnipotence. In *The Privacy of the Self*. New York: International Universities Press.

————. (1979). From masochism to psychic pain. In *Alienation in Perversions*, pp. 210–218. New York: International Universities Press.

————. (1980). *Alienation in Perversion*. New York: International Universities Press.

————. (1983). On lying fallow. In *Hidden Selves: Between Theory and Practice in Psychoanalysis*, pp. 183–188. New York: International Universities Press.

Killingmo, B. (1989). Conflict and deficit: implications for technique. *International Journal of Psycho-Analysis* 70:65–79.

Kinsey, A., Pomeroy, W., et al. (1948). *Sexual Behavior in the Human Male*. Philadelphia: W.B. Saunders Co.

————. (1953). *Sexual Behavior in the Human Female*. Philadelphia, PA: W.B. Saunders Co.

Kleeman, J.A. (1967). The peak-a-boo game: part I: its origins, meanings, and related phenomena in the first year. *Psychoanalytic Study of the Child* 22:239–273.

Klein, M. (1937). Love, guilt, and reparation. In *Love, Guilt, and Reparation and Other Works*, pp. 306–343. New York: Free Press, 1975.

————. (1940). Mourning and its relation to manic-depressive states. In *The Writings of Melanie Klein, vol 1, Love Guilt and Reparation*, pp. 344–369. London: Hogarth Press, 1975.

————. (1948). *Contributions to Psychoanalysis (1921–1945)*. London: Hogarth.

Knights, L.C. (1980). Poetry and "things hard for thought." *International Review of Psycho-Analysis* 7:125–136.

Koehler, K., Ebel, H., and Vartzopoulos, D. (1990). Lycanthropy and demonomania: some psychopathological issues. *Psychological Medicine* 20:629–633.

Kogan, I. (1990). A journey to pain. *International Journal of Psycho-Analysis* 71:629–640.

Kohut, H. (1971). *The Analysis of the Self*. New York: International Universities Press.

————. (1972). Thoughts on narcissism and narcissistic rage. *Psychoanalytic Study of the Child* 27:360–400. New Haven, CT: Yale University Press.

————. (1977). *Restoration of the Self*. New York: International Universities Press.

Kohut, H., Wolf, E. (1978). The disorders of the self and their treatment: an outline. *International Journal of Psycho-Analysis* 59:413–426

Kolansky, H. (1960). Treatment of a 3-year-old girl's severe infantile neurosis. *Psychoanalytic Study of the Child* 15:261.

Kolodny, S. (2000). *The Captive Muse: On Creativity and Its Inhibition*. Madison, CT: Psychosocial Press.

Kraepelin, E. (1919). *Dementia Praecox and Paraphrenia*. Transl. by Barclay R.M. and Robertson, G.M. Edinburgh: Livingstone.

Krafft-Ebing, R. von (1938). *Psychopathia Sexualis*. Stuttgart: Ferdinand Enke.

Kris, E. (1956). The personal myth: A problem in psychoanalytic techniques. *Journal of the American Psychoanalytic Association* 4:653–681.

Kritzberg, N.I. (1980). On patients' gift giving. *Contemporary Psychoanalysis* 16:98–118.

Kubler-Ross, E. (1969). *On Death and Dying*. London: The MacMillan Company.

Kulick, A., Pope, H.G., and Keck, P.E. (1990). Lycanthropy and self-idenfication. *Journal of Nervous and Mental Disease* 17:134–137.

Kupferman, K. (1977). A latency boy's identity as a cat. *Psychoanalytic Study of the Child* 32:363–385.

Kurtz, S. (1989). *The Art of Unknowing*. New York: Jason Aronson.

Lacayo, R. (1984). Meeting of two masters: Sir David Lean and Lord Snowdon take aim at *A Passage to India*. *Time*, August 27, pp. 54–55.

Langs, R. (1973). *The Technique of Psychoanalytic Psychotherapy*. vol. 1, New York: Jason Aronson

Laplanche, J. (1981). *Frontiers in Psychoanalysis: Between the Dream and Psychic Pain*. New York: International Universities Press.

Laplanche, J., and Pontalis, J.B. (1973). *The Language of Psychoanalysis.* Transl. D. Nicholson-Smith. New York: W.W. Norton.

―――. (1968). Fantasy and the origins of sexuality. *International Journal of Psycho-Analysis* 49:1–18.

Lazare, A. (1971). The hysterical character in psychoanalytic theory. *Archives of General Psychiatry* 15:131–137.

Leader, Z. (1991). *Writer's Block.* Baltimore, MD: Hopkins University Press.

Levinson, D. (1978). *The Seasons of a Man's Life.* New York: Alfred Knopf.

Lewis, A.J. (1936). Problems of obsessional illness. *Proceedings of the Royal Society of Medicine* 29:325–328.

Levy, S.T. (1987). Therapeutic strategy and psychoanalysis. *Journal of American Psychoanalytic Association,* 35:447–466.

Lichentenberg, J.D. (1983). *Psychoanalysis and Infant Research.* Hillsdale, NJ: The Analytic Press.

Lichtenstein, H. (1963). The dilemma of human identity: notes on self-transformation, self-objectivation and metamorphosis. *Journal of the Americna Psychoanalytic Association* 11:173–223.

Lockwood, R. (1994). The psychology of animal collectors. *Trends* 9:18–21.

Loewald, H.W. (1960). On the therapeutic action of psychoanalysis. In *Papers on Psychoanalysis.* New Haven, CT: Yale University Press.

Lower, R., Escoll, P., and Huxster, H. (1972). Bases for judgments of analyzability. *Journal of the American Psychoanalytic Association* 20:610–621.

Macaskill, N.D. (1987). Delusion parasitosis: successful non-pharmacological treatment of a folie-a-deux. *British Journal of Psychiatry* 150:261–263.

MacKinnon, R.A., and Michels, R. (1971). *The Psychiatric Interview in Clinical Practice.* Philadelphia: W.B. Saunders.

Madanes, C. (1990). *Sex, Love, and Violence: Strategies for Transformation.* New York: W.W. Norton Co.

Madow, L. (1997). On the way to second symbiosis: discussion of Cath's chapter "Loss and restitution in late life." In *The Seasons of Life: Separation–Individuation Perspectives,* eds. S. Akhtar, and S. Kramer, pp. 157–170. Northvale, NJ: Jason Aronson.

Magnan, V., and Saury, M. (1889). Trois cas de cocainisme chronique. *Comptes rendes, Seances et Memoires Societe Biologigue* 41:60–63

Mahler, M.S. (1958). On two crucial phases of integration of the sense of identity. *Journal of the American Psychoanalytic Association* 6:136–139.

―――. (1974). Symbiosis and individuation: the psychological birth of the human infant. In *The Selected Papers of Margaret S. Mahler,* vol. 2. New York: Jason Aronson.

―――. (1975). On the current status of the infantile neurosis. In *The Selected Papers of Margaret S. Mahler,* vol. 2, pp. 189–194. New York: Jason Aronson, 1979.

Mahler, M.S., and Furer, M. (1968). *On Human Symbiosis and the Vicissitudes of Individuation, Vol. 1:* New York: International Universities Press.
Mahler, M.S., Pine, F., and Bergman, A. (1975). *The Psychological Birth of the Human Infant.* New York: Basic Books.
Maier, C. (1987). The problem of parasitosis delusions. *Nervenarzt* 58:107–115.
Mailer, N. (1966). *Cannibals and Christians.* New York: Dial Press.
Maimonides, M. (1200). *Mishne Torah.* Translated by Eliyahu Touger. New York: Moznaim, 1989.
Maleson, F.G. (1984). The multiple meanings of masochism in psychoanalytic discourse. *Journal of the American Psychoanalytic Association* 32:325–356.
Malliaras, D.E., Kossovitsa, Y.T., and Dhristodoulou, G.N. (1978). Organic contributors to the intermetapmorphosis syndrome. *American Journal of Psychiatry* 135:985–987.
Maltsberger, J.T., and Buie, D.H. (1974). Countertransference hate in the treatment of suicidal patients. *Archives of General Psychiatry* 30:625–633.
Marks, IM. (1987). *Fears, Phobias, and Rituals,* pp. 372–442. New York: Oxford University Press.
Marneros, A., Deister, A., and Rohde, A. (1988). Delusional parasitosis. *Psychopathology* 21:267–274.
Masson, J.M. (ed.) (1985). *The Complete Letters of Sigmund Freud to Wilhelm Fliess: 1887–1904.* Cambridge, MA: Harvard University Press.
Masterson, J.F. (1993). *The Emerging Self: A Developmental, Self, and Object Relations Approach to the Treatment of the Closet Narcissistic Disorder of the Self.* New York: Brunner/Mazel.
May, W.W., and Terpenning, M. (1991). Delusional parasitosis in geriatric patients. *Psychosomatics* 32:84–94.
McCullough, M.E., Worthington, E.L., and Rachal, K.C. (1997). Interpersonal forgiving in close relationships. *Journal of Personality and Social Psychology* 73:321–336.
McMillen, D.L., and Helmreich, R.L. (1969). The effectiveness of several types of ingratiation tecniques following argument. *Psychonomic Science* 15:207–208.
McNally, R.J., and Steketee, G.S. (1985). The etiology and maintenance of severe animal phobias. *Behavior Research and Therapy* 23:431–435.
Mehler, J.A., and Argentieri, S. (1989). Hope and hopelessness: a technical problem? *International Journal of Psycho-Analysis* 70:295–304.
Mellor, C.S. (1988). Depersonalisation and Self perception. Second Leeds Psychopathology Symposium: The psychopathology of body image. *British Journal of Psychiatry* 153(Suppl):15–19.

Melville, H. (1851). *Moby Dick; Or, the Whale*. Berkeley, CA: University of California Press, 1979.

Merkur, D. (1981). The psychodynamics of the Navajo coyote ceremonial. *Journal of Mind and Behavior* 2:243–257.

Mester, H. (1975). Induced acaraphobia. *Psychiatria Clinica* 8:339–348.

Michels, R. (1983). The scientific and clinical functions of psychoanalytic theory. In *The Future of Psychoanalysis*, ed. A. Goldberg, pp. 125–135. New York: International Universities Press.

———. (1985). Perspectives on the nature of psychic reality. *Journal of the American Psychoanalytic Association* 33:515–519.

Mineka, S., Davidson, M., Cook, M., Keir, R., et al. (1984). Ovservational conditioning of snake fear in rhesus monkeys. *Journal of Abnormal Psychology* 93:355–72.

Mitchell, J., and Vierkant, A.D. (1991). Delusions and hallucinations of cocaine abusers and paranoid schizophrenics: a comparative study. *Journal of Psychology* 125:301–310.

Modell, A. (1976). The holding environment and the therapeutic action of psychoanalysis. *Journal of the American Psychoanalytic Association* 24:285–307.

———. (1983). Comments on the rise of narcissism. In *The future of psychoanalysis*, ed. A. Goldberg. New York: International Universities Press.

Moore, B., and Fine, B. (1968). *A Glossary of Psychoanalytic Terms and Concepts*. New York: American Psychoanalytic Association.

———. (1990). *Psychoanalytic Terms and Concepts*. New York: American Psychoanalytic Association.

Morris, M. (1991). Delusional infestation. *British Journal of Psychiatry* 159(Suppl):83–87.

Moses, R. (1999). Apology and reparation. *Presented at the 1st Izmir Conference on Psychotherapy and Psychoanalysis, Izmir, Turkey*, October 21–24th, 1999.

Mosher, P. (1991). *Title, Key Word, and Author Index to Psychoanalytic Journals—1920–1990*. New York: American Psychoanalytic Association.

Mouren, M., Ohayon, M., and Tatossian, A. (1980). Animals and their masters. Psychological and psychopathological aspects. *Annales Medico Psychologiques* 138:543–557.

Munro, A. (1982). *Delusional Hypochondriasis: A Description of Monosymptomatic Hypochondriacal Psychosis. Monograph Series 5*. Toronto, Canada, Clarke Institute of Psychiatry.

Musalek, M., Podreka, I., Walter, H., et al. (1989). Regional Brain Function in Hallucination: A study of reginal cerebral blood flow with 99m-Tc-

HMPA)-SPECT in patients with auditory hallucinations, tactile hallucinations, and normal controls. *Comprehensive Psychiatry* 30:99–108.

Myerson, A. (1921). Two cases of acaraphobia. *Boston Medical and Surgical
   Journal* 184:635–638.

Nelson, V. (1993). *On Writer's Block.* Boston: Houghton Mifflin Company.

Nemiah, J.C. (1967). Obsessive-compulsive reaction. In *Comprehensive Textbook of Psychiatry*, eds. A.M. Freedman, and H.I. Kaplan, pp. 912–927.
   Baltimore: The Williams and Wilkins Company.

Neruda, P. (1977). *Memoirs.* New York: Farrar, Strauss, and Giroux.

Neubeck, G. (1969). *Extramarital Relations.* Englewood Cliffs, NJ: Prentice-
   Hall.

Nietcshze, F. (1905). *Thus Spake Zarthustra.* New York: Modern Library
   Series.

Nooteboom, C. (1980). *Rituals.* New York: Penguin.

Norman, J.P. (1948). Evidence and clinical signs of homosexuality in 100
   unanlyzed cases of dementia praecox. *Journal of Nervous and Mental
   Disorders* 107:484–489.

O'Brien, T. (1998). *The Things They Carried.* New York: Broadway Books.

O'Malley, M.N., and Greenberg, J. (1993). Sex differences in restoring
   justice: the down payment effect. *Journal of Research in Personality*
   17:174–185.

Ohbuchi, K., Kameda, M., and Agarie, N. (1989). Apology as aggression
   control: its role in mediating appraisal and response to harm. *Journal of
   Personality and Social Psychology* 56:219–227.

Olinick, S. (1997). On writer's block: for whom does one write or not write?
   In *Work and Its Inhibitions: Psychoanalytic Essays*, eds. C.W. Socarides, and
   S. Kramer, pp. 183–190, Madison, CT: International Universities Press.

Ostapzeff, G. (1975). Parasitism. *Perspectives-Psychiatriques* 53:296–302.

Ostow, M. (2001). Three archaic contributions to the religious instinct:
   awe, mysticism, and apocalypse. In *Does God Help?: Developmental and
   Clinical Aspects of Religious Belief*, eds. S. Akhtar, and H. Parens, pp.
   197–234. Northvale, NJ: Jason Aronson.

Pacella, B. (1980). The primal matrix configuration. In *Rapprochement: The
   Critical Subphase of Separation–Individuation*, eds. R.F. Lax, S. Bach, and
   J.A. Burland, pp. 117–131. New York: Jason Aronson.

Pao, P.N. (1965). The role of hatred in the ego. *Psychoanalytic Quarterly*
   34:257–264.

Patronek, G.J. (1999). Hoarding of animals: an under-recognized public
   health problem in a difficult to study population. *Public Health Reports*
   114:81–87.

Paulson, M.J., and Petrus, E.P. (1969). Delusions of parasitosis: a psychological study. *Psychosomatics* 10:111–120.

Perkoff, G.T. (1992). To be a mentor. *Family Medicine* 24:584–585.

Piaget, J. (1936). *Origins of Intelligence in Children.* New York: International Universities Press, 1952.

Pietropinto, A., and Simenauer, J. (1976). *Beyond the Male Myth: What Women Want to Know About Men's Sexuality.* New York: Times Books.

Pine, F. (1995). On the origin and evolution of a species of hate: a clinical-literary excursion. In *The Birth of Hatred: Developmental, Clinical, and Technical Aspects of Intense Aggression*, eds. S. Akhtar, S. Kramer, and H. Parens, pp. 103–132. Northvale, NJ: Jason Aronson.

———. (1999). *Diversity and Direction in Psychoanalytic Technique.* New Haven, CT: Yale University Press.

Podoll, D., Bofinger, G., Von-der-Stein, B., Stuhlmann, W., et al. (1993). Delusional parasitosis in a patient with endogenous depression. *Fortschritteder Neurroligie Psychiatrie* 61:62–66.

Poland, W. (1975). Tact as a psychoanalytic function. *International Journal of Psycho-Analysis* 56:155–162.

———. (1977). Pilgrimage: action and tradition in self analysis. *Journal of the American Psychoanalytic Association* 25:399–416.

———. (1998). Plenary address. *Annual Meetings of the American Psychoanalytic Association,* Toronto, May, 12–16, 1998.

Pollock, G. (1975). On mourning, immortality, and utopia. *Journal of the American Psychoanalytic Association* 23:334–362.

———. (1977). The mourning process and creative organizational change. *Journal of the American Psychoanalytic Association* 25:3–24.

Pontalis, J.B. (1981). *Frontiers in Psychoanalysis: Between the Dream and Psychic Reality.* New York: International Universities Press.

Potamianou, A. (1992). *Un Bouclier dans L'Economie des Etats Limites L'Espoir.* Paris: Presses of the University of France.

Prego-Silva, L. (1978). Dialogue on "depression and other painful affects." *International Journal of Psycho-Analysis* 59:517–532.

Rachman, S. (1977). The conditioning theory of fear-acquisition: a critical examination. *Behavior Research and Therapy* 15:375–387.

Racker, H. (1953). A contribution to the problem of countertransference. *International Journal of Psycho-Analysis* 34:313.

———. (1957). The meanings and uses of countertransference. *Psychoanalytic Quarterly* 26:303–357.

Rado, S. (1933). The psychoanalysis of pharmacothymia. *Psychoanalytic Quarterly* 2:1–23.

Rajna, D.D., Guillibert, E., Loo, H., and Debray, Q. (1990). A case of bird metamorphosis delusion in a Buddhist schizophrenic. *Annales Medica-Psychologiques* 148:539–542.

Ramzy, I., and Wallerstein, R. (1958). Pain, fear, and anxiety: a study in their interrelationships. *Psychoanalytic Study of the Child* 13:147–189.

Rappaport, D. (1960). The structure of psychoanalytic theory. *Psychological Issues* 6:39–72.

Rappaport, E.A. (1968). Zoophily and zoerasty. *Psychoanalytic Quarterly* 37:565–587.

Redefer, L.A., and Goodman, J.F. (1989). Pet-facilitated therapy with autistic children. *Journal of Autism and Developmental Disorders* 19:461–467.

Reich, A. (1954). Early identifications as archaic elements in the superego. *Journal of the American Psychoanalytic Association* 2:218–238.

———. (1972). *Character Analysis* (original, 1933) 3rd edition, translated by Carfagno VR. New York: Farrar, Strauss, and Giroux.

Reilly, T.M. (1988). Delusional infestation. *British Journal of Psychiatry* 153 (Suppl): 44–46.

Ren, R., Yan, K., Su, Y., et al. (1991). The reconciliation behavior of golden monkeys (Rhinopiethecus roxellanae roxellanae) in small breeding groups. *Primates* 32:321–327.

Ressler, R., Burgess, A., Hartman, C., Douglas, J., and McCormack, A. (1986). Murderers who rape and mutilate. *Journal of Interpersonal Violence* 1:273–287.

Reynolds, P.P. (1994). Reaffirming professionalism through the education community. *Annals of Internal Medicine* 120:609–614.

Richardson, L.W. (1979). The other women: the end of the long affair. *Alternative Styles* 2:397–414.

Robertson, B.A., Kottler, A. (1993). Cultural issues in the psychiatric assessment of Khosa children and adolescents. *South African Medical Journal* 83:207–208.

Rogers, R. (1973). On the metapsychology of poetic language: modal ambiguity. *International Journal of Psycho-Analysis* 54:61–74.

Roheim, G. (1943). *The Origin and Function of Culture.* New York: Nervous and Mental Disease Monographs.

Rojo-Morenno, J. Rojo-Moreno, M. Baldemoro Garcia, C., Rojo Siwerra, M. (1990). The delusion of lycanthropic transformation. *Actas Luso-Espanolas de Neurologia, Psiguiatria y Ciencias Afines* 18:327–331.

Ronningstam, E. (1988). Comparing three diagnostic systems for narcissistic personality disorder. *Psychiatry* 51:300–311

Ronningstam, E., and Gunderson, J. (1989). Descriptive studies on narcissistic personality disorder. *Psychiatric Clinics of North America* 12:585–601

Rose, G. (1964). Creative imagination in terms of ego core and boundaries. *International Journal of Psychoanalysis* 45:75–88.

————. (1980). The power of form: a psychoanalytic approach to aesthetic form. *Psychoanalytic Inquiry* 49:1–17.

Rosenfeld, H. (1971). Theory of life and death instincts: aggressive aspects of narcissism. *International Journal of Psycho-Analysis* 52:169–183.

Rosenstock, H.A., and Bincent, K.R. (1977). A case of lycanthropy. *American Journal of Psychiatry* 34:1147–1149.

Ross, J.M. (1979). Fathering: a review of some psychoanalytic contributions on paternity. *International Journal of Psycho-Analysis* 60:317–327.

————. (1982). Oedipus revisited: Laius and the Laius complex. *Psychoanalytic Study of the Child* 37:169–192.

————. (1994). On the contribution of separation–individuation theory to psychoanalysis: developmental process, pathogenesis, therapeutic process, and technique. In *Mahler and Kohut: Perspectives on Development, Psychopathology, and Technique*, eds. S. Kramer, and S. Akhtar, pp. 19–52. Northvale, NJ: Jason Aronson.

Roth, H. (1934). *Call It Sleep.* New York: Avon Books, 1964.

Roux, G. (1988). Images of insects and psychosis. *Psychologie Medicale* 20:1129–1136.

Roy, A. (1997). *The God of Small Things.* New York: Random House.

Rycroft, C. (1968). *A Critical Dictionary of Psychoanalysis.* London: Penguin.

Sanders, K. (1995). *A behavioral study on forgiveness.* Senior thesis. Claremont McKenna College.

Sandler, J. (1960). The background of safety. In *From Safety to Superego: Selected Papers of Joseph Sandler*, pp. 1–8. New York: Guilford, 1987.

Sands, M. (1978). *The Mistress Manual.* New York: Berkley Books.

Schafer, R. (1985). The interpretation of psychic reality, developmental influences, and unconscious communication. *Journal of the American Psychoanalytic Association* 33:537–554.

Scheper-Hughes, N. (1999). Undoing: social suffering and the politics of remorse. In *Remorse and Reparation*, ed. M. Cox, pp. 145–170. London: Jessica Kingsley Publishers.

Scher, S.J., and Darley, J.M. (1997). How effective are the things people say to apologize? Effects of the realization of the Apology Speech Act. *Journal of Psycholinguistic Research* 26:127–140.

Schneck, J.M. (1974). Zooerasty and incest fantasy. *International Journal of Clinical and Experimental Hypnosis* 4:299–302.

Schneidman, E. (1993). *Suicide as Psychache.* Northvale, NJ: Jason Aronson.

Schowalter, J. (1983). The use and abuse of pets. *Journal of the American Academy of Child Psychiatry* 22:68–72.

Schulz, C., and Lewin, R.A. (1992). *Losing and Fusing: Borderline Transitional Object and Self Relations.* Northvale, NJ: Jason Aronson.

Schwaber, P. (1998). From whose point of view? The neglected question in analytic listening. *Psychoanalytic Quarterly* 67:645–661.

Searles, H.F. (1956). The psychodynamics of vengefulness. *Psychiatry* 19:31–39.

———. (1960). *The Non-Human Environment in Normal Development and Schizophrenia*. New York: International Universities Press.

———. (1986). *My Work with Borderline Patients*. Northvale, NJ: Jason Aronson.

Settlage, C. (1977). The psychoanalytic understanding of narcissistic and borderline personality disorders: advances in developmental theory. *Journal of the American Psychoanalytic Association* 25:805–833.

———. (1992). Psychoanalytic observations on adult development in life and in the therapeutic relationship. *Psychoanalysis and Contemporary Thought* 15:349–375.

———. (1993). Therapeutic process and developmental process in the restructuring of object and self constancy. *Journal of the American Psychoanalytic Association* 41:473–492.

———. (1994). On the contribution of separation–individuation theory to psychoanalysis: developmental process, pathogenesis, therapeutic process, and technique. In *Mahler and Kohut: Perspectives on Development, Psychopathology, and Technique*, ed. S. Akhtar, pp. 19–52. Northvale, NJ: Jason Aronson.

———. (2001). Defenses evoked by early childhood loss: their impact on life-span development. In *Three Faces of Mourning: Melancholia, Manic Defense, and Moving On*, ed. S. Akhtar, pp. 47–93. Northvale, NJ: Jason Aronson.

Shengold, L. (1967). The effects of overstimulation: rat people. *International Journal of Psycho-Analysis* 48:403–415.

———. (1989). *Soul Murder: The Effects of Childhood Abuse and Deprivation*. New Haven, CT: Yale University Press.

Sheppard, N.P., O'Loughlin, S., and Malone, J.P. (1986). Psychogenic skin disease: A review of 35 cases. *British Journal of Psychiatry* 149:636–643.

Siegel, R. (1978). Cocaine hallucinations. *American Journal of Psychiatry* 135:3.

Silk, J.B. (1998). Making amends: adaptive perspectives on conflict remediation in monkeys, apes, and humans. *Human Nature* 9:341–368.

Silk, J.B. Cheney, D.L., and Seyfarth, R.M. (1996). The form and function of post-conflict interactions between female baboons. *Animal Behaviour* 52:259–268.

Singer, M. (1977a). The experience of emptiness in narcissistic and borderline states, I: Deficiency and ego defect versus dynamic defensive models. *International Review of Psycho-Analysis* 4:459–470.

————. (1977b). The experience of emptiness in narcissistic and border-line states, II: The struggle for a sense of self and the potential for suicide. *International Review of Psycho-Analysis* 4:471–479.

Simopoulos, G. (1977). Poetry as affective communication. *Psychoanalytic Quarterly* 46:499–513.

Sizaret, P., and Simon, J.P. (1976). Presenile delusion of parasitosis. *Encephale* 2:167–175.

Skott, A. (1975). Delusions of parasitosis (parasitophobia) or Ekbom's syndrome: a literature survey. *Nordisk Psykiatrisk Tidsskrift* 29:115–131.

Slater E., and Roth, M. (1969). *Clinical Psychiatry*, 3rd ed. Baltimore: Williams and Wilkins Company.

Smolar, A. (2002). Reflections on gifts in the therapeutic setting: the gift from patient to therapist. *American Journal of Psychotherapy.*

————. (in press). When we give more: reflections on "gifts" from therapist to patient. *International Journal of Psychoanalysis.*

Sobel, E. (1978). Rhythm, sound, and imagery in the poetry of Gerard Manley Hopkins. In *Between Reality and Fantasy: Transitional Objects and Phenomena*, eds. S.A. Grolnick, L. Barkin, and W. Muensterberger, pp. 427–445. New York: Jason Aronson.

Socarides, C. (1966). On vengeance: the desire to "get even." *Journal of the American Psychoanalytic Association* 14:356–375.

Socarides, C., and Kramer, S. (1997). *Work and Its Inhibitions. Psychoanalytic Essays.* Madison, CT: International Univeristies Press.

Sohn, L. (1999). A defective capacity to feel sorrow. In *Remorse and Reparation*, ed. M. Cox, pp. 69–104. London: Jessica Kingsley Publishers.

Solzhenitsyn, A. (1969). *Cancer Ward.* New York: Farrar, Strauss, and Giroux.

Solyom, L., Beck, P., Solyom, C., and Hugel, R. (1974). Some etiologi-cal factors in phobic neurosis. *Canadian Psychiatric Association Journal* 19:69–78.

Spencer, J.H., and Balter, L. (1990). Psychoanalytic observation. *Journal of the American Psychoanalytic Association* 38:393–421.

Sperling, M. (1971). Spider phobias and spider fantasies: a clinical contribution to the study to symbol and symptom choice. *Journal of the American Psychoanalytic Association* 19:472–498.

Spiegel, L.A. (1966). Affects in relation to self and object: a model for the derivation of desire, longing, pain, anxiety, humiliation, and shame. *Psychoanalytic Study of the Child* 21:69–92.

Spitz, R. (1963). Life and the dialogue. In *Rene A. Spitz: Dialogues from Infancy*, ed. R. Emde, pp. 147–160. New York: International Universities Press, 1983.

Spitzform, M. (2000). The ecological self: metaphor and developmental experience. *Journal of Applied Psychoanalytic Studies* 2:265–286.

Spotnitz, H., and Freeman, L. (1964). *The Wandering Husband.* Englewood Cliffs, NJ: Prentice Hall.

Staercke, A. (1920). The reversal of the libido sign in delusions of persecutions. *International Journal of Psychoanalysis* 1:120–131.

Stein, M. (1988a). Writing about psychoanalysis: Analysts who write and those who don't. *Journal of the American Psychoanalytic Association* 36:105–124.

———. (1988b). Writing about psychoanalysis: Analysts who write and patients who read. *Journal of the American Psychoanalytic Association* 36:393–412.

Steiner, J. (1993). *Psychic Retreats: Pathology Organizations in Psychotic, Neurotic, and Borderline Patients.* London: Routledge.

Sterba, E. (1935). Excerpts from the analysis of a dog phobia. *Psychoanalytic Quarterly* 4:135–160.

———. (1940). Homesickness and the mother's breast. *Psychiatric Quarterly* 14:701–707.

Stern, D. (1977). *The First Relationship.* Cambridge, MA: Harvard University Press.

Stoller, R. (1976). *Perversion: The Erotic Form of Hatred.* New York: Pantheon Books.

Stolorow, R.D., and Grand, H.T. (1973). A partial analysis of a perversion involving bugs. *International Journal of Psychoanalysis* 54:349–350.

Stone, J. (1992). A psychoanalytic bestiary: the wolf woman, the leopard, and the siren. *American Imago* 49:117–152.

Stone, M. (1980). *Borderline Syndromes.* New York: McGraw Hill.

———. (1989). Murder. *The Psychiatric Clinics of North America* 12:643–652.

Strachey, J. (1934). The nature of the therapeutic action of psychoanalysis. *International Journal of Psycho-Analysis* 15:127–159.

Strean, H.S. (1980). *The Extramarital Affair.* New York: Free Press.

Strenger, C. (1989). The classic and romantic visions in psychoanalysis. *International Journal of Psycho-Analysis* 70:595–610.

Styron, W. (1990b). *Darkness Visible.* New York: William Morrow and Co.

Surawicz, F.G., and Banta, R. (1975). Lycanthropy revisited. *Canadian Psychiatric Association Journal* 20:537–542.

Szasz, T. (1955). The ego, the body, and pain. *Journal of the American Psychoanalytic Association* 3:177–200.

Tahka, V. (1993). *Mind and Its Treatment: A Psychoanalytic Approach.* Madison, CT: International Universities Press.

Talan, K.H. (1989). Gifts in psychoanalysis: theoretical and technical issues. *Psychoanalytic Study of the Child* 44:149–163.

Tartakoff, H. (1966). *The Normal Personality in Our Culture and the Nobel Prize Complex, in Psychoanalysis: A General Psychology,* eds. R.M. Lowenstein,

L.M. Newman, and M. Schure, et al., pp. 222–252. New York: International Universities Press.

Tavuchis, N. (1991). *Mia Culpa: A Sociology of Apology*. Palo Alto, CA: Stanford University Press.

Taylor, G.J. (1980). Splitting of the ego in transvestism and mask wearing. *International Review of Psychoanalysis* 7:511–522.

Tennyson, A. (1842). Break, break, break. In *Tennyson: A Selected Edition*, ed. C. Ricks, p. 165. Berkley/Los Angeles, CA: University of California Press.

Thomas, A., and Chess, S. (1977). *Temperament and Development*. New York: Brunner/Mazel.

Tobak, M. (1989). Lying and the paranoid personality. (Letter to editor) *American Journal of Psychiatry* 146:125.

Torch, E.M., and Bishop, E.R. (1981). Delusions of parasitosis: psychotherapeutic engagement. *American Journal of Psychotherapy* 35:101–106.

Trabert, W. (1991). Epidemiology of delusional parasitosis: psychotherapeutic engagement. *Nervenarzt* 62:165–169.

Traub-Werner, D. (1986). The place and value of bestophilia in perversions. *Journal of the American Psychoanalytic Association* 34:975–992.

Tseng, W., and McDermott, J. (1981). *Culture, Mind, and Therapy: An Introduction to Cultural Psychiatry*, pp. 47–48, 169–170. New York: Brunner/Mazel.

Turner, F., and Poppel, E. (1983). The neural lyre: poetic meter, the brain, and time. *Poetry* 2:277–309.

Tustin, F. (1980). Autistic objects. *International Review of Psychoanalysis* 7:27–35.

Tutu, D. (1999). *No Future Without Forgiveness*. New York: Doubleday.

Tyson, R. (1978). Notes on the analysis of a prelatency boy with a dog phobia. *Psychoanalytic Study of the Child* 33:427–458.

Tyson, R.H., and Sandler, J. (1971). Problems in the selection of patients for psychoanalysis: comments on the application of the concepts of "indication," "suitability" and "analyzability." *British Journal of Medical Psychology* 44:211–227.

Vaillant, G. (1977). *Adaptation to Life*. Boston: Little, Brown.

Valenstein, A. (1973). On attachment to painful feelings and the negative therapeutic reaction. *Psychoanalytic Study of the Child* 28:365–392.

van der Hart, O. (1981). Treatment of a phobia for dead birds: a case report. *American Journal of Clinical Hypnosis* 23:263–265.

Verbeek, E. (1959). Le delire dermatozoaire et le probleme de l'hallucinose tactile chronizue. *Psychiatrie et Neurologie* 138:217–233.

Verdoux, H., and Bourgeouis, M. (1993). A partial form of lycanthropy with hair delusion in a manic-depressive patient. *British Journal of Psychiatry* 163:684–686.

Volkan, V. (1972). The birds of Cyprus. *American Journal of Psychotherapy* 26:378–383.

———. (1972). *Linking Objects and Linking Phenomena.* New York: International Universities Press.

———. (1976). *Primitive Internalized Object Relations.* New York: International Universities Press.

———. (1982). Narcissistic personality disorder. In *Critical Problems in Psychiatry*, eds. J.O. Cavenar, and H.K.H. Brodie, pp. 332–350. Philadelphia, PA JB Lippincott.

———. (1987). *Six Steps in the Treatment of Borderline personality Organization.* Northvale, NJ: Jason Aronson.

———. (1995). *The Infantile Psychotic Self and Its Fates: Understanding and Treating Schizophrenic and Other Difficult Patients.* Northvale, NJ: Jason Aronson.

———. (1997). *Blood Lines: From Ethnic Price to Ethnic Terrorism.* New York: Farrar, Strauss, and Giroux.

———. (1973). Transitional fantasies in the analysis of a narcissistic personality. *Journal of the American Psychoanalytic Association* 21:351–376.

Volkan, V.D., and Akhtar, S. (1979). The symptoms of schizophreina: contributions of the structural theory and object relations theory. In *Integrating Ego Psychology and Object Relations Theory*, eds. L. Saretsky, G.D. Goldman, and D.S. Milman, pp. 270–285. Dubuque Iowa: Kendall/Hunt Publishing Co.

Volkan, V.D., and Luttrell, A.S. (1971). Aspects of the object relationships and developing skills of a "mechanical boy." *British Journal of Medical Psychology* 44:101–116.

Waelder, R. (1933). The psychoanalytic theory of play. *Psychiatric Quarterly* 2:208–219.

———. (1936). The principle of multiple function: observations on overdetermination. *Psychoanalytic Quarterly* 5:45–62.

Wallerstein, R.S. (1983). Self psychology and "classical" psychoanalytic psychology: the nature of their relationship. In *The Future of Psychoanalysis*, ed. A. Goldberg, pp. 19–63. New York: International Universities Press.

———. (1985). Concept of psychic reality: its meaning and value. *Journal of the American Psychoanalytic Association* 33:555–569.

Webster's Ninth New Collegiate Dictionary. (1987). Springfield, MA: Merriam Webster.

Webster's Ninth New Collegiate Dictionary. (1998). New York: Merriam Webster.

Weich, M.J. (1978). Transitional language. In *Between Reality and Fantasy: Transitional Objects and Phenomena*, eds. S.A. Grolnick, L. Barkin, and W. Muensterberger, pp. 413–423. New York: Jason Aronson.

Weil, A. (1970). The basic core. *Psychoanalytic Study of the Child* 25:442–460.

Weiss, E. (1934). Bodily pain and mental pain. *International Journal of Psycho-Analysis* 15:1–13.

Weiss, S. (1964). Parameters in child analysis. *Journal of the American Psychoanalytic Association* 12:587–599.

Werman, D.S. (1977). Normal and pathological nostalgia. *Journal of the American Psychoanalytic Association* 25:387–398.

Wheelis, A. (1966). *The Illusionless Man.* New York: Harper and Row.

———. (1990). *The Path Not Taken.* New York: Alfred Knopf.

Whitehurst, R. (1969). Extramarital sex: alienation or extension of normal behavior. In *Extramarital Relations,* ed. G. Neubeck. Englewood Cliffs, NJ: Prentice-Hall.

Winnicott, D.W. (1947). Hate in the Countertransference. In *Collected Papers: Through Paediatrics to Psychoanlaysis,* pp. 194–203. London: Hogarth, 1958.

———. (1949). Hate in the Countertransference. *International Journal of Psycho-Analysis* 39:69–75.

———. (1953). Transitional objects and transitional phenomena: a study of the first not-me possession. *International Journal of Psychoanalysis* 34:89–97.

———. (1958). *The Manic Defense.* London: Hogarth, 1958.

———. (1960a). Ego distortion in the terms of true and false self. In *Maturational Processes and the Facilitating Environment,* pp. 140–152. New York: International Universities Press.

———. (1960b). String: a technique of communication. In *The Maturational Process and the Facilitating Environment,* pp. 153–157. New York: International Universities Press, 1965.

———. (1963). The development of the capacity for concern. In *The Maturational Process and the Facilitating Environment,* pp. 73–82. New York: International Universities Press, 1965.

———. (1965). *The Maturational Process and the Facilitating Environment.* New York: International Universities Press.

———. (1971). *Playing and Reality.* New York: Basic Books.

Wolberg, L.R. (1954). *The Technique of Psychotherapy.* New York: Grune and Stratton.

Wolpe, J., and Rachman, R. (1960). Psychoanlaytic evidence: a critique based on Freud's case of Little Hans. *Journal of Nervous and Mental Diseases* 131:135–148.

Worth, D., and Beck, A.M. (1981). Multiple ownership of animals in New York City. *Transactions of the College of Physicians of Philadelphia* 3:280–300.

Wright, K. (1991). *Vision and Separation: Between Mother and Baby.* Northvale, NJ: Jason Aronson.

Wurmser, L. (1981). Phobic core in the addictions and the paranoid process. *International Journal of Psychoanalytic Psychotherapy* 8:311–335.

Yellowlees, P.P.M. (1989). Werewolves down under—where are you now? *The Medical Journal of Australia* 151:663–665.

Yeomans, F., Selzer, M., and Clarkin, J. (1992). *Treating the Borderline Patient: A Contract Based Approach.* New York: Basic Books.

Zavitzianos, G. (1972). Homovestism: wearing clothes of the same sex. *International Journal of Psychoanalysis* 53:471–482.

Zetzel, E.R. (1968). The so-called good hysteric. *International Journal of Psycho-Analysis* 49:256–268.

Ziskin, J., and Ziskin, M. (1973). *The Extramarital Arrangement.* London: Aberlard-Schuman.

INDEX

ABOUT THE AUTHOR

Salman Akhtar, M.D., is Professor of Psychiatry at Jefferson Medical College, Lecturer on Psychiatry at Harvard Medical School, and Training and Supervising Analyst at the Psychoanalytic Center of Philadelphia. He has served as an associate editor of the *Journal of Psychotherapy Practice and Research*, and member of the editorial boards of the *Journal of the American Psychoanalytic Association* and the *International Journal of Psycho-Analysis*. Currently he is the Book Review Editor of the *Journal of Applied Psychoanalytic Studies* and an editorial reader for *Psychoanalytic Quarterly*. He is the author of *Broken Structures* (1992), *Quest for Answers* (1995), *Inner Torment* (1999), and *Immigration and Identity* (1999). His more than 200 scientific publications also include nineteen edited or co-edited books. Dr. Akhtar is the recipient of the Journal of the American Psychoanalytic Association's Award (1995), the Margaret Mahler Literature Prize (1996), ASPP's Sigmund Freud Award (2000), the American Psychoanalytic Association's Edith Sabshin Award (2001), and IAPA's Scientific Achievement Award (2001). He has also published six volumes of poetry.